Wild Garden
weekends

wild-garden (*n.*):

1. A garden that is planted for biodiversity, to encourage pollinators and native wildlife species by providing food and habitat

2. A garden that thrives within its means and fits its natural landscape; one that doesn't need water where it is scarce or nutrients beyond compost and mulch

3. A garden that is productive, providing seasonal, healthy food to eat

4. A garden that is often naturalistic in style, inspired by plant communities in the wild

Explore the secret gardens, wild meadows and kitchen garden cafés of Britain

Tania Pascoe

Wild Garden

weekends

WILD THINGS PUBLISHING

Contents

Best for

Regions

Regions

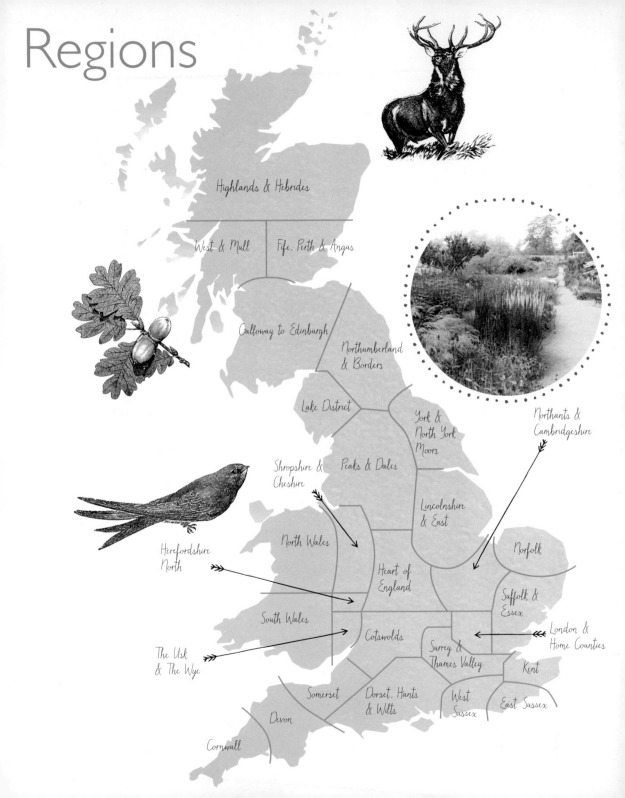

Highlands & Hebrides

West & Mull   Fife, Perth & Angus

Galloway to Edinburgh

Northumberland & Borders

Lake District

York & North York Moors

Shropshire & Cheshire

Peaks & Dales

Lincolnshire & East

Northants & Cambridgeshire

North Wales

Heart of England

Norfolk

Herefordshire North

Suffolk & Essex

South Wales

Cotswolds

Surrey & Thames Valley

London & Home Counties

The Usk & The Wye

Kent

Somerset

Dorset, Hants & Wilts

West Sussex

East Sussex

Devon

Cornwall

South West

South & East

Wales & Borders

Central & North

Scotland & Borders

Foreword

Stepping into my favourite gardens feels like entering a whole different world, and spending time in them is pure escapism. Gardens are never finished; they are always changing. Their moments are fleeting, determined by the hour and the season, the play of light, and the succession of blooms. No two days are ever the same. This is why garden visiting is so addictive.

The first hit is sensory and sometimes even emotional. After a time we can start to analyse and understand a garden, to think about why it works (or sometimes, why it doesn't). I have learned unexpected lessons from visiting gardens totally unlike my own. The late Derek Jarman made his small garden in the shadow of Dungeness power station, sprung out of shingle, driftwood, and poetry. It is powerful, moving, and bleak. There's never a bad time to visit the Phoenix garden, one of the most secret public spaces in central London and a wildlife haven where black-stemmed nettles jostle with scented regal lilies. I love historic walled kitchen gardens such Spetchley Park: abundant with vegetables, herbs, and flowers for cutting. Food doesn't come any more local, fresher, or delicious than from the garden where it has been grown.

It might seem unusual for a garden guide to list nature reserves, woods and meadows but with our ever-increasing interest in naturalistic styles of planting, it makes perfect sense. These wild and sensitively managed natural landscapes can be just as inspiring as formal gardens, and embracing a naturalistic approach starts with observing plants in the wild. Every April I rush to see damp grasslands covered in chequered snake's head fritillaries and in the early summer I seek out orchid-studded meadows. Tania's dedicated sleuthing means I now have a huge list of new locations to explore.

With this book in my hand I could spend years visiting new gardens, revisiting old favourites, eating well, and relaxing in some unique and wonderful locations. Tania has a natural instinct for finding special places and she has travelled the length of the country in pursuit of her passion for wild gardens. The result is a treasure trove that celebrates all that's great about Britain's gardens and natural landscapes.

Sarah Price, Chelsea Gold Medal-winning garden designer

Introduction

The beginnings

In the haze of my childhood memories, summers were spent rolling in flower-filled grass meadows and running after butterflies while my mother made wreaths of flowers for my hair. I grew up in Somerset and remember picking with abandon large bunches of cowslips from the hills and foraging for puffballs and field mushrooms. The buddleia in our garden was, in my imagination, a huge castle guarded by literally hundreds of butterflies of all kinds. I would collect their dead bodies, and use their wings as a very effective glittery eye-shadow. It was idyllic and bountiful and this world doesn't exist anymore. Now, with a young daughter of my own, I want to relive these precious moments and for her to experience the abundance and joy of nature, to know the smell of meadowsweet, to spend hours catching crickets or making the perfect posy of betony, daisies and clover.

Where have all the flowers gone?

My background is in corporate sustainability, travelling the world selling ethical strategy and responsible rhetoric. Yet, in my lifetime, the world has lost just over half of its biodiversity – 52% since 1970 (*Living Planet Report*, 2014 WWF). In the UK, 97% of our hay meadows and wild grasslands have been wiped out since the 1930s (The Wildlife Trusts) and 60% of all the UK species we know about are in decline (*National Ecosystem Assessment 2011*). If you look at the facts, the natural world looks to be teetering on the edge.

But there are also precious pockets of biodiversity that offer not only incredible natural spectacles but also seed banks, gene pools, and lessons on how we can reclaim such vital resources. These remaining fragments of our wild grasslands and semi-managed meadows – including traditional hay meadows and woodlands – are wildflower-rich landscapes that provide essential habitat and food for our insects, birds and small mammals.

We rely hugely on the breadth of our species. A rich biodiversity of plants and animals, as well as healthy soils full of micro-organisms and insects underpins our food systems and our environment. Healthy ecosystems ensure our waste is broken down, our water

supplies are regulated, and climate change-inducing greenhouse gases are absorbed. Traditional meadow flowers, and those that thrive in the field and woodland margins, feed our pollinators, which in turn benefit our farmland.

The decline of our pollinators and biodiversity is mainly due to modern agricultural practices and the conversion of hedgerows and meadows into arable land. Before the 1930s, farming was less intense and grazing allowed, and even enhanced, a rich diversity of flowering plants. Now, when only 3% of our flower-rich grasslands is all that remains, there is still hope that we can return from the brink. From gardeners to government, we are seeing a rise in meadow appreciation. Organisations including Plantlife, the Coronation Meadows project, The Wildlife Trusts, the RSPB, and the National Trust – and many more – are protecting, restoring, and providing access to these special places.

The pleasure of meadows

With my young family, I discovered many of the incredible flower-filled meadows teeming with the butterflies and birdlife that I remembered from my own childhood. It was a joy to walk in these vibrant places, which offer a rare insight into the landscape and farming heritage of our not-so-distant past. In the book you will find out where to see some of Britain's best wildflower displays: flower-covered dunes on Scotland's west coast (the machair); traditional hay meadows in Kent; shingle flora of Shoreham and Dungeness; and the minute alpine and arctic flora that survive high on our mountain tops. Also included are some of our island's best woodland flower 'shows', often occurring in the tiny fragments of our surviving ancient woodland. These sylvan wonderlands are some of the richest, most valuable wildlife habitats in the UK. Visit in spring and you will be rewarded with mists of native bluebells, old coppiced forests carpeted with celandines, anemones, primroses and violets, and mystical oak woods dripping in lichens and mosses.

A wild garden movement

As our wild places continue to be put under more and more strain, our gardens are turning into sanctuaries. There are about 16 million gardens in Britain and each has the opportunity to become part of a powerful network of wildlife habitats that nurture us as well as the birds and insects that share them. It's heartening to see that a wild-garden revolution is growing, spurred on by our need to reconnect to nature, marvel at its wonder, reclaim its rich biodiversity, and enjoy its mental and physical health benefits. People are creating their own meadows and increasingly we are choosing pollinator-friendly plants and gardening organically, without the use of pesticides and artificial fertilisers.

Setting out on a journey across Britain, from the Outer Hebrides to the Cornish coast, I discovered a country filled with incredible, bountiful wild gardens. Best of all, I discovered that we don't have to give up any of the beauty, artistry and romance that our British gardens are famous for. A 'wild garden' is arguably even more beautiful – one that audibly hums with life, planted with our wildlife in mind, and perhaps also providing us with delicious, fresh food. A wild garden is often naturalistic in feel, its design inspired by natural plant communities, and, luckily for us all, generally lower maintenance than perfectly manicured, species-poor outdoor spaces.

The art of travelling

Seeing so much beauty is hungry work, and with friends and family, I ate my way through some incredible home-made cakes, garden-fresh salads, quiches, soups and gourmet six-course meals. Each one of them was made with love and a respect for their provenance, which could often be measured in metres rather than miles. A wild garden is often a productive one, and many provided sustainable, super-local vegetables, fruit and honey, which visitors were often able to purchase to take home.

For overnight or longer stops, you will be spoilt for choice. The book contains a hand-picked selection of characterful, charming places set in wild flora-filled landscapes or lovingly tended gardens. You can camp in a traditional orchard in Cornwall or rent a rustic cottage set in its own small nature reserve in Pembrokeshire. There are farmhouse B&Bs, quirky boutique hotels, gypsy caravans, and yurts with wood burning stoves – all just waiting to be sampled.

All the entries in the book offer a taste of the good life, the good food and the beautiful places that our little islands are blessed with. I hope you find joy, solace and inspiration in discovering them too.

10 things you can do

1. Buy organic, chemical-free food and where possible, buy it locally and in season

2. Plant pollinator friendly, nectar-rich plants

3. Don't use pesticides

4. Plant a tree or native hedge

5. Build a wildlife pond

6. Compost and use mulch

7. Let your lawn (or a part of it) grow long

8. Don't cut back dead stems until spring

9. Buy peat free plants & compost

10. Join your local Wildlife Trust or one of the many other organisations

Treading gently

We are often asked why we want to tell people about these often-fragile places. There is an obvious argument that suggests that we should leave them alone. This is a valid point and in some cases and places, it's certainly the best strategy. Care has been taken to only include places that The Wildlife Trusts or other managing bodies recommend for public access. I believe that we need to build a relationship with these sacred places, and that means visiting them. The more we get out and value them, the more we will fight for them. Even so, every step we take can make an impact. 'Leave no trace' is as applicable whether you camp there for the night or are just passing by. Gain good karma by picking up any litter you find. Please stick to the paths and designated areas and when in doubt, stay out. Often certain times of year have restricted access due to breeding cycles or conservation demands. Please keep your dog on a lead or, even better, away from any places where there might be ground-nesting birds or animals. This is essential in spring and summer but can also mean life and death in winter when energy must be conserved. And finally, please ensure that no plant, whether in a garden or woodland or meadow is picked or harvested, unless it is absolutely known that there is a more-than-ample supply. Wild blackberries, for example, are plentiful and make for excellent foraging.

Finding your way

All the locations are provided with addresses, postcode and website. Meadows and wild places are often harder to find. Directions from main roads, details of parking, access and latitude and longitude have been included. The latter is given in decimal degrees (WGS84) and can be entered straight into any Smartphone, car SatNav, or any web-based mapping program, such as Google, Bing or Streetmap. The latter two also provide Ordnance Survey mapping. Print out a map before you go – or save a 'screen grab'. If you have paper maps, look up the equivalent national grid reference at nearby.org. Abbreviations refer to left and right (L, R) and north, east, south, west (N, E, S, W). Bring a map, compass and suitable clothing and always tell someone where you are going, don't rely on your mobile phone.

Where to find out more

There are lots of organisations that actively protect and promote our wild places and lobby for change. They can provide in-depth information on where to go locally and what you can do to help. You can find out about seasonal highlights, events and courses or gain some gardening tips. This list is not exhaustive but it's a great place to start if you want to find out more, visit more fantastic places and support the movement to restore our biodiversity.

 THE WILDLIFE TRUSTS wildlifetrusts.org

The 47 Wildlife Trusts across the UK work to inspire people to value our natural world and take action to protect and restore it. They manage thousands of nature reserves, run great events for adults and children and provide information on where to go and what to see locally.

 PLANTLIFE plantlife.org.uk

Plantlife is the organisation that is speaking up for our wild flowers, plants and fungi. They believe that wild flowers and plants play a fundamental role for wildlife, and their colour and character lights up our landscape. In 2012 they published 'Our Vanishing Flora' which clearly communicated the dramatic decline in our wild flowers. Plantlife runs campaigns, provides information and events and manages reserves that you can visit for free.

 CORONATION MEADOWS coronationmeadows.org.uk

His Royal Highness the Prince of Wales instigated the Coronation Meadows Project as a response to Plantlife's 2012 report on the loss of wild flowers across the UK. He brought together Plantlife, The Wildlife Trusts and the Rare Breeds Survival Trust to identify a Coronation Meadow in each county and use these flagship meadows as donors to provide seed to create other meadows locally.

 RSPB rspb.org.uk

The country's largest nature conservation charity, conserving, restoring and protecting British birds and wildlife and their habitats. Many of the RSPB reserves are incredible places to see wild flowers as well as the insects and birds that feed on them. The RSPB manages over 200 nature reserves and offers many events and education programmes for all ages across the UK.

WILD ABOUT GARDENS wildaboutgardens.org.uk

This is a great web resource helping gardeners to make their gardens more wildlife friendly. A joint project betwen the RHS and The Wildlife Trusts can find out about the biodiversity in your garden, provide tips on what plants to choose and ideas for quick and easy projects that will make a big difference.

NATIONAL TRUST nationaltrust.org.uk

The Trust is the UK's biggest land owner and strives to maintain it as an environment that supports a rich diversity of life. If you use it, National Trust membership offers great value access to hundreds of historic gardens, ancient woodlands and wildflower meadows, organic kitchen gardens, and cafes that serve their produce. They provide many wildlife-focused activities for children, encouraging us all to get out and have fun outdoors.

BEST FOR WILD FLOWERS

We have lost 97% of our traditional hay meadows and flora-rich grasslands since agricultural intensification started in the 1930's. Not only a beautiful cornerstone of the British landscape, they provide essential habitat and nectar for a diverse range of insects, that in turn offer food for our small birds and mammals. From the wildflower carpeted dunes of the machair on Scotland's West Coast to traditional hay meadows in Kent, walking in these flower-strewn places in spring and summer will not fail to inspire.

BEST FOR KITCHEN GARDEN FOOD

After visiting a garden, I love nothing more than sitting down to a home-cooked lunch lovingly made with their own vegetables freshly picked that morning. Ideally this would be accompanied by some award-winning local cheese and served on a sunny terrace with views of the garden. In cold weather, a roaring fire and some roast pork from the home-reared pigs would be much appreciated. We discovered a wealth of pubs, converted glasshouses and garden tearooms, all serving incredible food from their own plots or local farms.

BEST FOR BIRDS, BEES & BUTTERFLIES

Insects, including bumblebees, bees, hoverflies, moths, butterflies
and many others, are essential pollinators, ensuring we have
apples on our trees and vegetables on our plates. They also
provide food for our birds. There is nothing quite as magical
as a woodland dawn chorus or the song of a skylark in spring,
yet we've lost 55% of our farmland birds alone since 1970 and
insects have fared even worse. We must look to our gardens
and wild spaces to provide these essential habitats and you
can help by growing pollinator-friendly plants and creating a
pesticide-free environment. And the results can look stunning!

BEST FOR KIDS

Getting out into nature is essential for our well-being and
kids love nothing more than the chance to run free through
a meadow, or climb a tree. There are not many children who
get as excited as I do about visiting a garden, but choose your
destination carefully and they will be begging to see more.
We discovered many gardens and reserves that welcomed
children, inviting them to play in their tree-houses, explore
their pathways, and dip in their ponds. Nearly all the National
Trust sites offer inspiring outdoor activities ranging from seed
planting to beetle safaris. The Wildlife Trusts, too, often have
ranger-led, child-focused events.

BEST FOR KITCHEN GARDENS

More of us are either keen to grow our own fruit and vegetables or buy them from local markets and farm shops. In a window box or deep bucket, fresh salad leaves, herbs and potatoes can be harvested and served up within minutes. Nothing tastes better and nothing is better for your health or for our environment (especially if it's organic). Food in season anchors us to the time of year and reconnects us to our soil and heritage. From large walled estates to small, one-metre veg beds, we discovered exquisite heirloom varieties never found at the supermarket and bursting with unrivalled flavour. Whether you want to design your own productive garden or use vegetables and herbs ornamentally you'll find wheelbarrows full of inspiration.

BEST FOR URBAN ESCAPES

In the UK, 80% of us live in towns and cities, so you'll be glad to hear that there are some wonderful wild garden escapes within easy access of our urban centres. Whether you want to travel by tube, train, bicycle or bus, there are wildflower meadows, ancient forests, nature-filled gardens and fantastic cafés awaiting your discovery. Some you will find hidden behind high walls in the very heart of our cities; others lie a little outside the urban sprawl but feel like a million miles away. So grab some friends and try something different this weekend.

BEST FOR SECRET GARDENS

There is something extra special about feeling as if you are the
first person to discover a garden, pushing open that old door in
the wall and revealing a hidden wonderland of tumbling roses
and fruit-laden apple trees. Often the best Secret Gardens
come with an imbued sense of time having stood still and you
find yourself creeping quietly around corners, never quite
knowing what you will find next. I was entranced by these
charming places and amazed that they can be found in the most
surprising places.

BEST FOR ANCIENT FORESTS

Our ancient forests are the places of myths and legends and
offer enchanting wildlife-filled walks through their sylvan
cathedrals. The majority of our ancient forests were felled
during the Bronze Age clearances, and yet there are still many
easily accessible pockets of both virgin and managed woodland.
These provide some of our countryside's richest wildlife
habitats; spring time is heralded by carpets of anemones,
celandines, primroses and bluebells, accompanied by incredible
birdsong. Get out any time of year and you won't be
disappointed.

BEST FOR REALLY WILD GARDENS

Planted with nature in mind, a good wild garden is also a
beautiful place to be. For me there is no longer an excuse for
raggedy 'wildlife-friendly' gardens that are simply uninspiring.
These prove just how beautiful a garden can be that provides
a rich habitat and food source both for us and for our wildlife.
See how the large estates and small private gardens are pushing
the boundaries of garden design, as well as rediscovering the
ornamental and purposeful qualities of many plants previously
not considered garden-worthy. You will discover that there are
few strict rules in respect of what makes a great wild garden,
but a sense of place and a creative imagination are a must.

BEST FOR SPRING FLOWERS

After a cold, all-too-often wet and grey winter, there is nothing
like the unfurling of spring flowers to reawaken the spirit.
Whether it's a blanket of snowdrops illuminating a leafless
garden, theatrical displays of vivid tulips, or the mystical blue
haze of a May beech wood carpeted in bluebells, spring's
bright flowers inspire us to get up, get out, and start gardening
again. And if you need an injection of startling colour, visit the
rhododendrons and azaleas in Cornish valley gardens or the
plant-hunter glens of Argyll and Bute.

BEST FOR CAMPING & GLAMPING

For a real nature adventure you cannot beat a night under canvas. Whether you want to throw up a tarp for the night or prefer a double bed in a woodburner-warmed yurt, nothing beats camping. Spend your day lying in a flower meadow and the evening stargazing, hunting for glow-worms and cooking by campfire. At night go to sleep to the sound of the owls and wake to the joyful dawn chorus. We discovered some truly magical places where you can pitch your tent, rent sheepskin-strewn tipis on wild moors, sleep in shepherd's huts in ancient orchards, or hire gypsy caravans stranded in wildflower meadows.

BEST FOR INDULGENT GETAWAYS

Whether it's for a romantic weekend or a much-deserved week away, the UK is blessed with some outstanding secluded holiday cottages, as well as luxurious B&Bs and boutique hotels that offer slow-food dinners and a good night's sleep. I believe that character and charm go a long way and I met many hosts who treat their guests with the same care they lavish on their beautiful gardens. Often you can enjoy first-class suppers made from garden produce and breakfast eggs freshly laid by the chickens that peck around the orchard.

Cornwall

Make your way over rugged cliffs coloured with gorse and maritime flowers, along quiet lanes hung with campion and bluebells, to plant hunters' jungles.

Cornwall

The highlights

›› Gaze out over traditionally farmed arable fields, filled with corn marigolds and poppies (6)

›› Discover exotic jungle gardens filled with plant-hunters' treasures (1, 4 & 5)

›› Camp in an old apple orchard on the river Fowey and buy farm-raised meat for campfire suppers (11)

›› Wander along awesome cliff-top paths decorated with maritime flowers (8)

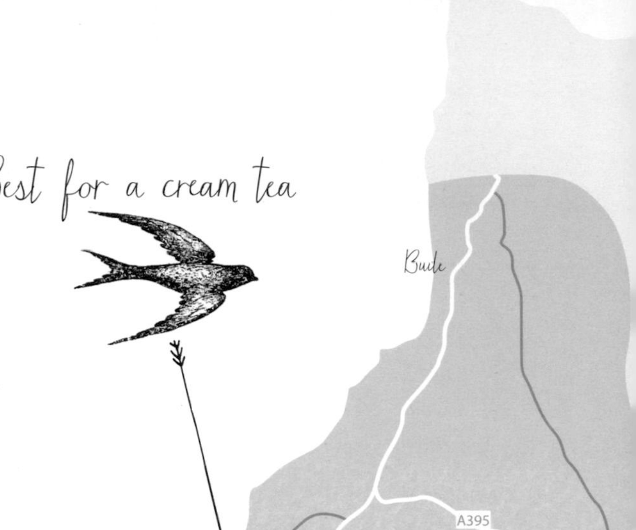

Best for a cream tea

The Eden Project

Best for an organic kitchen lunch

Stay on a traditional Cornish farm

Plymouth

There is something utterly romantic and nostalgic about rural Cornwall. Late spring in the lost world of the Roseland Peninsula, without the throngs of holiday makers, is a wonderland of wild spring flowers. Step back in time and discover sunken lanes that are feet deep in shades of pink, white, and blue, their steep sides erupting with miles of red campion, bluebells, and ramsons.

Along the stunning coastal section from Bude to the beautiful Rame Peninsula, a different range of wildflowers thrives on its cliff tops and sparse slopes. May is a dazzling brocade when the yellows of the bulbous buttercup and orange-tinged kidney vetch merge with pink cushions of sea thrift.

Maybe it's the remote location buffeted by Atlantic squalls, the mild climate, and lush, deep valleys; or maybe it's the inhabitants' instinctive connection with plants. Whatever the reason, almost every great Cornish garden feels distinctly wild.

In Cornwall's hidden valleys, jungle gardens are filled with champion trees, aged tree ferns, and specimens straight off Darwin's Beagle. Like the Scottish gardens full of Himalayan specimens, those of Cornwall are the showcases of the old-school plant hunters and their bountiful stock is breathtaking. The great and prolific Quaker gardening family, the Foxes, created the magical jungly valley gardens of Penjerrick, Trebah and Glendurgan in the 19th century. Each one is a completely different but wild experience.

When it comes to places to stay take me to Botelet Farm and leave me there. Outbuildings, wildflower meadows, doves, and wandering chickens drinking from stone troughs create the quintessential fairytale Cornish farmstead. In the same family since 1886, the stone farmhouse has been doing B&B since the Thirties. Step inside and you could have strayed into a photoshoot for *World of Interiors*: flagstone floor, cot hanging in front of the range, and a large farmhouse table. So simple and welcoming, and there's a very fancy stainless-steel coffee machine to help you wake up in case you think you are dreaming.

For delicious food I head straight for the Potager Glasshouse café. I could easily eat here every single day of the year, while dreaming of living in such a light- and plant-filled space. Choose a table in the big glasshouse with its exotic cacti, then play ping-pong or sleep off your spicy chickpea soup and home-made seed bread in one of the many garden hammocks.

I cannot mention Cornwall without highlighting The Eden Project, built in the old china clay pits; it is now a recognised icon for sustainable gardening—go and be inspired.

Gardens

1 PENJERRICK

Bring your wellies, plunge into the foliage, and enjoy a plant safari through the lost gardens of Penjerrick. There are very few gardens open to the public that allow a visitor to feel like a real explorer, but Penjerrick does. And it is magical: the towering gunneras and enormous tree ferns offer a kind of Alice in Wonderland experience. Following a long, warm summer of serious growth we were often unsure if we had lost the path. In the particularly wild Valley Garden, accessed over the wooden bridge, butterflies danced and peregrines screeched from the sky. There are some very mature trees each, no doubt, with its own plant hunter tale to tell. By the bridge is an elephant-sized brain coral that was given to Penjerrick by the captain of The Beagle. Both family and garden tell a story of exploration, discovery, and invention. Robert Were Fox, a geologist and inventor who made the garden in the early 19th century, is responsible for introducing many of the species we see today. Parking is along the monkey puzzle-lined drive, no loos.
→ Penjerrick Hill, Budock, Falmouth, TR11 5ED, 01872 870105 penjerrickgarden.co.uk
🕑 Mar–Sept, Sun, Wed, Fri 1.30–4.30pm
☕

1 PENJERRICK

1 PENJERRICK

2 CAERHAYS

Caerhays is one of Cornwall's most famous repositories of the plant-hunters' bounty. J C Williams of Caerhays, a keen plantsman, sponsored many expeditions, particularly to China, during the early 1900s. The seeds and plants that made their way back are still being used to create the celebrated, free-flowering, hardy camellias. Go very early in spring to see the magnificent national collection of magnolias. Dress warm, eat a hearty breakfast, and enjoy the two-hour guided tours from the head gardener (advance booking essential). There are over 80 species and more than 500 hybrids of magnolia alone to enjoy in this dramatic setting. From Caerhays Castle there are amazing views right down to sandy Porthluney beach.
→ Gorran, St Austell PL26 6LY 01872 501310 caerhays.co.uk
🕑 mid February–mid June daily 10–5pm
☕ 🌱 🏠 🍴 🌼

3 PINSLA GARDEN & NURSERY

Tucked away down winding lanes near Cardinham Woods you'll find the lovely cottage garden of Pinsla. Within lies a butterfly-filled maze of paths, woodland walks, open glades dotted with imaginative upcycled sculptures, and a beautiful stone circle set in long grass. Over the last 30 years, Claire and Mark have designed the garden around their gingerbread home in a naturalistic style to showcase the range of unusual plants sold in the nursery. A summer afternoon spent enjoying flowers that spill over on to paths, followed by their delicious homemade carrot cake is worth heading off the beaten track for.
→ Glynn, Nr. Cardinham, Bodmin PL30 4AY 01208 821339 pinslagarden.net
🕑 End Feb–Oct daily 9am–5.30pm
☕ 🍴 🌼

4 GLENDURGAN

On the northern banks of the Helford estuary, the warm microclimate and shelter belts have been brilliantly employed to create misty jungle gardens full of Himalayan rhododendrons and southern hemisphere mega-trees. The two best-known gardens, Glendurgan and Trebah, are both stunning, particularly when the rhododendrons, camellias and azaleas are at their frilly peak in late March. What I love about each is their romantic site: both gardens extend right down to the sea. Trebah has a particularly secluded and safe beach where, in the summer, you can spend a whole day swimming. At Glendurgan, apart from the superb champion trees, exotic palms, and mountain flora, there are exquisite wildflower glades that the National Trust has been nurturing over the years. Visit in late spring/early summer when swathes of bluebells and then columbines (*Aquilegia vulgaris*) cover the grass.
→ Grove Hill, Mawnan Smith, Falmouth, TR11 5JZ, 01326 252020 nationaltrust.org.uk
🕑 mid Feb–Oct Tue–Sun & BH 10.30–5.30pm (and Mon in Aug).
☕ 🌱 🍴 🌼

4 GLENDURGAN

3 PINSLA

5 TREGREHAN

With its rich horticultural heritage, Tregrehan is first and foremost a garden. It's also a specialist nursery and delightful place to stay, with accommodation in the characterful converted mews. Generations of the Carlyon family have been nurturing and enriching the park and garden since the 1600s, and the majority of the mature trees are well over a hundred years old . The family's relationship with New Zealand's flora continues and current members, Jo and Tom Hudson, are both knowledgeable plantspeople and keen to see Tregrehan's botanical heritage flourish. There are acres to explore, including the fantastic glasshouses where banana plants are literally bursting through the ceilings. Built in 1846, they are simply huge, and if it's raining you can quite happily luxuriate in this glorious space among the vines and rare plants.

Tregrehan House, Par PL24 2SJ 01726 812438 tregrehan.org

mid Mar–May, Wed, Thu, Fri, Sun & BH 10.30–5pm; Jun–Aug Wed, 1–4.30pm

The gardens at Enys
are among the oldest
in Cornwall and are
famous for their spring
bluebells

9 TREGOOSE

Meadows

6 WEST PENTIRE
The headland of Pentire Point West is awash with incredible displays of wildflowers throughout spring and summer. Early spring starts with cowslips and pyramidal orchids, then corn marigolds and poppies appear. All thrive on the thin, acid soils of this part of the north Cornish coast, which is now managed as an IPA (Important Plant Area) for its rare arable flora. Here and behind Holywell beach you can find other beautiful plants with wonderful names, including weasel's snout, shepherd's needle and Venus's looking-glass.
→ Start at West Pentire Road TR8 5SE following coast path around headland. At Porth Joke return via path across fields nationaltrust.org.uk 50.4041,-5.1303 ⤵

7 ENYS GARDENS
The gardens at Enys are among the oldest in Cornwall. The house and grounds were, in late 2014, part of an extensive restoration project yet there is still lots to see and this evocative location still feels like a lost world. Early May heralds the bluebell festival when the special draw is the massed bluebells that grow in the open meadow known as Parc Lye. There is a café serving cream teas and a small history museum in the coach-house.
→ St Gluvias, Penryn, TR10 9LB, 01326 259885 enysgardens.org.uk ⏰ Apr–Sept Tue,Thu, Sun 2-5pm; 1st wk May 11–4.30pm. 50.1818,-5.1078 ⤳ ⤵ 🍴

8 LIZARD NATIONAL NATURE RESERVE
In early summer, the dramatic cliffs between the Lizard and Kynance are a bright tapestry of pink sea thrift, bird's-foot trefoil, and numerous vetches. Rarer plants including green-winged orchids and wild chives thrive on the heathland, while harebells cover its ancient landscape, much of it protected. August is a great time to wander through the miles of purple heather – the whole area is open access so you are free to roam as you please.
→ Join coastpath NE towards Kynance. Lighthouse Road, Lizard, TR12 7NT the-lizard.org 49.9594,-5.2064 ⤵ 🍴

Accommodation

9 TREGOOSE B&B
Just five miles from Caerhays, Heligan, Trewithen, and the Eden Project, Alison O'Connor has created a beautiful Cornish garden around her elegant home. There are three sumptuous bedrooms with crisp linen sheets and on-request dinners, made with garden produce and local game. Alison is a trained horticulturalist (and cook) and an authority on Cornish plants. She is always more than happy to share her knowledge of the county's gardens and show guests around her own, which is overflowing with rare and interesting plants.

9 TREGOOSE

→ Signed off the A390 between Grampound and Probus. Grampound, Truro TR2 4DB, 01726 882460 tregoose.co.uk 🍷 🏠 🍴

10 BOTELET FARM

Lose yourself in the utter romance of this charming farmstead, situated in a wild flower-filled valley. In family ownership since the late 19th century, they have been offering farmhouse accommodation for over 80 years. Lovely Julie now runs the spot-on, rustic-chic B&B; or there is a choice of two yurts, each in their own meadow with their own woodburner, or gorgeous SC Cowslip Cottage . The gardens are a delight and merge with the bucolic landscape. There is an orchard planted with

The gardens are a delight and merge with the bucolic landscape. There is an orchard full of Cornish varieties.

local Cornish apples and the whole farm is self-sufficient in electricity. Sister-in-law Tia offers outdoor treatments and massages in the meadow, with the luxury of a heated blanket, or you can go inside and enjoy the warmth of the log fires.
→ Herodsfoot, Liskeard, PL14 4RD, 01503 220225 botelet.com 🍷 🐾 🏠

11 ST WINNOW

St Winnow is one of our favourite places to camp in Cornwall. The glorious orchard site, next to this remote hamlet's church, sits right on the river Fowey. This is true Famous Five territory: facilities are basic with a loo and a cold water tap but the location is simply magical. We like to go in May when the old apple trees are painted pink with blossom and the little lanes around Fowey are heavy with bluebells and spring flowers. Up at the farm, you will find a small yet charming vintage tractor museum, while Angie's kiosk sells sandwiches and farm-reared meat for your campfire supper.
→ St Winnow Barton, Lostwithiel PL22 0LF 01208 872327 🏠 🍴

11 ST WINNOW

Food

12 POTAGER GLASSHOUSE CAFE

Two beautiful light and airy glasshouses sit among the well-designed, highly productive, organic Potager gardens. Relax in one of the many hammocks, play on the lawn, or head inside for a game of post-lunch ping pong. The home-cooked food is incredible – many of the ingredients come from the café's organic gardens; all the rest are organic, wholesome and smothered in love. In winter, woodburners heat the interior and there are plenty of toys to keep the children happy. This is a truly sustainable and stylish project, and not to be missed.
→ High Cross, Constantine, Falmouth, TR11 5RF 01326 341258 potagergarden.org
☼ Easter–Oct Fri–Sun 10–5pm 🍷 🍴

13 DUCHY OF CORNWALL NURSERY

On the edge of Lostwithiel, up fern-clad sunken lanes, you'll find the Duchy of Cornwall Nursery lifestyle shop and café. Offering incredible views of ruined Restormel Castle, the nursery looks out over a valley with steep slopes covered in wild flowers and woods. Seating is indoors or out on the sunny terrace, where everything from just coffee to the freshest seafood, salads, and hearty lunches is on offer – all made with local, sustainable produce, according to the Duchy ethos. The café is fully licensed and on chilly days the woodburner is lit.
→ Cott Road, Lostwithiel, PL22 0HW, 01208 872668 duchyofcornwallnursery.co.uk
☼ daily 9–5pm (Sundays 10–5pm) 🍴 🌿

12 POTAGER GLASSHOUSE CAFE

10 BOTELET FARM

13 DUCHY OF CORNWALL NURSERY

14 PENCARROW PEACOCK CAFÉ

Approached along an ancient drive bordered by oaks, and with its own Iron Age hill fort, Pencarrow estate is straight out of Tolkien. The lovely Peacock café is housed in the 17th-century vaulted cottage to the back of the Georgian mansion. In the sheltered café gardens, peacocks roam the lawns and drape themselves elegantly over rose-covered arches. The café offers breakfast, lunch, and cream teas, all using the best Cornish produce. There are extensive gardens and wooded walks to explore, while an adorable slate-roofed wendy-house near the café will keep the kids amused for hours. The big house is also open for visits.

Old School Lane, Washaway, PL30 3AG, 01208 841369 pencarrow.co.uk April–Sept, Sun–Thurs 11–5pm

Devon

From the rugged lost world of the Hartland peninsula,
through rolling hills to the ancient moors, settlements,
and tors of Dartmoor, then down to sandy beaches
and the sunshine coast, Devon really has it all.

Devon

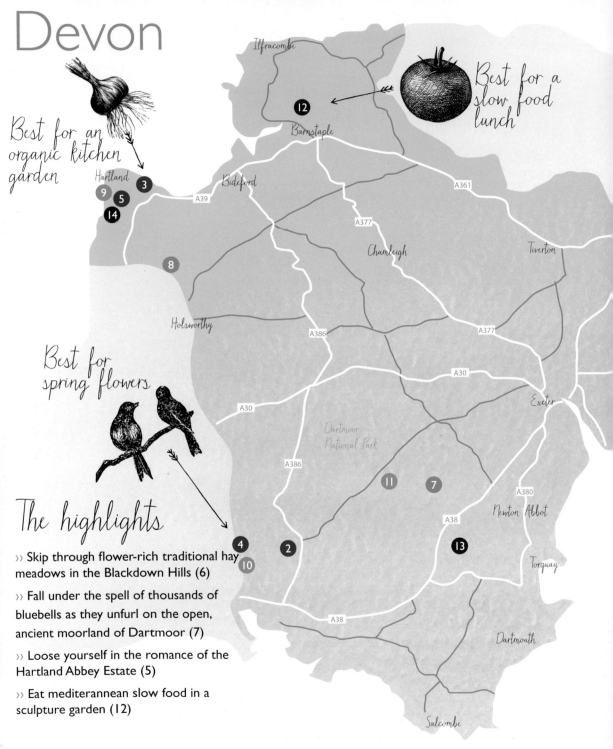

Best for an
organic kitchen
garden

Best for a
slow food
lunch

Ilfracombe

Barnstaple

12

Hartland

9 5

3

14

Bideford

A39

A361

8

A377

Chumleigh

Tiverton

Holsworthy

A386

A377

Best for
spring flowers

A30

A30

A386

Dartmoor
National Park

Exeter

11

7

A380

Newton Abbot

The highlights

A386

A38

13

Torquay

4

2

›› Skip through flower-rich traditional hay
meadows in the Blackdown Hills (6)

10

›› Fall under the spell of thousands of
bluebells as they unfurl on the open,
ancient moorland of Dartmoor (7)

A38

Dartmouth

›› Loose yourself in the romance of the
Hartland Abbey Estate (5)

›› Eat mediterannean slow food in a
sculpture garden (12)

Salcombe

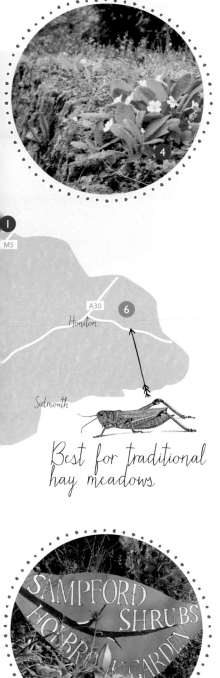

Devon's gardens flourish in quiet valleys and sheltered pockets. Farming dominates the county and organic producers, such as Riverford, have proved that good land husbandry can be sustainable. For a lovely day out, enjoy a communal meal at the Riverford café followed by a tour of the farm. And take inspiration from visits to the organic, walled kitchen garden at National Trust Knightshayes and the secret walled garden at Clovelly. There, you'll see how a productive kitchen garden can be a thing of beauty and abundance.

Spring always seem to arrive early in Devon and Dartmoor, in particular, is a great place to celebrate its reawakening. A haze of bluebells growing not in woodland but on open moor at Emsworthy Mire and Holwell Lawn forms a real spectacle. At Dunsford, native wild daffodils are preserved en masse, their delicate yellow heads making many garden hybrids look ungainly by comparison. Lydford Gorge is another favourite spot for walks and wildflowers; for local food and a cosy fire head to the nearby Elephant's Nest. And don't forget Dartmoor is one of the few places in England where wild camping is actively encouraged, so bring your tent and enjoy the stars.

Holbrook Gardens, near Tiverton, is one of my favourite small, wild gardens. It is a delightful experiment in naturalistic planting and the adjoining nursery is a treasure trove. The Garden House in pretty Buckland Monachorum, north of Plymouth, is a larger, but still intimate garden with meadows, overflowing cottage gardens, and woodland walks that merge with its valley landscape. For a perfect day combine it with a visit to lovely Cotehele and watch the sun setting over the Tamar.

A happy week could be spent exploring the wooded slopes of the River Dart. Enjoy lunch with views of the river from the fair-weather only Vineyard Café at Sharpham estate. Hamblyn's Coombe in Dittisham (NGS openings) is the garden of sculptor Bridget McCrum and exquisitely combines incredible river views, wildflower meadows, woodland gardens, and her own sculptures.

One of my favourite wild garden experiences was at Goren Farm, the home of Julian Pady and family. Their farm in the Blackdown Hills offered a window into a lost world of farming, and is open in summer for the NGS. Wander through ancient hay meadows filled with native wildflowers and drink in the special atmosphere of this truly bucolic idyll.

Best for traditional hay meadows

Gardens

1 HOLBROOK

If you want to buy plants and be inspired by some beautiful wild-style gardening, visit Holbrook, the home of the hugely knowledgeable owners of Sampford Shrubs nursery which is on site. Susan and Martin have created over two acres, a wildlife-rich oasis with innovative planting inspired by the communities that plants form in their natural habitats. The Stone Garden is a constantly evolving delight, showcasing a masterly mix of pollinator-friendly plants that just seems to get better and better as the season progresses. On my first visit in April, the clear spring light picked out the orange-peach tones of the wallflowers. These familiar plants looked truly glorious, the flowers standing out from their bed of blue bugle. Ducks wandered around the gardens, leading us past the open glades of primulas and fritillaries to damper ground. All was colour and life and birdsong. Sampford Shrubs holds the national collection of heleniums, which bloom in swathes throughout the garden in late summer.
→ Holbrook Hill, Sampford Peverell EX16 7EN, 01884 821164 holbrookgarden.com ☼ April–mid Sept Wed, Thur, Fri 10–5pm and many days for NGS 🥤🌿🌷

2 THE GARDEN HOUSE

2 THE GARDEN HOUSE

When I visited in April, many of Devon's trees were still tightly in bud, their branches gaunt and bare. But at the Garden House, spring was off to a thunderous start. The rhododendrons tried to steal the show with their frilly mountains of Barbara Cartland-

1 HOLBROOK

esque pink but they didn't. The stars were the delicate spring bulbs – erythroniums, snakeshead fritillaries, and anemones – naturalised in the grass. Outlined against the blue sky were magnolias covered in pure-white blossom and the church tower. It was idyllic. Everywhere I looked there were people sitting on benches drinking in the sun on that glorious spring day. In summer, the meadow becomes a waist-high tapestry of colour as perennials and annuals bloom among the long grass. As autumn approaches, the glowing acer glade continues the show. The tea room housed in the Old Rectory serves excellent home-made lunches and cream teas.
→ Pound Road, Buckland Monachorum PL20 7LQ, 01822 854769 thegardenhouse.org.uk ☼ Mar–Oct daily, 10.30–5pm (not Mon in low season) 🥤🌿🍴🌷

3 CLOVELLY COURT GARDENS

Leave the crowds at Clovelly village and head to the lovely organic, walled kitchen gardens at the top of the village, near All Saints Church. These truly are a delight to explore. Behind the old walls, the Victorian greenhouses and large open beds are packed full of heritage vegetables and fruits grown for the estate, its pub and cafés. We purchased courgettes, beans, tomatoes, and a beautiful bunch of cut flowers direct from the gardener in the small bothy near the garden entrance. The gardens benefit from the warmth created by the Gulf Stream,

the flowers and fruit clearly thriving here. You can walk down to the village from the garden and enjoy the sea views.
→ Off the B3237, Clovelly, Bideford EX39 5TA, 01237 431781 clovelly.co.uk ☼ daily, summer 9–6pm, winter 10–4pm 🥤

4 COTEHELE

After two weeks of unusually warm weather Easter day was cold and rainy. Yet even on such a gloomy day, Cotehele worked its magic. Nestled in a sheltered spot on the banks of the Tamar Valley, the setting on west-facing slopes is divided into the steep woodland glen and the formal gardens that rise up to the orchards. In April, the glen is a riot of fuchsia pink, white, purple and magenta, while the rhododendrons show off their blousy wares. Among the buildings you come across are a roundhouse topped with a frosting of the purest white doves and, through a maze of ferns and gunnera, a thatched rest-house above a lily pond. But my favourite part of the garden can easily be bypassed. Hidden behind the house to the east, spring bulbs massed under magnolias look like jewels in the grey mist. Mossy walls are blanketed with primroses and even the invasive Spanish bluebells put on a beautiful display.
→ St Dominick, Saltash PL12 6TA, 01579 351346 nationaltrust.org.uk ☼ daily dawn–dusk 🥤🍴🌷

4 COTEHELE

3 CLOVELLY COURT KITCHEN GARDEN

5 HARTLAND ABBEY

The Hartland peninsula is one of my favourite places in Devon – uncrowded, perfect for incredible coastal walks, and with an air of timelessness. Hartland Abbey and its estate, situated in a pretty, verdant valley that leads down to the Atlantic, enjoy the best of this wild landscape. One of our best-loved walks starts at the walled garden and then follows the wooded, marked path down to the beach. In spring, the woods are full of bluebells and joyful with birdsong. Walk past the parkland dotted with black sheep and you'll find the old gardens, sitting inland from the house. Sheltered behind skilfully renovated walls, the sloped gardens , which are backed by oak and native woodland, are simply charming. Each 'room' has a different feel and purpose: vegetables are grown in long beds and there are pretty flower gardens to enjoy. It's easy to lose yourself in this dreamy, romantic spot .

→ Hartland, Bideford, EX39 6DT,
01237 441496 hartlandabbey.com
end-Mar–Sep, Sun–Thu, 11.30–5pm

The farm sits comfortably among the rolling hills, its land a patchwork of ancient hay meadows.

9 BLACKPOOL MILL

Meadows

6 GOREN FARM

Open for the NGS in summer evenings, Goren Farm offers the opportunity to see what the ancient farming landscape of Devon would have looked like. The farm sits comfortably among the rolling hills, its land a patchwork of ancient hay meadows. These have never been ploughed and are used only for hay. The sheer abundance of flowers made the grass unsuitable for fodder and its floriferous diversity led to the creation of Stockland Seeds, a mail-order company selling hand-collected, unenhanced meadow seed. Walking through these fields in midsummer was heavenly.
→ Broadhayes, Stockland, Honiton, EX14 9EN, 01404 881335 goren.co.uk
🗓 June evenings 50.8147,-3.0901 🐦

7 EMSWORTHY MIRE & BECKA BROOK

Enjoy incredible displays of bluebells when they unfurl on this ancient, open moorland. Becka Brook is a river with a mystical atmosphere, its banks covered in mossy rocks and delicate woodland flowers. Crossing the footbridge you emerge onto bluebell-carpeted Holwell Lawn and the medieval ruins at Hound Tor. Bring a map and wear boots as it is often very muddy.
→ Car park on R, 300m W of Saddle Tor on B3387, Dartmoor TQ13 7TT. Start downhill NW for 100m to gate. 50.5716,-3.7692 🐦

8 DUNSDON NATURE RESERVE

Dunsdon is the single most important example of Culm grassland – a unique habitat – in England. A combination of marsh and heathland, Culm grassland has rapidly declined since the 1970s. Over 180 species of flowering plants have been recorded here and in spring and summer the grass is rich with orchids, ragged robbin, and devil's-bit scabious, as well as moths, butterflies, and birdlife. Light grazing by hardy cattle is followed by swailing, a controlled winter burning that removes dead grass and keeps vigorous grasses in check.
→ 30m S of Gains Cross, reserved parking on R. Pancrasweek, Holsworthy EX22 7JW devonwildlifetrust.org 50.8467,-4.4140 🐦

Accommodation

9 BLACKPOOL MILL

The best way to enjoy Hartland is to rent moody and rustic Blackpool Mill. Sitting on the sheltered valley bottom and overlooking the little cove, this 15th-century cottage has neither telephone nor television but lots of character and a woodburner for warmth. It's a great place to escape with friends and enjoy the coastal flora. The Abbey is open for visits and there is a tea-room serving home-made food, or you can visit the farm shop in Hartland village.
→ Bideford, Devon EX39 6DB 01884 860225 hartlandabbey.com 🏠 🐦

8 DUNSDON NATURE RESERVE

10 SOUTH HOOE COUNT HOUSE

We treasure our visits to the Count House with its wonderful views of the Tamar. The nature-tended gardens are home to large oaks, spring bulbs, and frothy mounds of cow parsley, and the grass is mown by the resident donkeys, Arabella and Willow. Owner Trish has created a cosy, light-filled hideaway complete with Rayburn, antiques, and fresh flowers, all in exquisite rustic-chic style. There are canoes to borrow or head to Tavistock for the market. The Count House is available for longer-term winter rental – perfect for that novel you've been meaning to write. The train station at Bere Alston is 2 miles away.

→ South Hooe Mine, Hole's Hole, Bere Alston, Yelverton PL20 7BW, 01822 840329
sawdays.co.uk

10 SOUTH HOOE COUNT HOUSE

11 WILD CAMPING DARTMOOR

Dartmoor National Park is one of the most accessible, truly wild areas in Devon. Its open moorland and magical, pixie-filled woods harbour incredible displays of wild flora set against a truly picturesque landscape. The woodlands erupt in early spring with delicate white wood anemones and wild daffodils, followed by miles of carpeting bluebells and foxgloves. The dark night skies are perfect for stargazing and it's one of the few places in England where we can legally wild camp. There are some rules to respect: no more than one or two nights with a small tent, and camp away from farmland and protected sites. To help you choose a good spot, the national park has created a map and offers guidelines on how to camp safely.

→ dartmoor-npa.gov.uk 01626 832093

10 SOUTH HOOE COUNT HOUSE

Food

12 TERRA MADRE AT BROOMHILL SCULPTURE GARDENS

We love the imaginative slow-food experience at quirky Broomhill sculpture gardens. Food is predominantly sourced from local farms or from their own vegetable garden and greenhouses, with Mediteranean-style dishes inspired by the owners' travels. First-class bakers, they make sourdough in their own wood-fired oven and delicious high teas can be pre-booked, Wednesday to Friday afternoons. If it's sunny, you can enjoy light menus on the outdoor terrace overlooking the garden and sculptures. The location, a deep valley with a river flowing through, is stunning. Broomhill is also a hotel and rooms overlook the gardens. Nearby is Marwood Hill Gardens.

→ Off the B3230 1.6 miles S of Muddiford, Barnstaple EX31 4EX, 01271 850262
broomhillart.co.uk

⏲ pre-booked lunch Wed–Sun, dinner Wed–Sat, high tea Wed–Fri 2.30–4pm

13 HILL HOUSE NURSERY

Hill House Nursery is a lovely place for a simple and delicious light lunch. In summer, enjoy your food on the sunny terrace behind the café and away from the nursery. Here, among mature trees and by the gothic house covered in climbing roses, you can enjoy home-made soups, creative salads, and vegetarian tarts, all served in generous portions. The café is unprentious, cosy and has a doll's house and toys which our daughter adored. The nursery is well stocked and has a good range of tree- and soft fruit, including some unusual varieties.

→ Landscove TQ13 7LY, 01803 762273 hillhousenursery.com
⏲ March–September 11–4.45pm daily

Food is predominantly sourced from local farms or from their own vegetable garden and greenhouses.

14 DOCTON MILL

13 HILL HOUSE NURSERY

14 DOCTON MILL

Enjoy award-winning Devonshire cream teas, salads from the garden, and light lunches in the pretty wildflower-filled gardens that surround renovated Docton Mill. The magical woodland walk is a delight in spring when bluebells, primulas, narcissi and camellias light up its steep, mossy slopes. The owners' overriding aim was to create a garden that in form and planting would be as close to nature as possible, and with a choice of plants dictated by the steep site dotted with rills and streams. Roses have been subtly introduced and there is an orchard and a magnolia garden. Paths are often steep, allowing for a good workout before heading to the tea room for refreshment.

Follow brown signs to Hartland, Lymebridge EX39 6EA, 01237 441369 doctonmill.co.uk
Mar–Sept 10–5pm

GREENCOMBE

Somerset & Exmoor

From the wild coast of Exmoor, to the fertile plains of the Mendips, to green valleys filled with cider orchards and romantic gardens of a time past.

Somerset

The highlights

›› Take tea or enjoy a wood-fired pizza in the utterly delightful walled garden at Mells (14)

›› Fall under the spell of Joan Loraine's magical Exmoor garden (1)

›› Stroll through the resplendent Peto gardens in the verdant Iford valley (3)

›› Discover over a thousand veteran trees in Britain's largest semi-natural, ancient woodland (6)

Best for ancient oak forests

Bristol

M49

M5

M4

Weston-super-Mare

A38

12

2

Mendip Hills

8

A37

Lynton

1

10

Minehead

6

A361

Exmoor National Park

M5

Glastonbury 361

A39

14

Dulverton

11

Bridgwater

4

A37

Taunton

5

A358

7

A303

M5

A303

Chard

Buy traditional cider

Best for a wild Italianate garden

Enjoy a kitchen garden lunch

Bath

13

9 3

A36

Warminster

The rolling hills and little lanes of Somerset are my home: its wooded forms and twisting river valleys are etched permanently in my mind.

But it has much more to offer. The land of the summer people is a diverse landscape where rural farmlands meet the Georgian splendour of Bath and Bristol, and the tiny city of Wells. Highpoints are the Mendip Hills, with their ancient barrows and field systems, and the sublime, flower-filled Cheddar Gorge. Cider orchards rise to the heath and woods of the Quantock Hills and further west to the wild moors and dramatic coastline of Coleridge's Exmoor. For me, it is a bohemian land, where art and landscape go hand in hand.

The most contemporary garden of note is Piet Oudolf's new perennial meadow gardens at the Hauser & Wirth rural art gallery near Bruton. It is gorgeous and worth a visit, not only because it injects a refreshing dose of slickness into the tumbling romance of the region's other 'wild' gardens. My favourite among these is either Cothay or Greencombe. Cothay is pure romance with luscious gardens surrounding the most beautiful moated medieval manor. But Greencombe is pure magic. I was transfixed during my almost spiritual, lily of the valley-scented journey through its mossy, woodland garden. The enormous rhododendrons, camellias, and azaleas create a colourful wonderland set against the backdrop of the Exmoor coast.

Fyne Court is a wonderful, really wild location that blurs the lines between garden and nature reserve. From spring through to summer and into autumn, it is a riot of wildflowers and woodland. Similar in feel, are the landscape gardens of Prior Park near Bath. This is an excellent spot for a February walk through the snowdrop-filled valley.

Another newish and fantastic wildlife-filled garden can be seen at Yeo Valley in the Mendips lowlands. It's the UK's first ornamental garden to be classified as organic by the Soil Association, and it's inspiring to see what can be created in just 20 years. There are lots of courses and events going on here, and a great garden café. And if you want to buy plants, you couldn't do better than head to Derry Watkins' lovely show garden and nursery north of Bath. Her special Tuesdays offer the best horticultural day courses around and the views are stunning.

Gardens

1 GREENCOMBE

If ever there was a secret magical garden, then this is it. Heading up the drive in early May, a sign directed me to 'ring with vigour' the heavy brass bell that lay on the little table. I was welcomed into the garden with directions and an almost overwhelming amount of information. Here were four national collections – erythroniums (dog's-tooth violets), vacciniums (the delicious edible whortleberries), gaultherias (low, berrying shrubs) and polystichums (shield ferns) – the largest champion holly in Britain, etc. etc. Rare species after rare species of camellia, rhododendron, azalea, fern, and lily rolled off the tongue of the venerable plantswoman Joan Loraine. This is the garden she planted and has nurtured over the last 50 years. Although now in a wheelchair and physically unable to garden, she describes the paths and flowers in bloom that day with astonishing accuracy.   This is a wild wild site. Exmoor sits directly behind and in front is Porlock Bay, the landscape of Coleridge. Fully organic, the garden makes and uses tons of leaf litter every year and its owner's love, care, and deep knowledge of plants have created an incredible garden. Paths carpeted with moss like the finest green moleskin led through a wonderland of tree trunks and enormous rhododendrons, the heady scent of lily of the valley adding to the enchantment.
→ Off the B3225 between Porlock and West Porlock, TA24 8NU, 01643 862363 greencombe.wordpress.com
🕒 April–July daily 2–6pm 🍵 🌱

2 YEO VALLEY ORGANIC GARDEN

At the home farm of Yeo Valley dairy are the beautiful, nature-inspired gardens of Sarah and Tim Mead. Over the last 20 years they have created the first Soil Association accredited organic ornamental garden and it's a stunning success. With a backdrop of the Mendip Hills and Blagdon Lake, the six and a half acres of fields have been transformed into an explosion of colour. When we visited in August, the meadow filled with annual yellow cosmidium

1 GREENCOMBE

created a magical late-summer display for our enjoyment as as well as their bees'. The prairie-style gravel garden is beautifully designed and its muted colours and mounded form flows effortlessly into the landscape. Food is delicious, home-grown and decorated with edible flowers. There is also a pretty woodland with native flowers that leads on to a natural hay meadow.
→ Holt Farm, Bath Road, Blagdon BS40 7SQ 01761 461650 theorganicgardens.co.uk
🕒 May–Oct, Thu & Fri 11–5pm
🍵 🐾 🍴 🌱

3 IFORD MANOR

In the beautiful Iford Valley, among rolling wooded hills and lush water meadows, sits a gorgeous Georgian manor. Here, Harold Peto, the celebrated 19th-century architect turned garden designer created an Italianate garden to house his incredible collection of European architectural finds. Inspired by William Robinson and Gertrude Jekyll it is a brilliant example of a successful marriage between formal and natural gardening. Lucky enough to live nearby, I often visit the garden and it is a joy throughout the seasons. In spring, naturalised bulbs, cow parsley and wild hedgerow flowers fill the lawns and steep wooded margins.   Martagon lilies catch the dappled light under the great trees and summer is a floral fantasia of ancient wisteria, irises and roses. The structure is grand and formal with terraces, broad walks, loggias and the cloisters, where operas are often heard drifting across the valley in summer. Planting is abundant and loose, and in this verdant valley setting, nature very much rules.
→ Iford Lane, Iford, Bradford on Avon, BA15 2BA, 01225 863146 ifordmanor.co.uk
🕒 April–Oct, Tue–Thu, Sat, Sun 2–5pm
🍵 🍴

4 FYNE COURT

The once-formal garden of Fyne Court tells the story of a rich family's decline and of an Arcadian garden's re-wilding. Owned by the poet, philosopher, and scientist Andrew Crosse, visitors included William Wordsworth and Frankenstein author Mary Shelley. Crosse was known as the Wizard of Broomfield on account of his experiments with thunder and lightning, and the grounds of his home still retain an air of magic. Beautiful follies, an ivy-covered boathouse and outbuildings are all that remains from the great fire that destroyed the house in 1894. Between these structures and the majestic trees, nature thrives. Birdsong, snowdrops, bluebells, ramsons and cow parsley light up the gardens through spring. There is a great dipping pond with little pontoons for insect-watching and numerous trails to follow.
→ Broomfield, Bridgwater TA5 2EQ, 01643 862452 nationaltrust.org.uk
🕒 daily dawn–dusk 🍵 🐾 🍴

2 YEO VALLEY

3 IFORD

5 COTHAY

Cothay is a dream of a garden. Down narrow winding lanes, the medieval manor rests resplendent in its timeless elegance. At once rustic yet grand, the house and its grounds have a special atmosphere. In spring we had the place almost to ourselves save a few gardeners, some lazy dogs and chickens. We started with tea and a sandwich as it was cold and we were hungry. 'This is the best Earl Grey' said the other tea-room visitor and we had the best home-made seeded rye open sandwich, ever. Revived, we stepped out into the gardens and experienced a whole 12 acres of changing stories. The romance of the 15th-century architecture is a perfect backdrop to the climbers and artfully controlled self-seeders that sprout from every crack. What I really like about Cothay is that wherever you are in the garden, particularly in the more formal garden rooms, there is always a window out into the wilder landscape – a window cut through the yew, an arch, or simply a gap in the hedge. You are always reminded that out there are trees, streams and uncontrolled beauty. The woodland walks are lovely, while informal plantings of camassias and tulips bloom in the spring meadows.

Piley Lane, Greenham, Wellington, TA21 0JR 01823 672283 cothaymanor.co.uk
Apr–Sep Tue, Wed, Thu, Sun & BH 11–5pm

Somerset is renowned for its cider and yet it's surprisingly hard to find orchards where you can see cider made in the traditional way. One of my favourite places is Burrow Hill in pretty Kingsbury Episcopi.

£10

Perry £2.40

8 CHEDDAR GORGE

Meadows

6 HORNER WOODS

Contained within the enormous National Trust Holnicote Estate, the ancient pastures of Horner Woods are full of bluebells in spring and rich with wildlife throughout the year. Classified as an Atlantic Oakwood, it is one of the largest wooded nature reserves in England and one of our best primary forests. The two metres of annual rainfall create a jungly Hobbit-like atmosphere, and there are bryophytes (mosses, liverworts, hornworts) hanging from 500-year-old sessile oaks.
→ A 1-hour, 2-mile loop start SW corner of Horner Village (opposite tea room). Exmoor National Park, Minehead TA24 8HY 51.1963,-3.5800

7 BURROW HILL CIDER ORCHARD

Somerset is renowned for its cider and yet it's surprisingly hard to find orchards where you can see cider being made traditionally. One of my favourites is Burrow Hill in pretty Kingsbury Episcopi where apples have been grown and pressed for cider for over 150 years. You can see the old presses and stills in the rustic barns and there is a lovely orchard trail. When sheep graze under the spring blossom or in the golden autumn light when the trees are heavy with fruit, the effect is pure Constable.
→ Burrow Hill, Burrow Way, Kingsbury Episcopi, TA12 6BU, 01460 240782 ciderbrandy.co.uk ☒ daily except Sunday 9am–5.30pm 50.9764,-2.8345

8 CHEDDAR GORGE

At over 120 metres deep and 3 miles long, Cheddar Gorge is spectacular. A good circular walk takes in the grassland of the limestone cliff tops. The walk is best done in summer when harebells, Cheddar bedstraw, and the rare Cheddar pink bloom among the scented marjoram and wild thyme.
→ Start up Cufic Lane off Cliff Rd, Cheddar BS27 3QE, take path R through wood, R with gorge on R to kissing gate. Descend on path R to road. Cross L and ascend bearing R at fork. Descend to start via Jacob's Ladder. 1.5 hours 51.2819,-2.7669

Accommodation

9 ABBOTSLEIGH COTTAGE

Abbotsleigh, a stylish holiday apartment in the glorious village of Freshford just outside of Bath, is the home of our friends Phil and Naomi. They have crafted everything to the highest standards and the views across the valley are divine, especially in winter. You are free to wander the sheltered garden and sit on the terrace. From the local train station, the city of Bath is just one stop.
→ Rosemary Lane, Freshford, Bath BA2 7UD 01225 722218 abbotsleighcottage.com

9 ABBOTSLEIGH COTTAGE

57

10 HINDON ORGANIC FARM

Perfectly suited for forays around Exmoor, Hindon is a working organic farm that is Soil Association certified. Arriving down a narrow lane you are greeted by a really rustic sight. The yellow farmhouse, complete with small cottage garden, is covered with wisteria and roses; there are geese, ducks, chickens, and a Morris Minor in the yard, as well as the all-important horse, head hanging over the gate. Hosts Penny and Roger are happy to introduce you to the new arrivals, such as calves and piglets, and breakfast includes farm sausage and eggs. Separate from the farmhouse, which does B&B, is a self-catering cottage with three bedrooms.

➔ Nr Selworthy, Minehead, Exmoor TA24 8SH 01643 705244 hindonfarm.co.uk 🏠

11 PARSONAGE FARM

Run on organic principles, idyllic Parsonage Farm is a flower-filled smallholding that aims to be as self-sufficient as possible. Here, bees and chickens forage among the fruit, vegetables, and flowers in the sunny south-facing walled garden. Breakfast includes home-made bread and home-grown produce as well as apple juice from the orchard. On request, you can enjoy a candlelit supper in front of the fire, or on summer Friday evenings, delicious wood fired pizzas in the garden. There are lots of wonderful walks in the area, including foraging for whortleberries on Quantock Common in August.

➔ Over Stowey, TA5 1HA, 01278 733237 parsonfarm.co.uk 🏠 🍽

10 HINDON ORGANIC

Food

12 THE ETHICUREAN RESTAURANT

The Ethicurean is one of our favourite places for a long lunch with friends. Settled at long wooden tables in the glasshouse, you will be served a consistently delicious, mouth-watering array of seasonal produce grown in the gardens, supplemented by local fare. Thoughtful food has won this young and friendly enterprise many accolades, and deservedly so. Local produce, including beers and ciders (and their cookbook), is available on site and if you live close by, a veg-box scheme runs from the restored Victorian kitchen garden, full of heritage and heirloom varieties.

➔ Barley Wood Walled Garden, Long Lane, Wrington BS40 5SA 01934 863713 theethicurean.com ⏰ All year Tue–Thu 11–4pm; Fri, Sat 11–11.30pm, Sun 10–5pm (afternoon tea Tue–Sun from 4pm) 🍷 🍽

13 SAM'S KITCHEN HOLT

At the stylish Glove Factory Studios, Sam's kitchen café serves everything from fantastic coffee right through to roasted suckling pig on Sunday. All food is home-made and sourced with an eye for quality, and artisanal care. It's a great place to bring the Sunday newspapers and then head across the road for a wander around the National Trust's Courts Gardens. Also nearby are the ancient gardens of Great Chalfield (and a fantastic B&B) and a little further, the divine Italianate Iford garden.

➔ Glove Factory Studios, 1 Brook Lane, Holt, BA14 6RL, 01225 784081 samskitchendeli.co.uk ⏰ daily 8–5pm (Sat 9–4pm, Sun 10–4pm) 🍽

I like to take my tea and cake to the sunny secret terrace overlooking the fields and grazing cattle.

12 THE ETHICUREAN

13 SAM'S KITCHEN

14 THE WALLED GARDEN MELLS

14 THE WALLED GARDEN MELLS

We just love the garden, food and ambience that fills the Walled Garden in the pretty Somerset village of Mells. Through the stone arches and within the old walls are large beds full of delightful cottage plants. The garden supplies cut flowers for weddings, and there is a charming florist's shop on site, where you can buy a bunch to take home. The excellent garden café serves home-made light lunches and teas, and at week-end lunchtimes they light the wood-fired pizza oven. Food can be enjoyed in the vintage finds-filled glasshouse or at any table within the garden. I like to take my tea and cake to the sunny secret terrace overlooking the fields and grazing cattle. A range of courses are offered, including planting design and art classes.

Rectory Garden, Selwood Street, Mells BA11 3PN 01373 812597
thewalledgardenatmells.co.uk
Mar–Oct daily 10–5pm

GILBERT WHITE'S HOUSE

Dorset, Hants & Wilts

Here rolling vales of Hardy's Dorset give way to the cliffs of the Jurassic coast. Journey through the wooded heaths of the New Forest to the chalk downlands that stretch across Dorset to Salisbury plain and beyond.

Dorset, Hants & Wilts

The highlights

>> Get far from the madding crowd and head to the enchanting valley at Mapperton (4)

>> Revel in the wildlife-rich meadows described by naturalist Gilbert White (1)

>> Rejoice in spring's glorious floral profusion at Cranborne Manor Gardens (5)

>> Count butterflies and glow worms at Kingcombe (7)

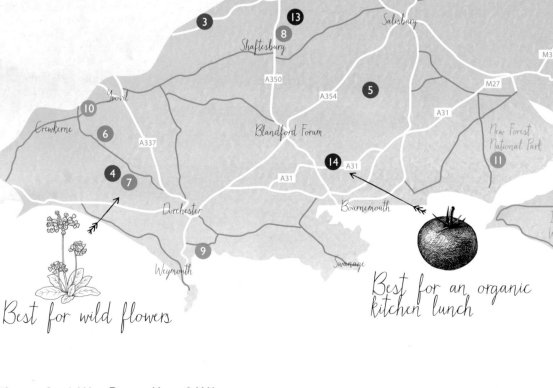

Best for wild flowers

Best for an organic kitchen lunch

This is a diverse and rich landscape packed full of wonderful wildflower meadows and secret gardens, just waiting to be discovered.

One of my most memorable summer days out was spent on Hampshire's South Downs and in the beautiful garden of naturalist and ecologist Gilbert White. Through his meticulous garden observations and recordings, White was to transform the way we look at the natural world. In 1770 he proclaimed: 'Earthworms, though in appearance a small and despicable link in the chain of nature, yet, if lost, would make a lamentable chasm. Worms seem to be the great promoters of vegetation, which would proceed but lamely without them'. Across from his garden, a stunning cricket- and butterfly-filled hay meadow was quivering with life.

After lunch we continued our day out exploring Selborne Common and its hanging beech woods. Derived from the old English word 'hangra', meaning a steep, wooded slope, the Hangers are a protected area and form two distinct 'steps' down from the chalk downland to the floor of the Weald. The Hangers Way is a 21-mile waymarked walk across the landscape or take the Zig-Zag or the Bostal path devised by White. Looked after by the National Trust, the area is renowned for its chalk grassland flowers. There are information boards that map out walks from the village.

For Dorset meadows we head to Ryewater Farm, Powerstock or Kingcombe where ancient hill forts and traditional hay meadows offer stunning views and richly biodiverse habitats. These are great places for spotting glowworm after watching the sunset.

Not far from from Kingcombe meadows is one garden that will surely fill your heart with joy. Mapperton nestles in a tiny coombe and within its boundary of trees is a magical country garden that balances its formal 'bones' with glorious tumbling climbers and wildflower banks. The Jacobean manor, its romantic gardens and bucolic farmland were used as the film set for Hardy's *Far from the Madding Crowd*. And you can also eat here: Sawmill Café serves delicious salads.

Basingstoke

M3

A31

M27

Portsmouth

Gardens

1 GILBERT WHITE'S HOUSE

Near species-rich Selborne Common amid a landscape of ancient woodlands, 18th-century naturalist Gilbert White planted his experimental garden and studied the insect-filled meadows. Much of the surrounding area is owned by the Natural Trust and is criss-crossed by footpaths through which you can walk and discover its incredible biodiversity. The garden is managed in accordance with the journals of Gilbert White and the 'Six Quarters Garden' is a showcase for the plants studied by White. A 'quarter' in the 18th century meant a flower bed, and in each was a particular seasonal display of native and common flowering plants. The wild garden areas remain unweeded and unmown, and among nettles and purple loosestrife is a natural pond with a viewing platform where children can see newts and dragonflies. There are kitchen gardens and orchards but my favourite place is Gilbert's Great Mead, a humming, traditionally managed meadow full of wildflowers and insects. A path takes you to the delightful barrel seat, created by White for its wonderful views. Set on its hillock, the seat turns through 360 degrees.
→ Selborne, Alton, Hampshire GU34 3JH 01420 511275 gilbertwhiteshouse.org.uk
⏱ Mid Feb–Oct, Tue–Sun 10.30–5.15pm (4.30pm in winter) 🍵 🌿 🍽 🌸

2 HEALE HOUSE

2 HEALE HOUSE

For quintessential Wiltshire romance, spend a summer afternoon wandering through the gardens of Heale House. The garden is perfectly situated and incorporates the meandering, shallow stream of the trout-filled river Avon into its natural design. Moving away from the attractive house, past nepeta (catmint) and the overflowing branches of roses, the garden becomes wilder and wilder. Roses cascade freely into walks of long grass, dotted with pyramidal and common spotted orchids. Along the chalk riverbank, the woodland garden is full of colour in spring and a verdant yet shady, secret place in summer. Follow the wide arbour of espaliered apples into the kitchen garden and you will be greeted by towering artichokes and scented towers of sweet peas. There is a simple and cosy tea room serving cakes and seasonal soups; pre-book for Sunday lunch.
→ Middle Woodford, Wiltshire SP4 6NT 01722 782504 healegarden.co.uk
⏱ April– Sept Wed–Sat, 10–5pm, Sun & BH 11–4pm 🍵 🌿 🍽 🌸

3 SNAPE COTTAGE

Up the road from Chaffeymoors and Abbey Plants nestles Snape Cottage. Pass the workshop where Ian makes Snape Stakes, down to where Angela's cottage garden unfolds. The cottage has been the couple's home for some 30 years and their garden is a relaxed space, planted in a naturalistic style, and holding a treasured collection of old-fashioned varieties, such as gentleman's button (a glossy, glorious double buttercup) and double red campions. Angela has always gardened in harmony with nature and takes a special interest in the history of plants.
→ Chaffeymoor Hill, Chaffeymoor, Dorset SP8 5BY 01747 840330 snapecottagegarden. co.uk ⏱ check website for opening times 🍵 🌿 🌸

4 MAPPERTON

Tucked away in the rolling Dorset Hills, Mapperton is a gorgeous Elizabethan manor and the family home of the Earl and Countess of Sandwich. Go through entrance gates crowned with eagle sculptures and enter an enchanted space. The garden seems to be surrounded and protected by the valley's trees, which provide a constant reminder of its bucolic location. The formal topiary garden with its water, statues, and follies is further enhanced by the carefree, self-seeding *erigeron* (fleabane), long-limbed hanging roses, and swathes of uncut meadow flowers. Water is a constant presence and trickles its way through lead and stone structures. Throughout the garden, birds, bugs and plantlife thrive under the love and care of the owners and David, the lovely head gardener. The intimacy of the space, unfussy and abundant plantings, and ridiculously pretty location make this one of my favourite gardens to visit. Excellent café.
→ Mapperton, Beaminster, Dorset DT8 3NR 01308 862645 mapperton.com
⏱ Mar–Oct, Mon–Sat, 11–5pm 🍵 🍽

4 MAPPERTON

3 SNAPE COTTAGE

5 CRANBORNE MANOR

The wild gardens of Cranborne Manor are among my favourite finds. The old kitchen garden is protected by medieval walls and doors open out into flower-rich meadows, where large bronze sculptures seemed to float upon floral seas. Visiting in May, new growth was unfurling at a phenomenal rate in the late spring sunshine. Cowslips, cow parsley, buttercups and bluebells created the floral understorey to the emerging trees and their blossom. The wide paths mown through the floral froth only seemed to intensify the impact of spring's bounty, while clipped yew and grand wrought-iron gates provided structure and a reminder that this was a cultivated garden. The orchard, my particular favourite, was definitely at its peak that day. Flower-smothered grass and blossom-covered trees made it hard to know where the ground stopped and the canopy began. The rest of the gardens are more formal and are designed to celebrate the ancient espaliered trees that give them structure. The Old Potting Shed tea room in the large plant nursery is open daily.

Cranborne, Wimborne BH21

5PP 01752 517248 cranborne.co.uk

Mar–Sep, Wed 9–4pm

Summer presented us
with butterfly-rich fields
blooming with delightfully
named corky-fruited water
dropwort, yellow rattle,
dyers greenweed and a few
remaining common spotted
orchids

8 OYSTERS COPPICE

Meadows

6 RYEWATER FARM SSSI

At Ryewater, long, thin hay meadows bordered by deep hedges and dotted with large oaks provide the perfect combination of meadow, hedge and margin loved by insects and butterflies. The farm is managed organically and the surrounding ancient woodlands add to its rich biodiversity. In spring, they are carpeted with wood anemones. Mid-summer presented us with butterfly-rich fields blooming with delightfully named corky-fruited water-dropwort, yellow rattle, dyer's greenweed, and a few remaining common spotted orchids.

→ No official parking at reserve, or village. 1st gate on R Ryewater Lane, Dorchester, Dorset DT2 0QF plantlife.org.uk. 50.8569,-2.6898 ⚐

7 KINGCOMBE MEADOWS

Step back in time and rejoice in the wild flowers and butterflies that thrive at Kingcombe. Along the little river Hooke, the patchwork of unimproved grassland, the old hedges, streams and ponds create a rich, thriving natural habitat. See cowslips in April, bluebells in May, and heath spotted orchids in the wet meadows in June. Nearby, on the wooded slopes of Powerstock Common you'll find the elusive bee orchid, massed bluebells, and fantastic views to the sea. End the day with a fresh-fish supper at the Three Horseshoes Inn in Powerstock.

→ Park at The Kingcombe Centre (great café) and follow meadow paths. Lower Porcorum, Dorchester DT2 0EQ 01300 320684 kingcombe.org 50.7892,-2.6334 ⚐ ⬤

8 OYSTERS COPPICE

I had written to Wiltshire Wildlife to see if the wild daffodils were still out. After a very damp winter with no real cold spells, spring was early and I did not want to miss their dainty display. I wasn't disappointed: the small oak wood was full of magic, birdsong and the promise of bluebells to come.

→ 4 miles NE of Shaftesbury. Britmore Lane, Gutch Common, Wiltshire SP7 9AZ wiltshirewildlife.org 51.0316,-2.1504 ⚐

Accommodation

9 EWELEAZE FARM

Camp, glamp, or rent a holiday cottage at this lovely, small organic farm where you can wander down flowery tracks with views of the sea and the rolling Dorset countryside. There is a private beach that is part of the Jurassic Coast World Heritage site and the SW Coast Path is minutes away. The onsite shop sells a wide range of produce from the nearby farms.

→ 2.7 mile walk from Weymouth train station E along coast path. Off A353 Osmington, Dorset DT3 6ED 01305 833690 eweleaze.co.uk 🏠 ⬤

9 EWELEAZE FARM

10 LOWER SEVERALLS FARMHOUSE B&B

It's not everywhere that you can expect to be welcomed by a large pig snorting happily around the garden. At this lovely 17th-century Ham-stone farmhouse B&B on the Somerset/Dorset border there are three acres of beautiful cottage gardens to explore, complete with pig. Your hosts, Mary and Mike, are experienced cooks and horticulturalists and as well as making you delicious breakfasts with their home-grown produce, will happily share their knowledge about the many fantastic local gardens and plant nurseries. We love visiting Picket Lane Nursery in summer, when you can wander through the flowery horse meadows.

→ I mile NE of Crewkerne off the A30. Lower Severalls, Crewkerne, Somerset TA18 7NX
01460 73234 lowerseverallsfarmhouse.co.uk

It's not everywhere that you can expect to be welcomed by a large pig snorting happily around the garden but you can at this lovely farmhouse B&B on the Somerset, Dorset border

10 LOWER SEVERALLS FARMHOUSE B&B

11 THE PIG HOTEL

Deep in the New Forest, at Brockenhurst, you'll come across The Pig. It's a great place to stay, relax, and wander around the wildflower orchard and kitchen gardens. Visit the pigs and chickens, and talk to the gardeners about what they have been growing for the kitchen or foraging for. There is even a smokehouse and a wood-fired pizza oven and although such things have become a bit of a cliché, The Pig just does them very well. The conservatory dining room is a beautiful space to enjoy a delicious lunch, or find a cosy spot by the fire and enjoy home-reared produce with a glass of red wine.

→ Beaulieu Road, Brockenhurst, Hampshire SO42 7QL, 01590 622354 thepighotel.com

Food

12 THE WELLINGTON ARMS

This excellent country pub (with two bedrooms) has won lots of awards and accolades for its unpretentious local food. Much of it comes from the garden, the polytunnel, or nearby organic farms. It is small, so do book ahead. In summer, eat outside in the garden and see many of the ingredients growing. The chickens and pigs

12 THE WELLINGTON ARMS

enjoy the vegetable peelings and the whole experience is of the super-slick good life.
Baughurst Road, Baughurst, Hants RG26 5LP, 0118 9820110 thewellingtonarms.com
🕐 daily (not Sun eve) 🍴 🏠

13 PYTHOUSE RESTAURANT

Within the beautiful 18th century walled gardens, the airy Pythouse restaurant is situated in the renovated glasshouse. Inside, the décor is bare wood, reclaimed furniture, and glowing woodburner. Outside, you can sit under the apple trees or on the sunny terrace. Food is a delicious offering of fancy, fully English breakfasts and gourmet burgers on Friday nights. Dictated by what is growing in the garden, the menu constantly changes and makes good use of flowers and herbs. Veg as well as local produce can be purchased from the shop and there are always cut flowers available.

→ Newtown, West Hatch, Tisbury, Wiltshire SP3 6PA, 01747 870444
pythousekitchengarden.co.uk
🕐 Apr–Sept Wed–Mon 9–5.30pm, Fri and Sat for dinner. Oct–Mar Wed–Sun 9–5pm

11 THE PIG HOTEL

13 THE PYTHOUSE RESTAURANT

14 SQUASH COURT CAFÉ

Enjoy delicious home-made quiches, salads, and hearty soups made with produce from the Deans Court Garden. Its serpentine-walled kitchen garden was the first organic garden in the country to be Soil Association accredited and a veg box scheme serves the local community. The 13 acres of kitchen garden, orchards, wild and more formal gardens are not open to the public except on a couple of days in summer for NGS. The cosy café is open and full of bohemian ladies, and there is a lovely courtyard where you can eat al fresco. A lifestyle shop opposite the café sells cut flowers, vegetables and eggs from the garden, and vintage homewares.

2 Deans Court Lane, Wimborne, Dorset BH21 1EE 01202 639249
deanscourt.org
Tues–Sat 10–4pm

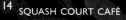

SNOWSHILL

Cotswolds

The Cotswolds is our island's largest Area of Outstanding Natural Beauty. Its romantic Arts & Crafts gardens, water meadows and woods are breathtakingly beautiful.

Cotswolds

The highlights

›› Discover the romantic walled garden and wild woodland walks at Cerney House (1)

›› Take a springtime walk through the South West's largest ancient woodland (6)

›› See eighty percent of Britain's wild snakes head fritillaries growing in the water meadows at Cricklade (5)

›› Indulge in a delicious Vegetable Garden Menu at Barnsley House Hotel (11)

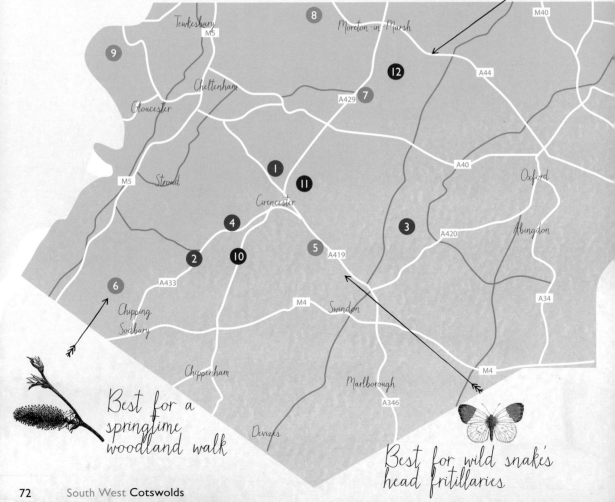

Best for a springtime woodland walk

Best for wild snake's head fritillaries

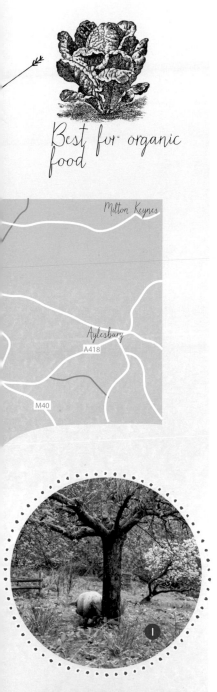

Best for organic food

The Cotswolds' oolitic limestone dominates and dictates the character of this region. It formed the rolling hills, and provided the raw material for the iconic dry-stone walls and honey-coloured houses. Pretty and prosperous, the area is still dominated by sheep and arable farming.

Over 50 per cent of the UK's total Jurassic unimproved limestone grassland is found within its stone walls and on its hills. Home to rare species of orchid, pasque flowers, and Cotswold pennycress, the total area of this precious wildflower grassland has declined dramatically over the last 90 years – from 40 per cent of the Cotswolds in the 1930s, to less than 1.5 per cent currently. Where it remains, such as at Cricklade and Greystone Farm, the land is protected and its seed used for the restoration of other meadows. The Cotswolds also possess horticultural riches: you can visit the world-famous gardens of Hidcote, Kiftsgate, and Highgrove, among many others.

Maybe it was on account of its accessibility from London, as well as its beauty, that that the area became the heartland for the hugely influential Arts and Crafts movement. Masterminded by John Ruskin and William Morris, the group placed a high value on craftsmanship, promoted the use of local materials, and favoured designs inspired by nature. William Morris chose Kelmscott Manor to be his country retreat, believing it to be a place of peace, in harmony with its surroundings, and a work of true craftsmanship. In its garden he found the inspiration to create some of Britain's most enduring floral designs. The garden, although small, presented a vision of simple, flowering beauty when we visited in spring and the museum is a lovely place to pay homage. For many, Morris's socialist and pro-environmental ideals remain equally relevant today.

For other glorious Arts and Crafts gardens that rejoice in the 'nature as divine leader' philosophy, head to Rodmarton and Asthall Manor. Both gardens, in different but equally glorious ways, use their fine bones and formal layout as excuse to relax and go a little wild with the planting.

Milton Keynes

Aylesbury

A418

M40

73

Gardens

I CERNEY HOUSE

The secret gardens of Cerney House exude romance. In the walled gardens and along the woodland paths, wildflowers, tangles of ivy and climbing roses create a scent-filled paradise, just waiting to be explored. We visited on a warm spring day, running for cover to the delightful bothy and tea room to hide from the April showers. Inside you are welcome to help yourself to home-made cakes and tea. There are jams and local cheeses for sale in the fridge and you can sit in the adjoining pottery and read vintage copies of *The Garden*. Outside, when the sun reappeared, the hidden garden was lit up in a rainbow of colour. A predominantly working kitchen garden, it was filled with a dazzling array of tulips, lilies, and lilacs growing between the bean poles. Roses tumbled from the arches and in the distance pigs snuffled in the blossoming orchard. Outside the walled garden, along little paths through acres of wild garlic and bluebells, sculptures seem to survey the wooded landscape or hide in the ivy-covered stone ruins. It is a loosely formal garden, with a wild yet nurtured feel, and full of interesting and rare plants.

→ Signed off A435. North Cerney, Cirencester, Glos GL7 7BX, 01285 831044 cerneygardens.com

⏰ Mid-Jan–Oct, daily 10–5pm 🍵 🌱 🍴

2 HIGHGROVE

At about £25, a ticket to Highgrove garden is very expensive and as you wander through the famous camassia-filled meadows you constantly feel you are being watched. Maybe you are, but don't let it put you off. All visits are led by knowledgeable and charming guides who unravel the story behind Prince Charles's lifelong mission to advance organic and biodiverse gardening and farming in every way he can. Personally, I admire him greatly for this. Highgrove provides a fascinating insight into what is essentially a private, experimental garden that aims to deliver beauty alongside a rich wildlife habitat. The iconic wildflower meadow really is as

I CERNEY HOUSE

beautiful as all the professional pictures you will see of it (note no photography). Managed as a traditional hay meadow, it begins the season with spring daffodils and then is continuously refreshed with a splendiferous array of naturalised bulbs and wildflowers native to the Gloucestershire area. There is much more to the gardens than just the meadows – a fantastical stumpery designed by the Bannerman duo, a fairytale treehouse, a smart kitchen garden, woodland and a thyme walk, as well as orchards and open glades filled with the national collection of beeches.

→ Doughton, Tetbury, Glos GL8 8TN 0207 766 7310 highgrovegardens.com

⏰ Apr–Oct 🍵 🌱 🍴 🌼

3 KELMSCOTT

3 KELMSCOTT MANOR

Artist, designer, writer, publisher, and socialist, William Morris was a highly influential figure. To visit his house, Kelmscott, and its gardens is to experience for yourself the beautiful location that inspired his designs and the 'honest craftsmanship' that he idealised. It was here that he and the Pre-Raphaelite artist, Dante Gabriel Rossetti, retreated when they wanted to escape London and immerse themselves in the natural world. The garden is not very big – in fact it is small – but it is lovely, especially in spring. In Morris's time, the garden would have been more cottagey in style and filled to the brim with food and flowers. Piece by piece, it is slowly being re-woven and re-planted following the evidence found in Morris's beautiful designs. Here you can see the range of plants that provided the content for the patterns, including roses, willow, fritillary and honeysuckle and the millefleurs of tiny meadow bulbs decorate the orchard again. The house is a delightful testament to his vision and art. After visiting, I experienced a renewed, if not somewhat rebellious, focus for my art as a gardener, a lover of beauty and of hand-made craft. Visit yourself and be inspired.

→ Kelmscott, Lechlade, Glos, GL7 3HJ, 01367 252486 sal.org.uk

⏰ Apr–Oct Wed & Sat 11–5pm 🍵 🍴

4 RODMARTON MANOR

I love the overflowing gardens that surround the Arts and Crafts manor of Rodmarton. Within its formal lines of clipped hedges, topiary, pleached limes, double borders and walls, is an unaffected profusion of wild plantings. The long terrace is a riot of self-seeded plants that have made their homes in the cracks and crevices, and it looks out over the ha-ha to the wildflower meadow and the fields beyond. In front of the topiary sits the delightful 'troughery' where miniature alpine gardens are laid out in weathered stone basins. Everywhere you look, there are paths too narrow to negotiate without pushing aside branches and boughs, moss-covered mill stones and high trees, and the whole effect is of a verdant country paradise. In the kitchen garden the battle between unruly nature and ordered vegetable gardening is very apparent. Ancient espaliered apples hold more moss than fruit ,and goldfinches feast on the thistles. The wonderful double borders lead the visitor from the rose-covered gazebo towards the stone dipping-pond surrounded by wild strawberries, ferns, and the froth of *alchemilla mollis.* The winning combination of rigid but mis-angled clipped yew and old walls and paths overhung with flowers works to delightful effect – almost a pastiche of what a Cotswold garden should be.

Off A433. Rodmarton, Glos GL7 6PF
01285 841442 rodmarton-manor.co.uk
May–Sep Wed, Sat & BH 2–5pm

There is something magical about the snake's head fritillary. It seems far too unusual and exotic to be one of our native wild flowers.

6 LOWER WOODS

Meadows

5 CRICKLADE NORTH MEADOW NNR

Intensive farming practices devastated the colonies of snake's head fritillary that thrived in damp lowland meadows. Thanks to its common-land status, Cricklade evaded the plough and now contains 80 per cent of Britain's wild stock. From April to May you can see the delicate flowers, which cover the reserve's 110 acres. The splendour continues into summer when other meadow flowers provide nectar for the rich insect life. Harvested in July, their seed is used for grassland restoration projects.
→ 20 mins walk NW of Cricklade or roadside parking near reserve entrance on High St, Cricklade, SN6 6DQ naturalengland.org.uk 51.6503,-1.8666

6 LOWER WOODS

The largest ancient woodlands in the South West are simply bursting with the magic only very old woods seem to retain. The medieval landscape of coppices, grassy lanes, known as 'trenches' and narrow strips of grazed common land has created a rich floral landscape. Coppiced once again, the woods are flourishing. Violets, bluebells, primroses, wood anemones, celandines and early purple orchids raised their tiny, joyful heads on our springtime walk.
→ Trails from Lower Woods Lodge car park, Inglestone Common, Wickwar, Glos GL9 1BY (track opp Inglestone Farm Cottages) 01452 383333 gloucestershirewildlifetrust.co.uk 51.5911,-2.3679

7 GREYSTONES FARM SSSI

Bustling Bourton-on-the-Water seems like a world away from nearby Salmonsbury Meadows, home to the farm. Information boards offer walks around Neolithic earthworks and the Meadows. Wildflower-rich Hypesleys Meads, along the river Eye, is grazed in late July by the longhorn cattle who digest the rough fodder. Their milk is used in organic single Gloucester cheese.
→ Greystones Ln, Bourton-on-the-Water, Glos GL54 2EN, 01452 383333 gloucestershirewildlifetrust.co.uk 51.8866,-1.7501

Accommodation

8 SNOWSHILL MANOR ESTATE

The National Trust holiday lets on the Snowshill estate are everything you would expect. The cosy, well-decorated cottages with terraced gardens and rose-covered porches, are set in a picture-book village, complete with good, local pub, on the top of the Cotswold escarpment. Best of all, you have access to Snowshill Manor, the incredible home and garden of artistic kleptomaniac, Charles Wade.
→ Snowshill, Nr Broadway, Glos WR12 7JU, 01386 852410 nationaltrustcottages.co.uk

8 SNOWSHILL

9 PAUNTLEY COURT

This part-Elizabethan, part-medieval, part-Georgian house is reputed to have been where Dick Whittington lived, before he departed for the gold-paved streets of London. Why would he leave such a stunning house, its garden filled with Elizabethan quinces and medlars, herb parterres, and pleached hornbeams. There is a lovely old mill pond where you can fish, take walks along the river Leadon, or hide out in the Bedouin tent in the garden. Accommodation ranges from scrumptious B&B bedrooms to a romantic self-catering holiday let.

→ Pauntley Court Drive, Redmarley, Glos GL19 3JA, 01531 828627 pauntleycourt.com

Food

10 THE POTTING SHED PUB

We love the cosy Potting Shed pub. Its food is delicious hearty fare, made with produce from the two-acre garden, plus local game, meats and cheeses. The menu changes according to the season, and I blame their divine rosemary and garden pear cocktails for the very unexpected marriage proposal I received one crisp All Hallows' Eve. Satisfactorily fed, I said yes. Although near a busy road, the garden is at the back well away from the noise and sheltered by apple trees. Dogs and wellies welcome. Off A429. The Street, Crudwell, Malmesbury, Wilts SN16 9EW 01666 577833 thepottingshedpub.com

> *Take time to wander around the gardens designed by Rosemary Verey, the kitchen gardens and the ancient meadows and romantic corners.*

11 BARNSLEY HOUSE

For a special lunch, choose something from the Barnsley Vegetable Garden Menu at the informally decadent Barnsley House hotel. Served every weekday and Saturday, in the garden or in the airy Potager Restaurant, dishes feature locally sourced, first-class produce with all vegetables home-grown in the hotel's garden. Take time to wander around the ornamental gardens designed by Rosemary Verey, the kitchen gardens, and the ancient meadows and romantic corners that make this such a special place.

→ Off the B4425 Barnsley, Cirencester, Glos GL7 5EE, 01285 740000 barnsleyhouse.com

11 BARNSLEY HOUSE

12 DAYLESFORD ORGANIC

Visit the award-winning café at Daylesford organic farm and enjoy delicious, and of course organic, food fresh from the market garden and pastures surrounding the café complex. It's all very stylish and the food is good, the deli excellent and if you have time, wander around Daylesford's Chelsea garden behind the pigs in their hazel coppice. The small garden is surrounded by apple trees, and in summer delicate ragged robin pokes its dotted through the long grass. A green oak, glass and sedum-roofed summerhouse sits in the centre and behind vegetable beds. Eat, drink, and be inspired but beware, a visit to the farm is never a cheap excursion. Daylesford, Nr Kingham, Glos GL56 0YG 01608 731700 daylesford.com Mon–Wed 9–5pm, Thu–Sat 9–6pm, Sun 10–4pm

9 PAUNTLEY COURT

HUGHENDEN ESTATE PARKLANDS

Surrey & Thames Valley

Dominated by the chalk ridge of the North Downs and by the towns and villages that mirror the winding course of the River Thames.

Surrey & Thames Valley

Best for birds and bees

The highlights

›› Learn about biodynamic farming at Waltham Place, with its inspiring approach to wild gardening (1)

›› Feel like Alice in Wonderland in the sylvan setting of the Hannah Peschar Sculpture Garden (4)

›› Enjoy a candlelit supper club at Brockdale Cottage, made with home-reared, home-grown produce (9)

›› Feel as if you're swimming in a sea of blue in one of Surrey's most magnificent wild bluebell woods (6)

Best for a garden tasting menu

Stay on a 16th century farm

Best for ancient oaks and bluebells

There is an incredible array of ancient forests, wildflower grasslands and garden oases to explore and enjoy here, even though this is a busy landscape, sometimes dominated by motorway, and not that far from London.

Here I discovered some radical and inspirational modern approaches to wild gardening. At Waltham Place, Strilli Oppenheimer and her dedicated team use the principles and philosophy of biodynamic farming to continue a legacy of nature-led experimental gardening. The result is an instructive and elevating garden that is beautiful, full of love and truly special. Plants self-seed in perfect harmony and the whole garden rustles with life. What we'd consider to be weeds, such as nettles or even hedge bindweed, have been allowed to play their part in the design. It's a rare delight to find a place that challenges our perceptions of what a garden should be.

Another refreshing surprise is the 'every colour as long as it's green' garden that landscape designer Anthony Paul has created at the home he shares with his wife, sculpture curator Hannah Peschar. Here, in wooded Surrey, the form and structure of verdant plants, let loose among the forest, create a magical wonderland in which the magnificent stone and metal sculptures shine. I'd love to rent the stylish fairy-tale cottage in the woods and see the place in the moonlight.

This area has many other charming places to stay, from those down tiny lanes in rural valleys, such as at

Nurscombe Farm, to urban oases, including the fantastic Brockdale Cottage and Black Pig Supper Club. Here, hidden away from the busy town of Bracknell, is a modern rural idyll. Tam and Mark Cowell keep bees and pigs, have an experimental micro brewery, and a garden overflowing with fruit and vegetables. All are used to creative design in their supper club evenings, which came about when they realised that butchering one pig produced too much meat for family and friends. So, in the bounty months, Tam and Mark use the overspill of asparagus, pork and greens in fantastic candlelit suppers. It's a great model, and I'd love to see more examples of it.

This part of the world also has some wonderful places to see naturalistic planting and wild flowers. Visit Inholmes garden (Woodlands St Mary, Berkshire, open under the National Gardens Scheme) to see inspirational planting and carpets of bluebells. Or head to Old Simms Copse to see Surrey's largest wild bluebell wood in gloriously-scented full bloom.

83

Gardens

1 WALTHAM PLACE

I have never been so challenged in my thoughts around gardening as I was when I had the privilege of a walk around the acclaimed gardens of Waltham Place with its head gardener Beatrice Krehl. With a mantra of 'working with nature', the garden and 88-acre working farm is run on biodynamic and organic principles. Under the vision of Strilli Oppenheimer, the original planting designs of the late Henk Gerritsen are honoured and expanded upon. Here they combine forces with nature and explore the boundaries between it and a garden. Any visit is an educational one and there are many inspirational courses to sign up to. Don't miss out on a delicious meal, cooked with home farm-raised produce, in the tea room. To visit the garden, you'll need to book in advance.
→ Church Hill, White Waltham, Berks SL6 3JH 01628 825517 walthamplace.com ⏰ mid May–Sep see website 🌱 🍴 🐝

2 GREYS COURT

In the picturesque setting of the rolling Chiltern hills, the gardens of 16th-century Greys Court are a wonderful place to visit. Magical garden rooms, managed on organic principles, are built among the ruins of medieval buildings. What a treat it was to climb up the steep Great Tower to enjoy a rare birds-eye view of the colourful planting and the 100-year-old wisteria walk that was at its peak on that midsummer's afternoon. In the kitchen garden the fantasy continues, and gnarly fruit trees provide structure to the edible fare. Planting is very

1 WALTHAM PLACE

much pollinator-focused and old varieties of borage and traditional herbs intermingle with artfully chosen herbaceous perennials.
→ Rotherfield Greys, Henley-on-Thames, Oxfordshire RG9 4PG 01491 628529 nationaltrust.org.uk ⏰ daily 10am–5pm (4pm winter) 🌱 🍴

3 LOSELEY PARK

Set in beautiful oak and chestnut parkland, the grand venue and its 2.5-acre walled gardens offer surprises for the lover of wilder styles of planting. Besides a rather regimented rose garden, the walled garden is an abundant explosion of perennials, herbs and vegetables all happily competing for space. The medicine garden is glorious and alive with bees and hoverflies. The organic vegetable garden leads on to a simple but beautiful nut walk and through to the long pond. Here, outside the garden's wall, the irises and waterlilies are guarded by the large and noisy dragonflies that weave their way among the plants.
→ Stakescorner Rd, Guildford, Surrey GU3 1HS, 01483 405112 loseleypark.co.uk ⏰ May–Sep Sun–Thu 11am–5pm 🌱 🍴

4 HANNAH PESCHAR SCULPTURE GARDEN

Walking into this incredible woodland is like walking into a stylish childhood fairy-tale. Hidden among the large leaves of gunnera and the towering umbels of the invasive, but here much-welcomed, giant

hogweed, you feel like Alice lost in verdant Wonderland. Each step offers a green-tinted spectacle of plant form and perfectly placed sculpture. Moleskin-soft mossy paths cup each step as you wander past the pond, past the river, past the charming black and white cottage to landscape designer Anthony Paul's delightful garden studio. This is a garden of combined creativity, Anthony creating the leafy backdrop to Hannah's curation of sculpture. Up the hill the magic continues with a private self-catering cottage in the woods. This is a magical garden to discover, or even to stay in.
→ Black & White Cottage, Standon Lane, Ockley, Surrey RH5 5QR, 01306 627269 hannahpescharsculpture.com ⏰ May–Oct Fri & Sat 11–6pm, Sun & BH 2–5pm 🌱 🐝 🏠

What a treat it was to climb up the steep Great Tower to enjoy a rare birdseye view of the colourful planting and the 100-year-old wisteria walk

2 GREYS COURT

2 GREYS COURT

3 LOSELEY PARK

4 HANNAH PESCHAR'S SCULPTURE GARDEN

At the very edge of the Chiltern Hills, this grassy landscape studded with giant trees and ox-eye daisies, rolls down to the Hughenden Valley bottom and stream below.

8 NURSCOMBE FARMHOUSE B&B

Meadows

5 HUGHENDEN ESTATE PARKLANDS

The parklands of Hughenden, once the country home of Victorian prime minister Benjamin Disraeli, are a lovely place to escape to, and one where children can roll around in the buttercups. At the very edge of the Chiltern Hills, this grassy landscape, studded with giant trees and ox-eye daisies, rolls down to the Hughenden Valley bottom and stream below. In the shallow water children splash about, enjoying the vast openness that feels far away from the busy town of High Wycombe.

→ Off the A4128 Valley Road, High Wycombe, Buckinghamshire HP14 4LA 01494 755565 nationaltrust.org.uk ☼ dawn–dusk 51.6495,-0.7556 ⏎

6 OLD SIMMS COPSE

On the White Downs, north of Abinger in Surrey, a lovely circular walk from White Down Lane car park offers one of the best displays of bluebells in the county. Old Simms Copse is one of Surrey's largest and most magnificent bluebell woods. Azure blue carpets lie under the new-leaved beach trees and ancient oaks on this easy walk through quiet glades. Surrey Wildlife Trust often arranges ranger-led walks during peak flowering season.

→ White Down Lane car park, Gomshall, N of Abinger, Surrey RH5 6SL surreywildlifetrust.org 51.2299,-0.41551 ⏎

7 ASTON ROWANT NATURE RESERVE

High on the beautiful Chilterns escarpment and with easy access from the M40 are the herb rich grasslands of Aston Rowant. You can hear the motorway traffic but all is forgiven as red kites soar high above your head. There are wonderful views north across the vale of Aylesbury, or you can head into the ancient beech woodland to see yellowhammers and green woodpeckers. Thirty species of butterfly have been recorded here, including grizzled skippers and chalkhill blues.

→ Bus from High Wycombe or Beacon Hill car park, off A40 near Stokenchurch, HP14 3YL chilternsaonb.org 51.6630,-0.9493 ⏎

Accommodation

8 NURSCOMBE FARMHOUSE B&B

In the Surrey Hills AONB, down a wooded lane in the birdsong-filled Thorncombe Valley, sits the ridiculously pretty farmstead of Nurscombe. It's a picture postcard perfection of tumbling roses and self-seeded cottage garden flowers. Old apple trees dot the grassy courtyard of the 16th-century wood-framed barns and farmhouse. Opposite the quiet lane, a white gate leads to mown paths through a meadow to a pretty pond complete with rowing boat. When we arrived the owner, Jane Fairbank, was baking delicious cakes for her guests.

6 OLD SIMMS COPSE

…wdenham Lane, Bramley, Guildford, Surrey GU5 0DB, 01483 892242 nurscombe.co.uk 🏠 🍵

9 BROCKDALE COTTAGE

Brockdale Cottage and The Black Pig Supper Club is the working vision of husband and wife team Mark and Tam Cowell. In their six-acre garden hidden on the outskirts of busy Bracknell they have created, from first principles, a stunning contemporary natural oasis. Rare breed pigs, organic vegetables, honey and beer from Mark's pilot brewery provide ingredients for their much applauded supper club and their family home. At the end of the garden sits a well-designed cruck-framed oak barn with its cosy wood burner. Here guests can stay, and enjoy evenings wandering around the pollinator-focused planting or join in the supper club merriments.

➔ Cricketers Lane, Warfield, Bracknell Forest, Berkshire RG42 6JR, 07775 993139 brockdalecottage.com 🏠 🍵 🍽️

9   BROCKDALE COTTAGE

10   WHITEHOUSE FARM COTTAGE

10 WHITEHOUSE FARM COTTAGE

Louise and Keir Lusby have created a floriferous escape within the gardens of their cosy farm cottage. Roses, clematis and flowering trees create a petalled cocoon from the busy world outside. Two outbuildings, The Old Forge and Garden Cottage, offer cosy country-style self-catering or there is B&B in the ceramics-filled house. This is not a place for children to run around, more a place to bring a book and glass of wine and enjoy the pretty garden. The owners are both knowledgeable plantspeople and have planted with care all the trees and flowers that you see.

➔ Murrell Hill Lane, Binfield, Bracknell, Berkshire RG42 4BY, 01344 423688 sawdays.co.uk 🏠 🍵

Food

11 MEDICINE GARDEN & THE HOTHOUSE CAFE

This newly-restored walled garden in Cobham is home to a collective of offerings focused around health and heart. The Hothouse café serves nutritious hearty home-made food or you can collapse on a sofa with a coffee from the vintage airstream caravan outside or enjoy a picnic. The Larder is a farm shop cooperative selling a good choice of locally reared meats, pastries and cheese. The walled garden itself is a work in progress. Currently a large green space in which to run around, it will be planted to encourage wildlife and will include herbs and vegetables for the café.

➔ Downside Road, Cobham, Surrey KT11 3LU 01932 862562 themedicinegarden.com ⏰ Mon–Sat 9am–5pm Sun 10am–4pm (and some Fri evenings, booking essential) 🍵 🍽️

12 GREAT FOSTERS

If you are looking for a real treat, head to the former royal hunting lodge that is now Great Fosters hotel and indulge in a first class lunch, afternoon tea or supper. If the weather is fine you can sit on the terrace in summer and enjoy views of the garden. Chefs design the daily menus, and divine tasting menus, based on what's growing in the kitchen garden and around locally sourced fresh produce. An even better way to enjoy the gardens, with their mix of wild flower meadows, beehives and Italianate pomp and glory, is to stay at the luxury hotel and wander the many acres at your leisure.

➔ Stroude Road, Egham, Surrey TW20 9UR 01784 433822 greatfosters.co.uk ⏰ daily 🍽️ 🏠

Myth has it that here in the brick walled garden 17th-century gardener John Rose grew the first pineapple

Companion Planting

Companion	Companion for	Benefit
Onion family	Many Vegetables	Disguises the scents of other vulnerable harvests, ie. protecting carrots from carrot fly
Borage	Tomatoes, squash	Attracts pollinating insects and repels tomato worm
Nasturtiums	Brassicas	Attracts cabbage white butterflies away from brassicas + lettuces
Basil	Tomatoes, aubergine	Attracts aphids away from more vulnerable harvests
Marigolds (Tagetes sp.)	Most vegetables	Produces chemicals in its roots, which deter nematodes, slugs and wireworms
Coriander	Most vegetables	Repels aphids + carrot fly + attracts bees when in flower
Mint	Cabbage,	Deters cabbage white butterflies, aphids

13 DORNEY COURT

The café and plant nursery at Dorney Court Kitchen Garden is a great choice if you want to eat delicious seasonal food made using home-grown produce. The garden once served historic Dorney Court manor house (now open separately). Myth has it that here in the brick walled garden, 17th-century gardener John Rose grew the first pineapple in the country and presented it to King Charles II. Although no exotics are grown today, what is grown is a productive array of vegetables that head straight to the kitchens and shop. It's a beautifully presented garden mixing flowers (available in the nursery shop) and edible produce.

Court Lane, Dorney, Berkshire SL4 6QP 01628 669999 dckg.co.uk
daily 9am–5pm

West Sussex

Dominated by the South Downs National Park, this is a rich landscape with ancient forests, flower-rich downland, swathes of parkland and shingle-covered coastline. According to the Met Office, it's also, officially, the sunniest county in the UK.

West Sussex

The highlights

>> Be inspired by Arundel Castle's stunning kitchen garden that's run on organic principles (1)

>> Discover the Loder Valley and over 450 acres of ancient forests and wildflower grasslands (2)

>> Wend your way through herb-rich and fragrant grassland at Ebernoe Common (6)

>> Go to the seaside at Shoreham, where the beach is a wildflower tapestry that defies salty sea gales (7)

5

Haslemere

10

Horsham

A23

6

A272

Petersfield   A272

13

9

South Downs National Park

A24

4

11

3   8

5

A283

14

1

A280

A27   7

Chichester   A27

Worthing

Bognor Regis

Selsey

Best for walled
kitchen garden

7

Best for a
special lunch

A22

East Grinstead

12

15

2

Best for
prairie
planting

Brighton

Best for
shingle beach
flora

Here in West Sussex you'll find some of the oldest living things in Britain – the ancient yews of Kingley Vale near Chichester. Their knarled, thick trunks, holding lifetimes of stories, are approached through lanes lined with flowers and glades filled with butterflies.

Wild flowers thrive in the many areas of rolling chalk grassland in West Sussex. Its biscuit-thin soil was created by the calcite deposits of millions of sea-living micro-organisms deposited over tens of thousands of years. Cleared of forests by the first settlers, these green hills still offer fine grazing to cattle, sheep and deer. They also offer fantastic forage to a wealth of insect and bird life. Make sure your visits to the best wildflower areas, such as Harting Down, Ebernoe Common and Levin Down, are in summer when they are at their peak. Then, you will be rewarded with the magic of a field hazy with hoverflies, bumblebees and butterflies. For a knockout spectacle, head south to Shoreham Beach for the astounding tapestry of wild flowers growing on its shingle sands.

Sussex's rich natural flora is matched by that of its cultivated gardens, many of which are managed to enhance the wildlife – especially pollinating insects. Near East Grinstead sits Gravetye Manor, a luxurious country house hotel that was once the home of William Robinson. His influential book *The Wild Garden*, published in 1870, advocated a more naturalistic and natural approach to gardening. It was revolutionary, moving from constricted and formal Victorian practices towards a cottage garden style of planting that enhanced nature's beauty rather than trying to force its surrender.

William Robinson's principles live on strongly in the gardens of this sun-drenched corner of Southern England. Parham House is one of my favourite private country gardens, where hens forage in long grass in the orchard and walled gardens are planted with naturalistic borders. Wakehurst Place is another haven of wild flowers, and home to Kew's Millennium Seed Bank as well as acres of planted and natural wildflower meadows. There are also charming and productive gardens found in the grounds of the picturesque castle of Arundel. Its organic kitchen garden is so alive with insects that it's almost deafening. It's a triumphant reminder of the benefits of organic methods of gardening.

1

Gardens

1 ARUNDEL CASTLE GARDENS

What a surprise location for a wild garden. This stunning organic kitchen garden is bursting with flowers, fruits and vegetables in beds and greenhouses towered over by the castle's impressive cathedral. The journey to the kitchen garden first passes deep patches of campion and ox-eye daisies and a magnificent cork oak. Through the door in the wall you are presented with a garden created by designers Isabel and Julian Bannerman, with oak structures, lush planting and gushing water. Walk through the willow arch and you emerge into a richly planted stumpery that gives the effect of being in a strange jungle. The contrast of the fanciful structures and the bounty of the garden is topped off by the sheer number of pollinators that clearly enjoy the planting as much as the visitors. (Within walking distance is a lovely place to stay, Billycan Camping at Manor Farm).
➜ Arundel, West Sussex BN18 9AB
01903 882173 arundelcastle.org
⏰ End Mar–Oct Tue–Sun & BH 10–5pm (and daily in Aug) 🥖 🍴 🌿

2 WAKEHURST PLACE & LODER VALLEY

Wakehurst Place and its secret Loder Valley deserve a full day's exploration. With more than 460 acres it is a large area to cover, so be prepared and wear comfortable shoes. Acres of excellent planting merge into protected and habitat-rich wildflower meadows and ancient forests. Spend the whole day wandering the acres of nature's incredible show, see how the Millennium Seed Bank works to conserve plants,

1 ARUNDEL CASTLE GARDENS

experience life in a traditional hay meadow, or simply call into the main entrance, collect your pass and details and head straight to the Loder Valley. Visitors to this special nature reserve are limited to 50 a day but even at the meadows' floral peak in June we felt as if we had the whole place to ourselves.
➜ Ardingly, Haywards Heath, West Sussex RH17 6TN, 01444 894066 kew.org
⏰ daily 10–6pm (4.30pm in winter)
🥖 🍴 🌿 🌸

3 WEST DEAN GARDENS

Set in beautiful South Downs parkland, alongside the pretty Lavant River, is the impressive restored walled kitchen garden at West Dean. We visited on a beautifully warm and golden day in March. The low sun was gleaming through the daffodils. Naturalised bulbs of scillas, narcissi, fritillaries and primroses created a dreamy vision below a thatched lodge. The sunny terrace restaurant serving breakfasts, lunches and tempting teas is a destination in itself, but it is the walled garden that is the main draw. The incredible heritage collection of trained apples and pears looked like sculptures without their dressings of leaves. In their skeletal form you can see in detail the diverse ways in which fruit trees may be trained, such as into pyramids, goblets and espaliers. Each of the impressive glasshouses is home to its own congregation of plants. Don't miss the

beehives, or the head gardener's tiny bothy, filled with the art of crafted and oiled tools.
➜ West Dean, Chichester, West Sussex PO18 0QZ, 01243 811301
westdean.org.uk ⏰ Feb–Dec 10.30–5pm (4pm in winter) 🥖 🍴 🌿 🌸

4 SUSSEX PRAIRIE GARDEN

In a six-acre field in verdant Sussex, Paul and Pauline McBride have created, from scratch, an enviable prairie-style show garden using stock from their farm nursery. Wandering through the tall massed perennial plantings and billowing grasses, you can instantly see the attraction of this extended season planting style. Naturalistic in spirit, the garden feels modern and exciting. Above all it feels very full of life, due to the continual movement of both the plants and the insects that happily exist in this colourful oasis. In the tea room Pauline's mother serves delicious home-made cakes and artisan ice cream from Brighton. Plant stock from the garden is available for purchase from the nursery.
➜ Morlands Farm, Wheatsheaf Road, Henfield, West Sussex, BN5 9AT
01273 495902 sussexprairies.co.uk
⏰ Jun–mid Oct daily (except Tue) 1–5pm
🥖 🍴 🌸

2 WAKEHURST PLACE

5 PARHAM HOUSE

3 WEST DEAN GARDENS

5 PARHAM HOUSE

Parham is a glorious private family home, a 16th-century manor house set in rolling parkland that is studded with majestic oaks. The gardens are romantic, tranquil and generously planted. The large walled garden contains an excellent plant nursery with artful displays and it has a stall selling vegetables from the kitchen garden. In the traditional orchard, mown paths meander through the long grass, and running ducks and chickens forage under the old apple trees. There is a large ornamental vegetable garden with a happy blend of vegetables, herbs and flowers. Don't miss the Wendy House, a charming two-storey children's cottage. Outside the garden walls, planned vistas draw the eye to the wilderness beyond. In the Big Kitchen restaurant, enormous home-made meringues with strawberries and cream compete with the light lunch offerings.

Storrington, near Pulborough, West Sussex RH20 4HS, 01903 742021 parhaminsussex.co.uk   May–Sep Wed–Fri & Sun, Apr & Oct Sun & BH 12–5pm

Enjoy walking through
beautiful herb-rich
grassland Sweet briar
bushes dot the walk
and their apple scented
leaves and pretty flowers
tumble into the grass

7 SHOREHAM BEACH

Meadows

6 EBERNOE COMMON
From pretty Ebernoe Church, with its graveyard full of poppies, spotted orchids and ox-eye daisies, follow a signed path to the meadow. Enjoy walking through its beautiful herb-rich grassland. Sweet briar bushes dot the walk and their apple-scented leaves and pretty flowers tumble into the grass. A stunning diversity of insect life.
→ Car park next to church off Streel's Lane, 3 miles N of Petworth GU28 9JY sussexwildlifetrust.org.uk 51.0417,-0.6085 ⤴

7 SHOREHAM BEACH
This is a rare, and internationally significant habitat that is a joy to visit in summer. The vegetated shingle beach, ravaged by salty winds, is home to a diverse display of hardy, and legally protected, wild flowers. It is the only place in the UK where starry clover can be seen. Rare yellow horned poppy, white-flowering sea kale, and masses of pink and white valerian all create a colourful tapestry in the seascape.
→ Park at W Beach Road. Walk E along beach. Shoreham-by-Sea BN43 5LY fosbeach. com 50.8274,-0.2756 ⤴

8 LEVIN DOWN
With a name derived from 'leave-alone hill' this terrain was too steep for intensive agriculture, which is probably why it is now so rich in wildlife. The chalk grassland and scrub, today a reserve and SSSI, has orchids, clustered bellflowers and green and brown hairstreak butterflies.
→ Walk from Charlton or park in small lay-by at crossroads. Follow public footpath directly across field to reserve. PO18 0HX sussexwildlifetrust.org.uk 50.9128,-0.7418 ⤴

9 HARTING DOWN
Leave the chalky South Downs Way and drop down into the valley: it's an incredible habitat where you'll hear skylarks overhead. The wildflower-rich grassland includes the deep blue 'Pride of Sussex' round-headed rampion and the rare blue carpenter bee.
→ NT car park off B2141, 1.3 mile S of South Harting GU31 5PN 50.9622,-0.8731 ⤴

Accommodation

10 CANFIELDS FEATHER DOWN FARM
Head past the farm and cottages to the luxury safari tents set out in a large flower-filled hay meadow. Nestled between the North and South Downs in the village of Rudgwick, this lovely organic beef farm offers lots to explore. Without electricity, you can set yourself free from your mobile phone. There are bluebell woods to play in, lambs to feed and eggs to collect.
→ Lynwick Street, Horsham, West Sussex RH12 3DL 01420 80804 featherdown.co.uk 🏠 ⤴

10 CANFIELDS FEATHER DOWN FARM

11 STANE HOUSE B&B

Handsome Stane House, a period property, has three en-suite four-star bedrooms. It sits in its own lovely garden, which is tended by the owner. It's set in the pretty village of Bignor, home to Bignor Roman Villa and local vineyard. There are several outdoor seating areas dotted around the flower-filled garden, the perfect place for enjoying your bottle of the vineyard's wine.

→ Bignor, West Sussex RH20 1PQ
01798 869454 stanehouse.co.uk 🍵🏠

12 ASHWOOD FARM CAMPING

Park at Ashwood Farm (home of Trefoil Montessori Farm School – you may see their tipis). Then, you can either grab a wheelbarrow or pay £5 and get taken by the farmer on his vintage Massey Ferguson tractor to a secret, secluded field and your camp. The site is located near the National Trust's Standen House, where you can often buy kitchen garden harvest from their vegetable barrow in summer. East Grinstead train station is only 25 minutes walk away and you'll get a discount at the campsite if you don't drive.

→ Ashwood Farm, West Hoathly Road, East Grinstead RH19 4ND, 01342 316129
woodlandcampingeco.wordpress.com 🏠🔖

11 STANE HOUSE

Hammocks hang from the apple trees, sheepskin rugs cover the benches and chickens wander at will in the garden

14 DENMANS

Food

13 HORSEGUARDS INN

Hammocks hang from the apple trees, sheepskin rugs cover the benches and chickens wander at will in the garden of this pretty inn. Filled with roses, and lit by lanterns as dusk falls, it's a delightful setting, day or night. Inside, the eclectic theme continues in the relaxed restaurant and its bedrooms. The food is delicious, local, and bursting with flavour. Nearby are the historic parklands of the National Trust's Petworth, filled with wildlife.

→ Upperton Road, Tillington, West Sussex GU28 9AF, 01798 342332
thehorseguardsinn.co.uk 🕐 daily 🍵🍴🏠

14 DENMANS

Denmans is the home of the renowned garden designer and author John Brookes. Rambling roses scramble in the trees above the popular garden café and the outdoor seating area is filled with bird song. Inside, a piano and operatic glitz fill the conservatory. Enjoy aubergine bakes, burgers or fishcakes finished off with ridiculously enormous puddings. The show garden, plant nursery and gift shop are all just steps away. Although entry to the café is free, there's a small charge for the garden (it's an RHS Partner Garden).

→ Denmans Ln, Fontwell, Arundel, BN18 0SU, 01243 542808 denmans-garden.co.uk
🕐 daily 10–4pm 🍵🍴🌷

15 GRAVETYE

Gravetye is perfect for a special day out. Once the home of William Robinson, whose work *The Wild Garden* revolutionised early 20th century gardening, Gravetye is now a hotel. You can enjoy delicious lunches with produce from their unique oval-shaped walled kitchen garden (booking essential). On fine days these are served on a terrace overlooking meadows filled with butterflies. Garden visits are by prior arrangement and the best way to experience Gravetye is as a hotel guest. Wander through the gardens down to the lakes where tumbling roses climb through the trees.

→ Vowels Lane, West Hoathly, East Sussex RH19 4LJ 01342 810567 gravetyemanor.co.uk
🍵🍴🏠

GREAT DIXTER

East Sussex

From chalk hills to clay vales, this is a landscape saturated in rich natural flora and artistic gardens.

East Sussex

The highlights

›› See British gardening at its best at Great Dixter, a heady mix of romantic planting and wild flowers (5)

›› Find inspiration for naturalistic planting schemes at Marchants Hardy Plants (4)

›› Climb the hills of the South Downs and discover rare orchids in ancient wildflower meadows (6)

›› Discover King John's Nursery and stay at this gorgeous family run secret (10 & 13)

Best for a plant nursery

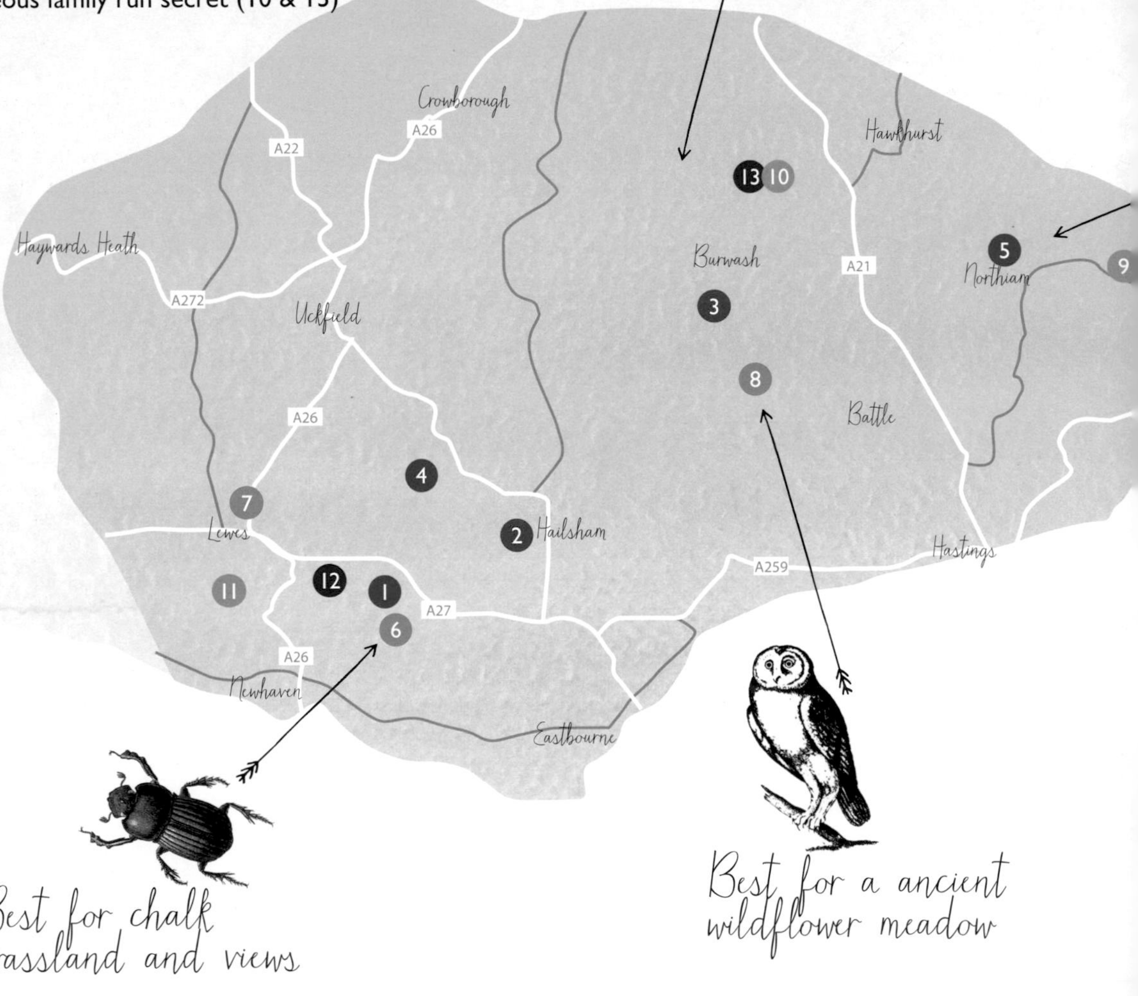

Best for chalk grassland and views

Best for a ancient wildflower meadow

Crowborough

Hawkhurst

A22

A26

Haywards Heath

A272

Uckfield

A26

Burwash

A21

Northiam

13 **10**

5

9

3

8

Battle

4

7

Lewes

2 *Hailsham*

Hastings

A259

11

12

1

A27

6

A26

Newhaven

Eastbourne

Artistry and enchantment seem to permeate every garden and chalk-covered ridge of East Sussex.

Here, in the early 20th century, the writers, thinkers and artists of the Bloomsbury set retreated from stuffy London to find solace, peace and pleasure in these rolling hills and pretty river valleys. Inspired by their love of the landscape, their ideas created an artistic movement that still strongly resonates today. Their quest for colour, freedom, and simplicity can be seen in their former homes and gardens. Their passions play out in the small garden of Monk's House, once home to Virginia and Leonard Woolf, and at inspirational Charleston, home to Vanessa Bell and Duncan Grant. In 1936 Bell wrote about 'lying about in the garden which is simply a dithering blaze of flowers and butterflies and apples'.

In the 1950s, Christopher Lloyd's passion for colour and floral experimentation found expression at his family house, Great Dixter. His determined garden writing, his creativity with 'unfashionable' plants, and the love of his mother's wildflower meadows left a lasting impression. It's a legacy that continues to evolve under the stewardship of Fergus Garrett. Great Dixter is a perfect English country garden, abundant, unrestricted, and deeply romantic. What I love most are its meadows, filled with orchids and brimming with meadow brown and peacock butterflies, moths and bees, all savouring its delights. The topiary meadow is magical and an icon for the new wild garden. Anchored by its yew hedges it symbolises how we can

have it all: a wild, free meadow of our childhood dreams and the grown-up clipped humour of the mature garden. If all agree (and most do) that Great Dixter is British gardening at its best, then I hope more of us can be inspired to abandon our limitations and embrace wild flowers in all their unkempt, unruly beauty.

To see how nature does it very well on her own, head to the UK's newest national park, The South Downs. The area is a tapestry of landscapes, where in the chalk grassland meadows of Bo Peep or Malling Down you can experience the beauty of some rare native flora in their wild environment.

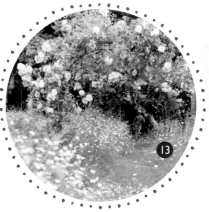

For exquisite ox-eye daisy meadows in a garden setting, visit King John's Lodge in summer. For even more inspiration, and to buy plants, visit the beautiful show garden of Marchants Hardy Plants to see wild flowers and grasses used in naturalistic flowing scenes. On a practical note, don't miss the talks or courses held by writer, gardener and wild flower advocate Sarah Raven, at her gorgeous garden, Perch Hill.

Best for a wild garden

Gardens

1 CHARLESTON HOUSE

A tour of the bohemian house of artists Vanessa Bell and Duncan Grant is not to be missed, and neither is a wander around the garden. Walk past the naïve Greek-inspired urns and the artistry and inspiration for many of their paintings continues throughout the outdoor spaces. As you enter the small walled enclosure, you will be invited to push back the cottage garden conquerors that invade the path. Roses tumble from all sides and from the laden apple trees. Faces and carvings catch your eye as they battle for attention with their petalled neighbours. In the far corner sits a productive and very pretty kitchen garden. The overall experience is one of carefree abandon and a love of form and colour (as also seen in the house). It's a small garden but packed full of passion and delight. There is a simple café serving delicious home-made drinks, cakes and light lunches. Come and be inspired.

➜ Firle, Lewes, East Sussex BN8 6LL
01323 811265 charleston.org.uk
⏰ end Mar–Oct Wed–Sat 1–6pm (Jul–Sep from 12) Sun & BH 1–5.30pm 🍽 🍴

2 MICHELHAM PRIORY

Michelham is a fairytale castellated priory surrounded by a tranquil water-filled moat, the longest in England. Once through the high stone gatehouse you emerge into a protected island of gardens planted for bees and butterflies. The moat itself is managed as a conservation area and its banks are covered in wild flowers. Much of the garden

1 CHARLESTON HOUSE

is in essence a recreation of the medieval garden that once existed there, and includes a small physic garden with medicinal plants. The 800-year-old priory would have needed to be largely self-sufficient and this is reflected in the kitchen garden and the superbly varied orchard, where in spring the ground beneath the medlars, mulberries, quinces, walnuts, apples, and pears is carpeted with delicate bulbs.

➜ Upper Dicker, Hailsham, East Sussex BN27 3QS 01323 844224 sussexpast.co.uk
⏰ mid Feb–mid December 10.30–5pm (11–4pm in winter) 🍽 🍴 🌱

3 SARAH RAVEN'S PERCH HILL FARM

Set in the grounds of a charming Sussex farmhouse, Sarah Raven's garden is open only a couple of days a month for visits and courses, with dates given on the website. During open days you can explore the abundant flower and vegetable packed oast gardens, hear talks from Sarah, and see how she expertly combines her productive kitchen vegetables with herbs and flowers for cutting and to give an explosive display of colour. Delicious light lunches and teas and cakes are available on the day using seasonal garden produce based on recipes from her cookbooks. There is a small, well-stocked gift shop and plant sales.

➜ Perch Hill Farm, Brightling, Robertsbridge TN32 5HP, 0845 092 0283 sarahraven.com
⏰ several open days throughout the year, including for the NGS 🍽 🍴 🌱

4 MARCHANTS HARDY PLANTS

This beautifully designed and planted nursery show garden with delightful views of the South Downs should be a destination in itself. Owner Graham Gough and his team propagate all their own hardy pollinator-friendly plants and have artfully designed a tempting nursery: you may find it is an expensive yet valuable outing. In the small but densely planted garden, expertly chosen wild flowers and long grasses wind their way among the curved beds. Instead of different 'garden rooms' the beds merge seductively into each other, from naturalistic wildflower meadow to prairie to dry gravel garden.

➜ 2 Marchants Cottages, Mill Lane, Laughton, East Sussex BN8 6AJ
01323 811737 marchantshardyplants.co.uk
⏰ May–mid Oct Wed–Sat 9.30–5.30pm
🍽 🌱

2 MICHELHAM PRIORY

5 GREAT DIXTER

If there was just one garden you could visit in this country it would have to be Great Dixter. It is inspiring to think that a garden with such heritage can continue to be so fresh and relevant. It is also surprisingly intimate in its experience, despite its many pilgrims. On a sunny afternoon in June I often found myself alone, with just five little wide-mouthed swallows in the rustic eves of an outbuilding for company. The gardens are relaxed and informal, set among picturesque sagging barns and a house adapted by architect Lutyens from a Tudor manor. The planting, by Fergus Garrett and team, is wonderful. The garden is filled with planting ideas that seem to know no bounds: it is the garden's structured chaos that delights the eye. There is a small café serving baguettes, teas, coffees and tempting cakes and a restored old oast house is open to visitors. The plant nursery is open all year.

Great Dixter, Northiam, Rye, East Sussex TN31 6PH, 01797 252878 greatdixter.co.uk
end Mar–Oct Tue–Sun & BH 11–5pm

High up in the South Downs, with superb views over the surrounding countryside, this grassland ridge is a wonderful place to see rare wild flowers

6 BO PEEP

Meadows

6 BO PEEP

High up in the South Downs, with superb views over the surrounding countryside, this grassland ridge is a wonderful place to see the wild flowers that grow in the remaining three per cent of pristine chalkland preserved in their honour. It's one of the few places to spot round-headed rampions in June and July but although trying hard, we found none. Fragrant and common spotted orchids and even the rare burnt-tip orchid can be seen in summer. The colour continues into autumn with the purple haze of scabious. At the southern tip of Bo Peep Lane is a car park, the start for a good walk along the South Downs.

→ Bo Peep Lane, Alciston, East Sussex BN8 6PA 50.8256,0.1199

7 MALLING DOWN

In walking distance of boutique-filled Lewes, and towering over the town and countryside beyond, is Malling Down. Its deep valley and rolling chalk downs twist themselves over humps and bumps. It's worth the steep climb for the scented carpets of wild thyme, lady's bed-straw dotted with orchids and the stunning views.

→ Walk up from the town or park at small car park at the top of Mill Road, off Malling Hill, Lewes BN7 2RU
sussexwildlifetrust.org.uk 50.8828,0.0212

8 COACH ROAD FIELD

This ancient wildflower meadow is a Coronation Meadow, designated in 2013 on the 60th anniversary of the Queen's coronation. Farmed in traditional ways since time immemorial, it has never been ploughed: its historic haymaking tradition has ensured a species rich display of native Weald wild flowers and insects. In summer, beautiful quaking grass, ox-eye daisies, orchids and dyer's greenweed provide a flush of pollinator-covered colour that continues until knapweeds take over in August.

→ The old coach road gives access through the meadow. 0.5 miles W of Penhurst, 1st track on R (after Peen's Farm). Battle, East Sussex TN33 9QR 50.9247,0.3974

Accommodation

9 MEADOW KEEPER'S COTTAGE

Enjoy quirky, chic glamping on a quiet family run farm set in 40 acres of wildflower meadows and woods. Managed wholly for conservation, the meadows will surely be a highlight of your summer stay. The utterly charming hand-crafted cottage on wheels is off-grid so you can enjoy the peace and quiet. There is a tiny honesty-box farm shop on site selling eggs and produce from the kitchen garden.

Swallowtail Hill Farm, Hobbs Lane, Beckley, East Sussex TN31 6TT, 01797 260890
canopyandstars.co.uk

7 MALLING DOWN

10 KING JOHN'S LODGE

King John's Nursery and Lodge is a real find. Jill Cunningham runs the handsome Jacobean King John's Lodge B&B with its oak beams, leaded windows and comfortable rooms. Her son and daughter-in-law run the plant nursery, gift shop and café (see food listing). The garden is glorious, in a tucked away position in the High Weald. Large oaks stalk the meadow while statues peek out from behind their mighty trunks. We visited in June when the rose arbours tumbling into the oxeye daisy meadows were at their peak. Next door at the nursery you can find a good selection of garden statuary, home-propagated plants, and proper coffee.

→ Sheepstreet Lane, Etchingham, East Sussex TN19 7AZ, 01580 819232 sawdays.co.uk

11 MONK'S HOUSE GARDEN STUDIO

The garden studio is set in the country garden that once belonged to the Bloomsbury set's Virginia and Leonard Woolf. The studio was Leonard's writing retreat, an intimate and unaffected place, and is now a National Trust holiday stay. The plot is a simple cottage garden with a small orchard, which has beehives, and Leonard's vegetable patch. Beyond it there are stunning views of the South Downs. Silent statues hide in the greenery and when we visited, the little pond was alive with frogs. Both house and garden are full of bohemian artistry and demonstrate the love of colour that these artists shared. The little studio, with its large window overlooking the garden, is the perfect way to experience this charming place that is laden with literary associations.

→ Rodmell, Near Lewes, East Sussex BN7 3HF 0344 335 1287 nationaltrustcottages.co.uk

10 KING JOHN'S LODGE

11 MONK'S HOUSE GARDEN STUDIO

Food

12 THE RAM INN, FIRLE

The flint covered Ram Inn is a picturesque village pub with cosy rooms in the pretty village of Firle, well positioned for exploring the South Downs or the historic country retreats of the Bloomsbury set. Hidden within the walled gardens, you can sit under the fruit trees and enjoy delicious, super-fresh seasonal produce with meat from the local farm, game from Firle Estate and wild mushrooms foraged from the Downs. Our food was fresh, simple and impeccably prepared. Inside, fires warm the resting walkers and at the front there's a sunny courtyard where the friendly locals mix with the Bloomsbury tourists.

→ The Street, Firle, East Sussex BN8 6NS 01273 858222 raminn.co.uk
⏰ daily 9–11pm 🍴 📷

13 KING JOHN'S NURSERY

Harry & Harry (Harriet and Henry) live in a fairytale cottage in the woods with their children and run King John's Nursery. As well as propagating all their own plants (all peat-free), they artfully curate the gift shop and run the cosy, chic tearoom in the former chicken sheds of King John's Lodge. Choose which beautifully decorated room to hide away in and have lunch. Or take your coffee and cake and enjoy gorgeous views of the High Weald. The gardens surrounding the handsome Jacobean manor are stunning, particularly when the climbing roses are running riot in the orchard.

→ Sheepstreet Lane, Etchingham, TN19 7AZ 01580 819220 kingjohnsnursery.co.uk
⏰ Feb–Dec daily (except Tue) 10–5pm (4pm in winter) 🍴 📷

The gardens surrounding the handsome Jacobean manor are stunning, particularly when the climbing roses are running riot in the orchard.

12 THE RAM INN, FIRLE

13 KING JOHN'S NURSERY

13 KING JOHN'S NURSERY AND LODGE

GODINTON

Kent

The Garden of England, once renowned for hops
and orchards, is now more famous for the gardens
and meadows that enjoy its sun-baked climate.

Kent

The highlights

›› Hunt for the elusive bee orchid in the wildflower meadows at Godinton House (1)

›› Enjoy a woodland walk in the quirky and wildlife-friendly gardens of Marle Place (5)

›› Spot half of Britain's native flower species growing in the harsh seaside landscape at Dungeness (8)

›› Fall asleep to the sound of owls and wake to the scent of bluebells at Badgells Wood campsite (11)

Best for bluebells and nightjars

Best for a wild garden

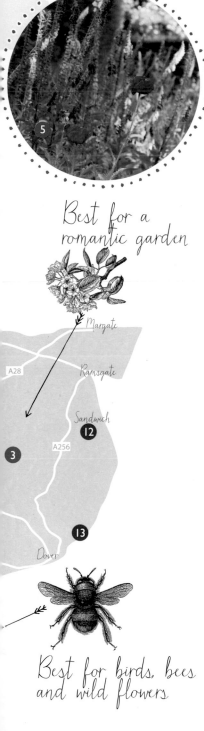

Best for a
romantic garden

Margate

A28

Ramsgate

Sandwich
12

3

A256

13

Dover

Best for birds, bees
and wild flowers

Traditional orchards are superb habitats for wild flora and fauna, so it's a sad fact that Kent lost more than 92 per cent of its orchards from the late 1950s to early 1990s. Happily, our appreciation of orchards is on the rise again.

If you love orchards, you can visit Britain's National Fruit Collection at Brogdale. Or head to one of the growing number of community-owned orchards that are preserving Kent's special agricultural and cultural history, as well as providing valuable community space. Common Ground is a great organisation to seek out if you want to discover more. No Man's Community Orchard, accessed through the recreation ground in Chartham Hatch, was the first orchard in the UK to be designated as a Local Nature Reserve. Its old apple trees, many planted in the 1940s, are home to rare lichens and mosses. They help ensure that local heritage varieties such as Flower of Kent and Kentish Fillbasket continue to be enjoyed.

Despite its proximity to London, Kent manages to retain its quaint village atmosphere and picturesque market towns. Here, in the mild climate, inimitable gardeners such as Vita Sackville-West created gardens in its chalk, greensands and clay soils that are still famous. The National Trust gardens of Knole, Scotney Castle and Stoneacre or the private gardens of Goodnestone and Godinton House each, in their own way, offer a sense of romance and wilderness.

One of my favourite Kentish wild gardens is Marle Place. Here, among cobnuts and sculpture, the impression

is one of relaxed artistry and a love of wildlife. It is an appealing example of how a garden focused on nature can also be a truly beautiful one. It also has a first class tea room. But above Kent's cream teas and oast houses, what I love most are its pockets of glorious wild flowers. Drive past Love Lane in Aylesham in summer and a streak of red poppies brightens the fields.

As I travelled across the UK looking for the country's best meadows, I found what I was looking for – at Polebrook Farm. This could have been the setting of my childhood dreams On my visit, the summer sun beat down and lit up the richest natural

English flower meadow I had ever seen. I watched in a halcyon daze as my young daughter ran in carefree abandon along its narrow paths trying to catch crickets. At Polebrook, or at Plantlife's Ranscombe Farm, in the bluebell woods of Blean Wood and even on the shingle coast of Dungeness, a grand show of wild flowers is always incredibly uplifting.

Gardens

1 GODINTON

Godinton is a handsome house, near the pretty Kent village of Great Chart. As we walked into the walled kitchen garden in June, our jaws dropped at the sight of the vibrant colour within its walls. The rows upon rows of sweet peas, vegetables and cottage garden herbs and flowers were impressive but couldn't compete with the almost unnatural blues and indigos of the magnificent Delphinum Society collection that is housed here. Doves and chickens wander in and out of their charmingly weathered homes. With its rows of veg, highly-bred perennials and productive glasshouses, the walled garden is a scene of industry. Heading away from it all into the wild garden the contrast is immediate. Here among the lyrical bird chatter, martagon lilies naturalise in long grass alongside the often-elusive bee orchid. Near the pond, roses tumble with carefree abandon into the grass and seem much happier than their showy neighbours trapped in the formal rose garden.

→ Godinton Lane, Ashford, Kent TN23 3BP
01233 643854 godintonhouse.co.uk
🕑 Mar–Oct daily 1–6pm 🍽 🍴 🌱

1 GODINTON

2 DOWN HOUSE

Nestled in the rural Kent village of Downe, Down House is where the naturalist Charles Darwin wrote his revolutionary *On the Origin of Species*. Here in his garden laboratory, through the study of plants you can see growing at the site today, he set out to amend the way that humanity understood our natural world. In his greenhouse you

3 GOODNESTONE PARK

can see collections of the carnivorous sundew plants (*Drosera*) that he studied. My favourite time to visit is in spring when the bulbs unfurl to carpet the budding orchard with native species of primroses, daffodils and snowdrops. Later in the season cow parsley, bluebells and buttercups fill the meadow and woods alongside Darwin's Sandwalk, the path of his daily meditational walks and where his world-shaking theories were born.

→ Luxted Road, Downe, Kent BR6 7JT
01689 859119 english-heritage.org.uk
🕑 Apr–Sep daily 10am–6pm, Oct 10am–5pm, Nov–Mar Sat & Sun 10am–4pm 🍽 🌱

3 GOODNESTONE PARK

There is the magical charm of a lost world that surrounds Goodnestone, perhaps because it has been in the same family, the FitzWalters, for generations. During my visit, cricket was being played at the front of the house beyond the ha-ha. Cricketers in whites and the sound of clapping as willow met leather added to the idyllic ambience. The garden is home to a magnificent 400-year-old sweet chestnut whose textured bark demands to be stroked. In the arboretum, which has a large *cornus* collection, there is another champion specimen – an ancient cedar of Lebanon. To the back of the house ox-eye daisy-filled meadows lead to the wilder gardens and new gravel gardens. The renowned walled garden is overflowing with roses and deep

herbaceous borders and has a picture postcard view of the church. There is a simple tea room and gallery in the stables.

→ The Street, Goodnestone, Kent CT3 1PL
01304 840107 goodnestoneparkgardens.co.uk
🕑 Apr–Sep Thu–Sat 11am–5pm, Sun & BH 12–5pm, Oct Sun only 🍽 🍴 🌱

4 KNOLE

Hidden away in Sevenoaks lies the enormous 600-year-old house complex of Knole, one of the nation's largest country houses. The approach is through beautiful rolling medieval parkland. Huge herds of deer, descendants of those hunted by Henry III, bask in the sun among foxgloves and bracken. The site is designated an SSSI for its acidic grassland, rare dung beetles and fungi. In the garden, native orchids thrive in meadows alongside the miles of mown paths that meander through the trees. For such a grand house full of so many treasures, the wilderness gardens are a peaceful escape. Heading towards the ponds, the planting gets more colourful and combines wild bog-loving flowers with complementary perennials. In Lord Sackville's private walled gardens, open only at certain times, you will find the longest wisteria in the country. Almost 200 years old, it is a perfumed delight in May.

→ High Street, Sevenoaks, Kent TN15 0RP
01732 462100 nationaltrust.org.uk
🕑 park daily dawn–dusk, walled garden
Apr–Sep Tue only 11am–4pm 🍽 🍴 🌱

4 KNOLE

5 MARLE PLACE

5 MARLE PLACE

Marle Place gardens are the life's work of
the owners. Glorious wild elements merge
effortlessly with bold and creative planting.
Roses ramble through specimen trees.
Sculptures surprise at every turn and add to
the garden's sense of humour and artistry.
In the native cobnut orchard rests an old
tractor, while rare breed chickens hide
among cherries in the potager garden. The
tearoom is a delight, with home-made cakes
and light lunches in its cosy surroundings
or out in the sunny walled garden. There's
a woodland walk that's at its best in spring,
while in summer, the mature trees (some
more than a century old), the ponds, and
meadows are full of life. Everywhere you can
enjoy an incredible orchestra of bird song.
Nesting peregrine falcons, as well as little
and tawny owls, have all made this their
home. This is a garden that is, deservedly,
recognised for its wildlife.

Marle Place Rd, Brenchley, Kent TN12 7HS
01892 722304 marleplace.co.uk
Apr–mid Sep daily (except Thu) 11am–5pm

Polebrook farm's unimproved neutral grassland is thought to have remained unchanged for more than seven hundred years.

7 RANSCOMBE FARM

Meadows

6 POLEBROOK FARM SSSI

Polebrook's unimproved natural grassland is thought to have remained unchanged for more than 700 years. You first enter a small wet field that, in June, is dominated by clouds of southern marsh orchid. The next field, however, takes your breath away. Crickets jump from your footsteps. The grass is alive with meadow browns dancing amongst the small ox-eye daisies, orchids, field buttercups and yellow rattle. It is a diverse and rich habitat and a delight to experience such an abundance of life.

→ 2.5 miles SW of Bough Beech Visitor Centre, Winkhurst Green, Ide Hill TN14 6LD kentwildlifetrust,org.uk Follow road S. 1st L onto Bore Place. After 0.1 mile FP on R through cottages. 1st style on L, past house via permissive path 51.2086,0.1545 ↴

7 RANSCOMBE FARM

Enjoy beautiful walks through peaceful ancient woodland and farmland that is now a 500-acre country park reserve that acts as a visual reminder of the diversity of colour and species that existed before modern farm practices took over. In summer, poppies and viper's bugloss add vibrant splashes of colour to the arable fields. Ranscombe is the home farm of Plantlife, the organisation that speaks up for wild flora, and it holds guided walks focusing on the season's highlights.

→ Ranscombe Farm, Cuxton, Rochester, Kent ME2 1LA 01722 342742 plantlife.org.uk 51.3838,0.4577 ↴

8 DUNGENESS RSPB

This RSPB reserve is a special place to visit for its incredible wild flowers as well as its famous birds. Here, in the harsh sea-assaulted landscape, the summer spectacle of massed viper's bugloss, wild carrot, rare yellow horned poppy and biting stonecrop is a joy to discover. Half of all Britain's native flower species can be found growing here. There are often ranger guided walks, or just head out on your own. Nearby is the late Derek Jarman's much-acclaimed wild garden, not open to visitors. The film-maker created a garden anchored in its natural context using natural shingle and native wild flowers – an icon of how to garden in harsh surroundings.

→ Boulderwell Farm, Dungeness Road, Romney Marsh, Kent TN29 9PN 01797 320588 rspb.org.uk 50.9398,0.9336 ↴

BLEAN WOOD RSPB

Home to the song of nightingales, nightjars and woodcocks, a walk here will always enchant. This ancient woodland is managed by the RSPB for its wealth of birds but it's also a haven for dragonflies and butterflies including one of the largest colonies of rare heath fritillary butterfly. Dominated by oaks, sweet chestnuts and beech, which enjoy the heavy acidic clay soils, the forest has been coppiced for a thousand years and this ancient management has ensured its wealth of biodiversity. Visit in spring for the deep carpets of bluebells that cover the woodland floor.

→ Rough Common Road, Rough Common, Port Ellen, Kent CT2 9DD 01227 464898 rspb.org.uk 51.2941,1.0408 ↴

12 SECRET GARDENS OF SANDWICH

Accommodation

10 PRIEST'S HOUSE, SISSINGHURST

No visit to Kent's gardens should miss the romantic, world-famous Sissinghurst. But the best way to experience the passionate displays of Vita Sackville-West's unequalled garden creation is to stay in Priest's House. Here, when the light is low and at its finest, you can wander without the crowds through Vita's inspired and abundant planting. Windows overlook the famous white garden, which was originally designed to be enjoyed by moonlight, and there is a private garden to retreat to when the crowds descend.

→ Biddenden Road, Cranbrook, Kent TN17 2AB, 0344 3351287 nationaltrustcottages.co.uk

🐾 🍴 🏠

11 BADGELLS WOOD CAMPING

Dens and hideouts abound in this lovely back-to-nature woodland campsite. Pitch your tent among beautiful coppiced sweet chestnuts or, in May, amid scented bluebells. The quiet woods border a Site of Special Scientific Interest where you can see owls and peregrine falcons and listen to bird song. At the campsite there are composting loos and the free range chickens that scratch about provide eggs for breakfast. As it is off-grid, light comes from the campfire or stars. There are bushcraft lessons to be had and it's simply a great place for children to run free.

→ Whitehorse Rd, Meopham, Kent DA13 0UF 07528 609324 badgellswoodcamping.co.uk

🏠 ♻

11 BADGELLS WOOD CAMPING

Food

12 SECRET GARDENS OF SANDWICH

The Secret Gardens of Sandwich are home to the luxurious Salutation B&B and tea room. It's a real haven from the tourist bustle of Sandwich. Designed by architect Lutyens, with planting inspired by Gertrude Jekyll, the gardens offer some lovely surprises. A stunning rose sculpture rests in the flower meadow and the tumbling rose arbour cries out for a good book and cushion. The tea rooms, serving lunches and proper cream teas, are unfortunately not on the garden side but the terrace overlooks the handsome house. Knightrider St, Sandwich, Kent CT13 9EW 01304 619919 the-secretgardens.co.uk ⏰ Mar daily 10am–4pm, Apr–Sep daily 10am–5pm, Oct–Dec daily 11am–4pm

🐾 🍴 🏠

13 THE PINES TEA ROOM

High above windy St Margaret's at Cliffe on the edge of England, overlooking the Channel, nestles The Pines Tea Room. It's part of the charitable trust that also

A stunning rose sculpture rests in the flower meadow and the tumbling rose arbour cries out for a good book and cushion

runs the eco Pines Garden opposite. The tea room is deservedly popular and full of chatter. Home-grown and home-made salads, quiches, focaccia breads and soups are enjoyed in the garden yurt, café or terrace. Other food options in the area just don't compete and there's lots of outdoor seating if the weather is fine.

→ Beach Road, St Margaret's Bay, Dover, Kent CT15 6DZ 01304 853173 pinesgarden.co.uk ⏰ Apr–Sep daily 10am–4.30pm, Oct–Mar Wed–Sun 10am–4.30pm

🐾 🍴 ❀

14   GREAT COMP TEAROOM

14   GREAT COMP SALVIA NURSERY

14   GREAT COMP TEAROOM

The garden of Great Comp, surrounding a 17th-century manor house, is known for its planting among ruins, its bold Italian gardens and its specialist salvia nursery. But it's also home to the delightful Old Dairy Tearoom. Run by two lovely ladies, the cosy vintage feel is a welcome reward for the weary garden visitor. Retro crocheted rugs cover comfortable sofas, and nostalgic finds are for sale in the adjoining gift shop. Delicious cream teas, home-made cakes and lunches are served outside on the terrace or in the cosy tea room. Or discover the covered hideaway with its toybox, doll's house and ample seating.

Comp Lane, Platt, Kent TN15 8QS
01732 885094 greatcompgarden.co.uk
Apr–Sept daily 11.30am–4.30pm
(Oct 12–4pm)

London & Home Counties

Escape the city and discover tranquil oases of inspiring
green spaces, rich with unexpected wildlife.

London & Home Counties

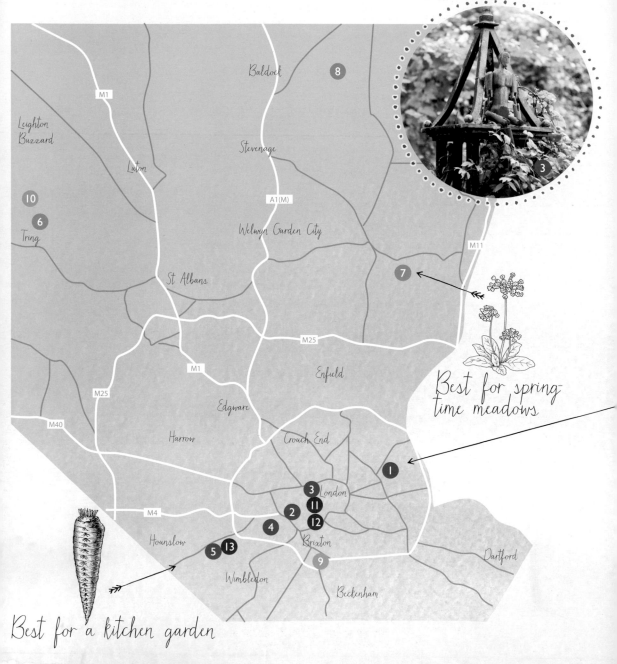

Best for spring-time meadows

Best for a kitchen garden

The highlights

>> Discover plants from all over the world growing in their natural communities in Stratford (1)

>> Enjoy delicious vegetarian food in an atmospheric old church garden in Lambeth (11)

>> Wander along miles of lakeside pathways, through meadows alive with butterflies and wild flowers (6)

>> Indulge in delicious Italian slow food in a Richmond glasshouse filled with tree ferns (13)

Best for miles of meadows and gardens

With over 8 million people living in the capital city today, the need for accessible green spaces is obvious. But there is a difference between a green space and a wild one. There is no doubt that London's green spaces are beneficial for mind, body, and spirit, but hidden amongst the city's streets are many quite wild, accessible pockets where nature thrives.

One of the smallest of these might be the Phoenix community garden between Leicester Square and Tottenham Court Road, where, in a tiny wildlife pond – a very small fragment of habitat – a community of frogs survives. On a larger scale, the London Wetlands Centre in Barnes is a contemporary wildlife haven that in the last 15 years has built up its flora and fauna to become one of London's biodiversity hotspots.

Valuable sites in this region include Kew Gardens, which plays a key role in global plant conservation, and London's first botanic garden, the historic Chelsea Physic Garden. Both offer hours if not days of rich horticultural discoveries, but they also come at a price that's prohibitive for a quick drop-in unless you invest in membership.

For a free adventure, there are multiple huge open spaces just bursting with natural wonders. Epping Forest's staggering 6,000 acres is rich with wildlife from small stag beetles to huge, antlered stags, and two thirds of it is now designated an SSSI. The reinvigorated Lee Valley regional park is Greater London's largest parkland,

covering an even larger area of 10,000 acres. It extends from Ware in Hertfordshire right down to Stratford and the Olympic Park.

Three years after the Olympic Games of summer 2012, their legacy, in gardening terms, has been far-reaching. The Queen Elizabeth Olympic Park, which re-opened in spring 2014, now extends over 500 acres of riverside and parkland, and its glorious gardens opened up naturalistic planting styles and meadows to the wider public. To the north of the capital, the chalk grasslands of Hertfordshire and Buckinghamshire offer meadows filled with the song of skylarks in spring and the chirping of crickets in summer. And Hunsdson Mead SSSI at Roydon, Essex, is only half an hour by train from Liverpool Street Station.

Gardens

1 QUEEN ELIZABETH OLYMPIC PARK

The infuence of the planting in London's Olympic Park continues in the gardens and nurseries of the UK. At its core, the park focuses on biodiversity and precious ecological networks. To the north are acres of wild wetlands, meadows, newly planted woodlands, and nature trails. To the south, are the new pleasure gardens and the original 2012 gardens. The latter, created by designer Sarah Price with Professors Nigel Dunnett and James Hitchmough of Sheffield University, introduced a fresh, new style of planting – particularly for public green spaces. Nearly a mile of paths floats through four continents of plant communities. Matrix plantings of grasses and perennials offer us a glimpse of the wild meadow habitats found across the globe, as well as insights into the origins of many of the ornamental plants that we grow in our gardens. In the newer gardens through Canal Park, Piet Oudolf's highly acclaimed prairie plantings are a perfect counterbalance to the concrete.

→ Tube Stratford or Hackney Wick. London E20 2ST 0800 0722110 queenelizabetholympicpark.co.uk ⏱ open access 🥡 ♿ 🍴

1 QUEEN ELIZABETH OLYMPIC PARK

2 CHELSEA PHYSIC GARDEN

Screened from the bustle of the city's streets, the Chelsea Physic Garden conceals a prodigious hoard of plants. Established in 1673 by the Worshipful Society of Apothecaries, its purpose was the study of useful plants. One hundred years after it was founded it was to become the world's

2 CHELSEA PHYSIC GARDEN

most important botanic garden. Although the site is smaller than its original layout, there are still three acres to explore, and it really does feel like you've stumbled into an oasis. The mood one sunny October morning was of quiet contemplation and learning. School children were silent as mice and local residents seemed to be popping in for a wander and lunch on the terrace. Throughout the year, a diverse range of events is on offer, from prehistoric plant history to compost clinics, from art to herbalism and everything green in between. The cafe is excellent.

→ Tube Sloane Sq. 66 Royal Hospital Rd, Chelsea SW3 4HS 0207 3525646 chelseaphysicgarden.co.uk ⏱ Apr–Oct, Tue–Fri, Sun & BH 11–6pm; Nov–Mar, Mon–Fri 9.30–dusk 🥡 🍴 🌷

3 PHOENIX GARDEN

Since 1984, the small sliver of green in London's frenetic West End has offered its many appreciative visitors a space for rest and reflection, and some creatures have made it their home. In early spring, frogs raucously search out their mates in the small wildlife pond. In the autumn sunshine, office workers take time out – heads back, eyes closed, their ears picking out birdsong from the background hum. It is a true wild garden. Ivy covered in foraging bees hangs from the fencing, and inside wildflower seedheads tangled themselves up with velvet roses and bright salvias. This is

a community garden, created and managed using sustainable techniques. Plants are chosen so they require no watering. There are no 'weeds' and no 'pests'.

→ Tube Tottenham Ct Rd. Enter off St. Giles Passage. 21 Stacey St, London WC2H 8DG thephoenixgarden.org ⏱ daily 8.30–dusk 🥡

4 LONDON WETLAND CENTRE

When it comes to biodiversity in the capital, the Wetland Centre probably takes the lead – a remarkable feat when you consider that just 15 years ago the site was a mass of concrete reservoirs. Once drained, the concrete was crushed for paths, and lakes now fill the clay membranes. The open marshes, reedbeds and wet fenland meadows now offer habitat to a vast array of wildlife. Sir Peter Scott's vision of a wetland centre in the heart of the city has been joyously realised. Ignore the constant sound of planes overhead and and explore miles of paths against a shifting backdrop of wild gardens and marshy banks of native plants. The spring display in the fritillary meadow is the result of hundreds of native bulbs, including southern marsh orchids, all planted by hand. There is also a collection of sustainable gardens including a rain garden by Nigel Dunnett, whose planting designs integrate ecology and aesthetics.

→ Bus Hammersmith tube or 15 min walk from Barnes Station. Queen Elizabeth's Walk, Barnes SW13 9WT 0208 4094400 wwt.org.uk ⏱ daily 9.30 - 6pm (5pm winter) 🥡 ♿ 🍴

3 PHOENIX GARDEN

4 LONDON WETLAND CENTRE

5 HAM HOUSE

From Richmond tube, walk along the river bank past Petersham Nurseries (see Food) to beautiful Ham House. Overhead, the skies are filled with the chatter of green parakeets. The walled kitchen garden is one of the most productive in London, supplying the newly renovated orangery cafe with an array of unusual produce, including salsify and skirret. The Wilderness and the acres of meadows, divine in early summer, are now managed to enhance their grass and flower diversity. Don't miss the little library at the far end of the café, which is full of old and new gardening books. A cosy woodburner makes this a great place to hide away in if the sun isn't shining on the terrace outside.

1.5 miles by riverside footpath from Richmond Tube. Ham Street, Ham, Richmond TW10 7RS 0208 9401950 nationaltrust.org.uk
daily, 10—5pm

Surrounding the lakes,
are miles of paths, where
you can stroll through
a fantastic display of
wild flowers.

7 HUNSDON MEAD

Meadows

6 COLLEGE LAKE

The wildlife trust-run nature reserve outside Tring, set within the now-flooded chalk quarry, is predominantly for wildfowl. Surrounding the lake are miles of paths, where you can stroll through a fantastic display of wild flowers. Primroses and cowslips start the season, followed by a combination of annual meadow plants. In June and July, the rough chalk grassland is dotted with orchids, including the elusive bee orchid. This is also a good time to enjoy the stunning 'cornfield flower' project that started 30 years ago. It's a great place to take children, with lots of nature-focused activities including butterfly spotting. There is a small café in the sedum-roofed eco-centre. For the less able, there are mobility vehicles and some wheelchair access.

→ Park at visitor centre (parking charge). Signed off Upper Icknield Way B488, Tring HP23 5QG 01442 826774 bbowt.org.uk
⏰ daily 9.30–5.30pm (4pm in winter)
51.8161,-0.6444 ⚐ 🍴

7 HUNSDON MEAD SSSI

The flood meadows along the river Stort are some of the best-preserved, unimproved grasslands in Hertfordshire. Hunsdson Mead offers easy access (some wheelchair access along towpath) and a fascinating glimpse into our colourful farming history. Carpets of cowslips, lady's smock, and marsh marigolds welcome spring to the meadows. From April through to the end of July, you can see a range of wild flowers while listening to the call of the skylark.
→ Roydon station, Harlow, Essex CM19 5EH 01727 858901 hertswildlifetrust.org.uk walk 1 mile E twds Harlow along R. Stort towpath. Info sign shows permissive paths. 50.7762,-0.0511 ⚐

8 BLAGROVE COMMON SSSI

Blagrove is one of the only places in this area to see large swathes of ragged robin, as well as early marsh, southern marsh, and common-spotted orchid as they emerge from the damp commons in May and June. Wear boots as it can get very muddy. Throughout the summer, butterflies and birds feast on the rushes and tufted hair grass (*Deschampsia*), and the exotic spotted flycatcher sometimes breeds here. In late, July the grass is cut and raked to ensure the rushes don't take over, and handsome longhorn cattle are let in to graze.
→ Limited parking on edge of green on Beckfield Ln. Follow signposted FP on R (next to white house). Green End, Nr Sandon, Herts SG9 0RG
hertswildlifetrust.org.uk 51.9851,-0.0676 ⚐

Accommodation

9 THE GARDEN B&B

The B&B in this airy Victorian villa is worthy of its name and although you can't sleep in the garden, you can tiptoe through the tulips and breakfast in its verdant oasis. With four perfectly formed, mature garden rooms there are lots of places to hide away with a book and tea, and forget that you are in the city. Your host, Winkle, a trained horticulturalist, can offer advice on gardens and green spaces to visit in the capital. Inside objets d'art, collected over the years and on their travels by Winkle and Philip, fill the house and add to the wonderfully warm ambience of their home.

→ 4 min walk from Streatham Hill overground station. 38 Killieser Avenue, Streatham Hill, London SW2 4NT 0208 6714196 thegardenbedandbreakfast.com

For other places to stay in London I highly recommend airbnb. There are so many fantastic quirky places, including yurts in gardens and houseboats on the river near Kew Gardens.

10 WESTEND HOUSE B&B

Richard and Sue are wonderful hosts who are happy to share their lovely two-acre garden as well as their stories of running a rare-breed smallholding. Breakfast is served in the conservatory of the converted Tudor cottages, which overlook the garden and its sculptures. Home-reared meat and garden vegetables are on the menu at Sue's delicious dinners and suppers, but do book in advance. The garden is full of surprises, including a large wildlife pond complete with painted summerhouse designed for candlelit suppers overlooking the rowing boat and pontoon.

→ West End Road, Cheddington, Leighton Buzzard, Bucks LU7 0RP 01296 661332 westendhousecheddington.co.uk

11 THE GARDEN MUSEUM

Food

11 GARDEN MUSEUM

One of the nicest places for a simple lunch in central London is the Garden Museum café in Lambeth. In historic surroundings that include the carved tomb of John Tradescant, the 15th-century plant hunter, the 17th century style knot gardens, and the ivy-clad abandoned church of St Mary's, the grounds offer more than just a breath of the sweetest air around. Outside and in, superior vegetarian and vegan dishes are

10 WESTEND HOUSE B&B

served along with cakes and coffee – with much of the produce from the on-site kitchen garden. The museum is a treasure trove. It puts on exhibitions and offers a programme of thoughtful talks and events on what gardening is and what it means.

→ Thames South Bank next to Lambeth Palace. Lambeth Palace Road, London SE1 7LB 0207 4018865 gardenmuseum.org.uk ⏰ daily 10.30–5pm (Sat & Sun 4pm)

12 BONNINGTON CAFÉ

Just round the corner from Bonnington Square community garden in Vauxhall is the lovely Bonnington café, a co-op offering vegetarian and vegan fare. Providing healthy, cheap food for the community from a squat in the 1980s, the café grew and still serves delicious, excellent-value dishes. The menu is very varied: the café's cooks hail from all over the world, adding their own spice to this leafy corner. It's cash only, unlicensed, and very popular, so book a table and bring your own bottle.

→ Tube Vauxhall. 11 Vauxhall Grove, London SW8 1TD 07552 475535 bonningtoncafe. co.uk ⏰ daily 12–2pm, 6.30pm–10.30pm

11 GARDEN MUSEUM

12 BONNINGTON CAFÉ

13 PETERSHAM NURSERIES

Petersham Nursery has become something of an institution for food-loving gardeners. It can get busy, but choose your time and enjoy a delicious, relaxed lunch with friends in the wonderful indoor-garden spaces. Lunch consists of a few first-class, hand-picked Italian slow-food seasonal dishes that utilise the heritage produce from the walled kitchen garden. For simpler but still delicious meals or maybe just a coffee, head to the equally attractive Teahouse. Supper clubs are sometimes held at the café in the evening and I can only imagine how bewitching the place must look illuminated by candlelight.

Signed off Petersham Road, Richmond TW10 7AB 0208 9405230 petershamnurseries.com Tue–Sun, 10–4.30pm (Sun 11am)

KENTWELL

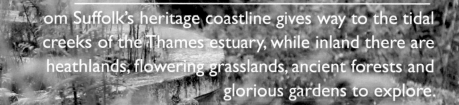

Suffolk & Essex

om Suffolk's heritage coastline gives way to the tidal creeks of the Thames estuary, while inland there are heathlands, flowering grasslands, ancient forests and glorious gardens to explore.

Suffolk & Essex
The highlights

›› Eat and drink local, then sleep in a special cabin designed just for star-gazing (9)

›› Find enchantment in a kitchen garden contained within a moated castle (1)

›› Wander through one of Britain's finest ancient woodlands (6)

›› Indulge in a long vintners' lunch accompanied by some excellent British wine (13)

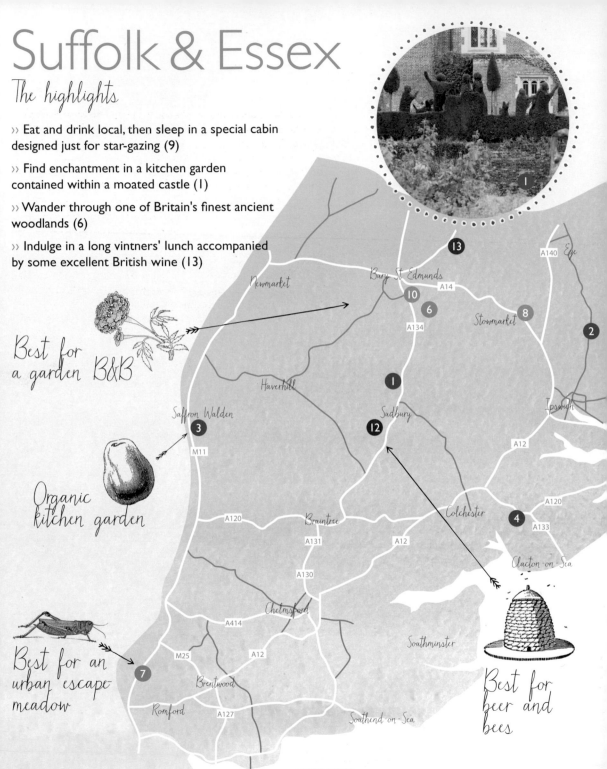

Best for
a garden B&B

Organic
kitchen garden

Best for an
urban escape-
meadow

Best for
beer and
bees

Newmarket
Bury St Edmunds
A14
A140   Eye
Stowmarket
A134
Haverhill
Saffron Walden
Sudbury
Ipswich
M11
A12
A120
Braintree
Colchester
A120
A131
A12
A133
A130
Clacton-on-Sea
Chelmsford
Southminster
A414
M25
A12
Brentwood
Romford
A127
Southend-on-Sea

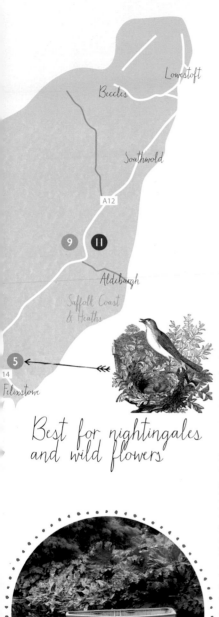

Lowestoft

Beccles

Southwold

A12

9 11

Aldeburgh

Suffolk Coast
& Heaths

5

14

Felixstowe

*Best for nightingales
and wild flowers*

Within easy reach of the capital and blessed with wonderful coastlines and ancient forests, the counties of Suffolk and Essex are full of surprises. Bradfield Woods nature reserve is considered one of England's finest ancient woodlands and home to hundreds of species of birds, fungi and flowers. For bluebells, head to Captain's Wood and experience the largest expanse of spring-time blue in the county. Other meadows not to be missed include delightful Newbourne Springs, Arger Fen and Spouse's Vale reserve, Martin's Coronation Meadow, and Mickfield meadow where snake's head fritillary – rare in Suffolk – can be seen in glorious profusion. Wildflower-rich Shut Heath nature reserve is said to have glow-worms but they proved elusive when we visited. The local wildlife trusts' websites offer lots of information and there are guided walks with the knowledgeable and often-charming rangers.

To see the beautiful results of a garden designd and planted along ecological lines, visit Beth Chatto's famous gardens near Elmstead in Essex. Here in the 1960s, Beth and her late husband created an oasis on an unpromising site, following the principle of using only plants that were naturally suited to the conditions. Moisture-lovers flourish in the boggy areas, while plants in the dry garden thrive without water and with minimal maintenance.

If you long for romance, you'll find it at the glorious gardens of moated Helmingham Hall and Kentwell Hall. The walled gardens of Kentwell were stunning even in the pouring rain.

We spent a perfect summer Saturday wandering around the lovely farmers' market held at Wyken Hall Vineyards. After filling my basket with local plums, cheeses, vegetables and meats we treated ourselves to lunch at the excellent Leaping Hare restaurant. Here, in an ancient timber-framed barn you can choose from the vintners' menu and do some wine-tasting. There are woodland walks to help you digest, but pretty Wyken Hall gardens are not open on Saturdays. If you miss the farmer's market, home-reared organic meat, flour and vegetables can be bought from Maple organic farm where you can see very happy hens and pigs and meet the equally happy farmer.

4

11

Gardens

1 KENTWELL

Even in the rain Kentwell has the air of a lost garden paradise. Looking for shelter, we went in search of coffee in the charming converted stables. Sitting in an old armchair, I enjoyed the fluffiest Victoria sponge smothered in freshly whipped cream while the chickens and peacocks looked on hungrily. There are heritage breeds of pigs, sheep, and donkeys at the Tudor farm, but the real draw for us was the mysterious walled garden. We visited in August when the pears and apples clung tightly to their old, mossy espaliers, the restrained geometry of the branches contrasting with the bounteous herb and vegetable beds. In the summer rain, the place was ours and the romance level was off the scale. Vines as thick as an elephant's leg burst out of the tumbledown vine houses, while roses draped themselves over arched, studded doorways. And all this beauty was displayed against the backdrop of gorgeous, moated Kentwell Hall. At the house, which is open for visits, you can take a peek into a 500-year-old family home. Looking out of the window, you catch sight of a topiary pied piper who seems to be playing to the potager beds bursting with borlotti beans and artichokes, together with their happy audience of leaves.
→ Long Melford, Sudbury, Suffolk CO10 9BA 01787 310207 kentwell.co.uk
⏱ various days from mid Feb–mid Sept check website for details 🥤 🍴

1 KENTWELL

2 HELMINGHAM HALL

2 HELMINGHAM HALL

This beautiful Suffolk estate, home of designer Xa Tollemache, has it all – historic moated house, huge oaks, wild meadows, bridges, orchards, tumbling roses, and a lovely vegetable garden. Inquisitive highland cattle and deer wander in the Tudor parkland, then you cross the moat to the wildflower garden and orchard. There, paths cut through the spring-flowering cowslips and primroses, which make way for a beautiful show of ox-eye daisies and meadow orchids later in the summer. There are many formal garden rooms to discover nearer the house but our favourite was the vegetable plot in the walled garden. Hanging from the rusted pergola, lanterns of gourds added colour and interest to the other rampant climbers, and vegetables mingled with abundant cottage-garden flowers. The stable shop sells surplus vegetables and that day visitors walked out with bags of beans for their supper. The Coach House tea room serves proper afternoon tea, or indulge in soups and salads fresh from the garden.
→ Helmingham, Stowmarket, Suffolk IP14 6EF 01473 890799 helmingham.com
⏱ May–Mid Sep Tue, Wed, Thu, Sun & BH 12–5pm 🥤 🐾 🍴

3 AUDLEY END WALLED GARDEN

Within the palatial grounds of Audley End, well away from the house and the (to my taste) vulgar Victorian parterre, is the grand walled kitchen garden. Run on organic principles, it is a showcase for life in a Victorian kitchen garden and vividly described in the detailed diary of William Cresswell, gardener, in 1874. In the vast glasshouses, the cultivation of grapes, peaches and figs, as well as strawberry forcing, was a serious business. There are over 150 varieties of apples to discover and 60 varieties of tomatoes. Visit the potting shed to buy some of the fresh produce or, if you live locally, sign up for a veg box.
→ London Rd, Saffron Walden, Essex CB11 4JF 0870 3331181 english-heritage.org.uk
⏱ Nov–Mar, Sat & Sun 10–4pm; Apr–Oct daily 🥤 🍴 🌸

4 THE BETH CHATTO GARDENS

The gardens of pioneering plantswoman Beth Chatto display a deep understanding of both the local environment and plant ecology. Faced with an overgrown site and poor soil in an area with very low rainfall, the Chattos combined their knowledge and sought plants from around the world that would thrive under specific conditions. Beth's first book, *The Dry Garden* was published in 1978, and the stunning gravel garden is testament to her low-maintenance, drought-resistant planting. The woodland garden is magical in spring and the nursery is renowned for its special plants.
→ Elmstead Market, Colchester, Essex CO7 7DB 01206 822007 bethchatto.co.uk
⏱ daily 9–5pm (Sunday 10–5pm); until 4pm in winter 🥤 🐾 🍴 🌸

4 THE BETH CHATTO GARDENS

3 AUDLEY END WALLED GARDEN

Leaf Beet Rf

Leaf Beet Swiss Chard

1 KENTWELL

Ancient trees, butterflies
and beautiful show of
ragged robin, water avens,
and common twayblade
– all thrive in this
magical wooded valley.

6 BRADFIELD WOODS NATURE RESERVE

Meadows

5 NEWBOURNE SPRINGS

Ancient trees, butterflies, and a beautiful show of ragged robin, water avens, marsh marigolds and common twayblade – all thrive in this magical wooded valley. Listen to the call of the elusive nightingale in spring, or on balmy summer nights, if luck is on your side, you might see glow-worms.
→ Look for nature reserve signs, car park and entrance on Woodbridge Lane, Newbourne, Ipswich, Suffolk IP12 4NY 01394 411019 suffolkwildlifetrust.org. Follow marked trail 52.0411, 1.3151 ⚲

6 BRADFIELD WOODS NATURE RESERVE

Ash trees have been coppiced here for over a thousand years and this traditional method of woodland management provides a haven for wildlife. Considered by many to be among the most wildlife-rich woods in Britain, the reserve contains over 370 species of flowering plant and 420 different fungi. Here in the wide cut grassy paths I saw the startling caterpillar of the elephant hawkmoth hanging on a rosebay willowherb stem. There is a designated, well-signposted butterfly glade, and it's worth stopping at the visitor centre to find out which species the rangers have spotted.
→ Felsham Rd, Bradfield St George, Bury St Edmund's, Suffolk IP30 0AQ 01449 737996 suffolkwildlifetrust.org. 52.1863,0.8300 ⚲

7 RODING VALLEY MEADOWS SSSI

The unimproved meadows of the Roding valley comprise the largest surviving area of traditionally managed, flood-plain hay meadow in the South East. From May, the mosaic pattern of meadows and old hedgerows erupts with wild flowers, creating a peaceful haven away from busy Chigwell. Southern marsh orchids, devil's-bit scabious, and great stands of purple loosestrife decorate the pretty valley.
→ Chigwell Tube 25 min walk to Grange Farm Centre (parking). Grange Farm Lane, High Road, Chigwell, Essex IG7 6DP 0208 1274323 grangefarmcentre.co.uk. Waymarked FP crosses M11 following river valley. 51.6325,0.0763 ⚲

Accommodation

8 THE GIG HOUSE COLUMBINE HALL

Once the stable for Suffolk heavy horses, the Gig House is now a stunning three-bedroom holiday cottage with its own private garden. Its soft colours, exposed beams and white-painted wooden floors, at once rustic and luxurious, display the design flair of the hall's owners. The interiors and gardens of the moated hall have received much acclaim and the gardens are sometimes open for NGS.
→ Stowupland, Stowmarket, Suffolk IP14 4AT 01449 612219 columbinehall.co.uk ⚱ 🏠

8 THE GIG HOUSE

9 ALDE GARDEN

Hidden behind the Sweffling pub is a fantasy camping world filled with happy families and rosy-cheeked children. It's a small plot with a big heart and great community spirit. Accommodation is an eclectic mix of gypsy caravans and quirky sheds – one is designed specifically for star gazing – or you can bring your own tent and pitch it under the apple trees among the wild flowers, geese, and funny feathered ducks. The communal areas are well-equipped with proper loos and sparkling showers. Head to the friendly pub for supper where almost 70 per cent of the food and drink is locally sourced.
→ Off the B1119 between Framlingham and Saxmundham. Low Road, Sweffling, Suffolk IP17 2BB 01728 664178 aldegarden.co.uk

9 ALDE GARDEN

This is how a rural farm shop should be. Two black labs lay asleep in the sun, the old barns in the courtyard filled with apple presses and vintage tractors.

10 LUCY REDMAN'S GARDEN

Stay in the colourful and cosy thatched home of Lucy Redman. The garden is a creative explosion of reclaimed finds, innovative plantings and a keen and quirky eye for design. Her much-loved garden is open to visitors on Fridays throughout the spring and summer but B&B guests get to enjoy it in the evening and morning light. Breakfast is a hearty spread of eggs from their chickens, sausage and bacon from their pigs, and tomatoes from the garden. Lucy also runs a variety of design and horticultural courses and you will definitely not leave uninspired.
→ 6 The Village, Rushbrooke, Bury St Edmunds, Suffolk IP30 0ER 01284 386250
lucyredman.co.uk

Food

11 MAPLE ORGANIC FARM

We stumbled upon idyllic Maple Farm on our way to the coast, and what a find! It is my idea of the perfect rural farm shop: two black labradors lay asleep in the sun, there were apple presses and vintage tractors in the courtyard barns, and a fantastic, bijou farm shop. It's not often that a single organic farm offers such an incredible range of organic, home-grown produce. We

11 MAPLE ORGANIC FARM

bought just about everything we needed: organic flour ground on site, apple juice, sausages from the happy pigs, potatoes, eggs, heritage tomatoes, multi-coloured beans, and a large bunch of flowers. If only shopping could always be such fun.
→ East Green Kelsale, Saxmundham, Suffolk IP17 2PL 01728 652000
maplefarmkelsale.co.uk daily

12 THE PHEASANT INN

In the pub's one-acre, organic kitchen garden, chickens and beehives are tended by chef, owner, and former landscape gardener, James Donoghue. He and his wife Diana have even installed a smokery where they cold oak-smoke everything from local rape-seed oil, to fish, game, and even the hops for their own Pheasant beer. Food is fresh and seasonal and sourced, where possible, from within a ten-mile radius. From the garden, there are lovely views to the fields beyond. At their boutique hotel down the road, there is a choice of five rooms.
→ Church St, Halstead, Essex CO9 3AU 01787 461196 thepheasant.net
daily 12–12.30pm & 6.30–9pm

10 LUCY REDMAN GARDEN

13 LEAPING HARE AT WYKEN HALL

13 LEAPING HARE AT WYKEN HALL

Wyken Vineyards is not only a fantastic foodie destination, it also boasts a well-curated bookshop and homeware store as well as a lovely restaurant in the estate's 400-year-old timber barn. Home of Carla Carlisle, her book, *South Facing Slope*, records how the family planted Wyken's vines. Their excellent red, white, and sparkling wines can be enjoyed alongside special vintners' menus or just with cake. In the gardens, which are open to visitors (not Saturdays), peacocks and guinea fowl wander among the topiary and flowers. And if you haven't yet worked up an appetite, there are lovely woodland walks to enjoy. Visit on a Saturday morning and shop at the excellent farmers' market, which is held weekly and brings together local producers.

Wyken Vineyard, Stanton, Bury St Edmunds, IP31 2DW 01359 250287 wykenvineyards.co.uk   daily lunch 12 – 2.30pm & Fri, Sat eve from 7pm

HOLKHAM HALL

Norfolk

Famed for its wildlife-rich fens, crabs and picturesque villages, Norfolk also possesses an incredible diversity of enchanting wild gardens.

Norfolk

The highlights

›› Visit the romantic moated gardens at Hindringham and Mannington Hall (3 & 5)

›› See bountiful allotments growing in the walled garden at Felbrigg (4)

›› Learn about the history of Holkham's beautiful relic walled gardens (1)

›› Go butterfly spotting in Norfolk's largest remaining chalk grassland (6)

Norfolk's largest wildflower meadows

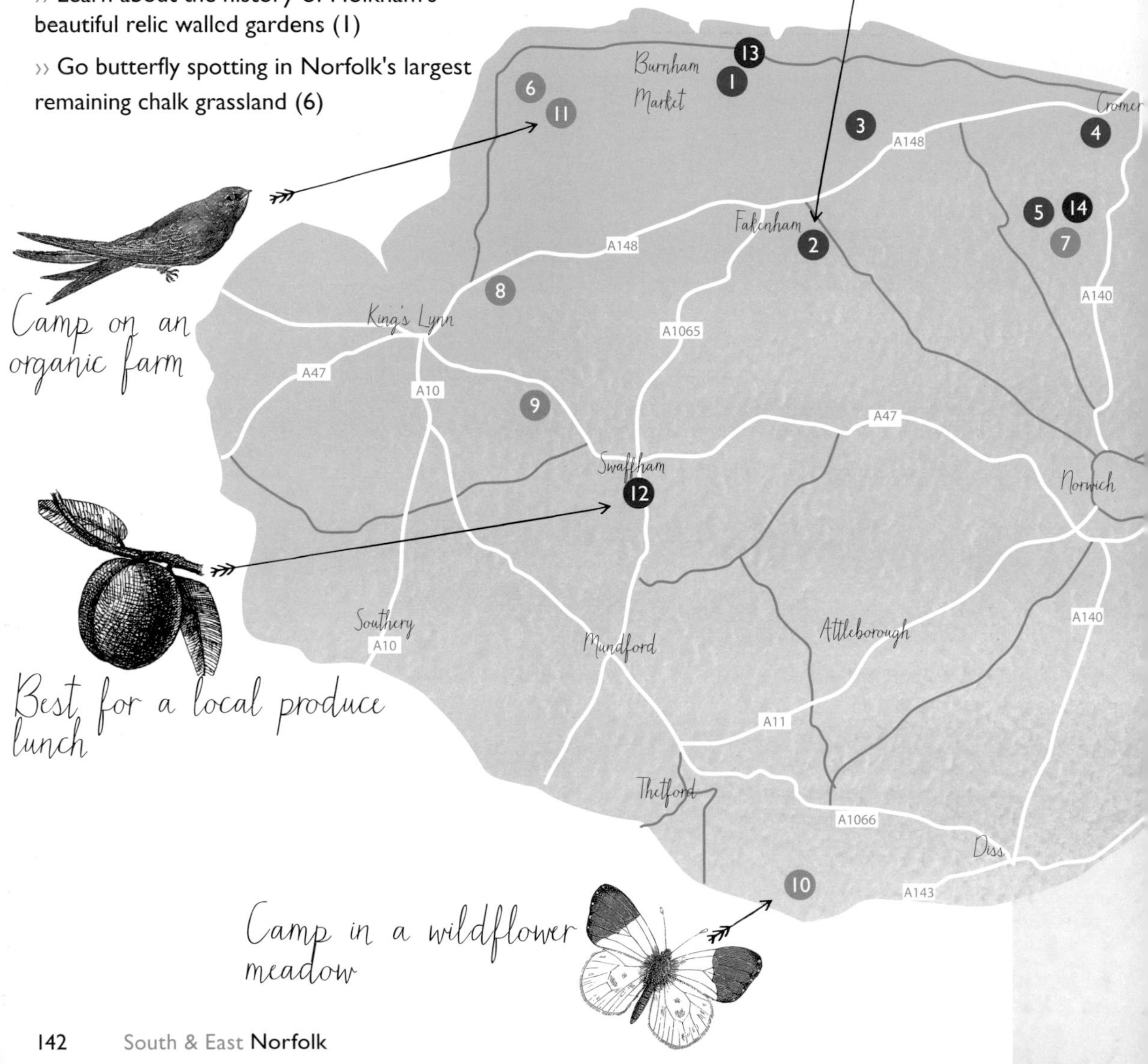

Camp on an organic farm

Best for a local produce lunch

Camp in a wildflower meadow

Burnham Market

Cromer

Fakenham

King's Lynn

Swaffham

Norwich

Southery

Mundford

Attleborough

Thetford

Diss

A148

A148

A1065

A47

A10

A47

A140

A140

A10

A11

A1066

A143

In an area famed for its rich fenland habitat and marine bounty, I was surprised to hear of the sad state of Norfolk's wildflower meadows. Their decline has been so extreme that the county's Coronation Meadow is now reduced to a roadside verge along Wood Lane in Long Stratton, near Diss. According to Plantlife, we now have more wildflower-rich roadside verges nationally than we do wildflower meadows. In Norfolk's Wood Lane, the seeds of the scarce sulphur clover and dyer's greenweed will be harvested and used to restore the meadows of neighbouring farms.

For a spectacular display of shingle coastal flowers, it's worth heading to RSPB Snettisham to see horned poppies and viper's bugloss thriving in defiance of the coastal winds. Or visit the wildlife gardens and café of award-winning Natural Surroundings in the lovely Glaven Valley. Another fantastic place to walk among the wild flowers is on the public and permissive paths of Courtyard Farm in Ringstead, an arable farm that displays the highest organic standards. There is a bunkhouse and simple camping should you wish to stay longer. At Pensthorpe Natural Park, visit the large wildflower meadow on the reserve and admire Piet Oudolf's rich planting designs, which perfectly echo the colour, form, and movement of the native meadows.

For beautiful gardens with wild hearts seek out deeply romantic Hindringham Hall with its geese, moat, and organic kitchen garden. Holkham Hall walled garden is

another gem, although on an altogether grander but equally romantic scale. Once Europe's largest productive walled garden, it is now a beautiful restoration project. Swathes of globe thistle (*Echinops*) and fennel look as if they could have planted themselves, and the crumbling glasshouses add to the romance.

Norfolk is a food-lover's paradise. If you are in busy Swaffham, head directly to CoCoes deli and café, or try and the more rural Saracen's Head inn, which has local food-hero status. At the attractive community allotments in the walled garden at Felbrigg you can pick up freshly harvested produce from the vegetable cart, then wander through the peaceful orchard, where hens wander freely and bees buzz around the hives.

Stalham

Great Yarmouth

Gardens

1 HOLKHAM HALL

This monumental Palladian house and its fertile farmland was the home of Thomas William Coke – Coke of Norfolk' – the 18th-century promoter of innovative agricultural techniques. He encouraged field rotation, ensuring that the soil was not exhausted and the tradition of good husbandry lives on at Holkham. The huge walled garden, once the largest in Europe, comprises six and a half acres of hollow, red brick walls that were heated from the inside to ward off frosts and ensure a plentiful supply of produce for the house. Once maintained by a staff of 50, this is now a peaceful and beautiful garden looked after by just two full-time gardeners and six volunteers. The restoration of the vast glasshouses (for vines, melons, and pineapples) within the mellow, great walls is currently a major project for the Holkham estate. Planting varies according to the individual garden 'rooms', but is generally informal, naturalistic and rich in colour and texture. In its current rather derelict state, with vines bursting through broken glass, the garden is a very romantic place.
→ Holkham Hall, Wells-next-the-Sea NR23 1RH 01328 710227 holkham.co.uk
⏰ Apr–Oct daily 10–5pm 🍴 ♟ 🍽

1 HOLKHAM HALL

2 PENSTHORPE

2 PENSTHORPE

Walk through one of Norfolk's largest flower meadow, visit Piet Oudolf's stunning Millennium Garden and learn about the wild flowers that thrive in the glorious Wensum Valley. Once through the car park and the crowded entrance gate, there is plenty of room for everyone to wander around at their leisure and enjoy the flowers, rare butterflies, and red squirrels. The traditionally managed hay meadow is a must-see. Grazed in autumn by Norfolk longhorns, the meadow in spring and summer buzzes with insects and offers the most delicate and perfect display of wild flowers. There is a good tea room and the kids loved the noisy adventure playground.
→ Fakenham Road, Fakenham NR21 0LN 01328 851465 pensthorpe.com
⏰ daily 10–5pm (4pm Jan & Feb)
🍴 🦢 🍽

3 HINDRINGHAM HALL

In a lovely rural location, close to Norfolk's wild coast and pretty villages, moated Hindringham Hall is a truly enchanting place to visit. From the moment you begin your walk up the drive, the view is bucolic. Black-horned sheep forage under the trees and geese patrol the orchard. A painted cart with plants for sale is the first indication of the attention to detail that you will find everywhere in the garden and little tea room. The sunny vegetable garden is organic and roses tumble from beautiful old walls. There is a Victorian nut walk, a wild garden and a water garden along the bank of the moat. Tea and delicious cake is served in bone-china cups and you can enjoy it out on the terrace. There are three delightful holiday cottages to rent on the estate.
→ Blacksmiths Lane, Hindringham, Near Fakenham NR21 0QA 01328 878226 hindringhamhall.org
⏰ Apr–Sept Sun 2–5pm & Wed 10–1pm
🍴 🏠 🍽 ❦

4 FELBRIGG HALL

Extensive woodland walks and rolling parkland are just two of the reasons to visit Felbrigg, but the walled garden is quite another. Contained with in it are the beautiful, bountiful, and very tidy allotments of the local residents. The setting is perfect – old red-brick walls covered with espaliered figs and even a working hexagonal 1750's dovecot. At the end of the garden lies a gate to the secluded orchard. On our visit here in August we were greeted by an idyllic scene. A hen with her young brood foraged in the long grass, bees buzzed in their hives, and the fruit trees were heavily laden with ripe yellow and purple plums, mulberries, apples and pears.
→ National cycle route 30. Off B1436 Felbrigg, Norwich NR11 8PR 01263 837444 nationaltrust.org.uk
⏰ Mar–Oct 11–5.30pm, Nov & Dec Thu–Sun 11–4pm (3pm in Dec) 🍴

3 HINDRINGHAM HALL

4 FELBRIGG HALL

5 MANNINGTON GARDENS

Beautiful, medieval, moated Mannington Hall, home of Lord and Lady Walpole, makes an elegant backdrop for your walk around the wildflower meadows that separate the lake from the moat. Next stop is the pretty Greedy Goose café for a generous ploughman's or home-baked cake. If the weather is good, sit outside on the sunny terrace, relax, and take time to drink in the wonderful views. In autumn, you can enjoy one of the more energetic wildlife walks – the area is groaning with a rich diversity of fungi, birds, and flora. There is glamping in the fields and a small children's playground. Nearby, Walpole Arms is a good place for refreshment or visit Norfolk's smallest café in the village and purchase some local vegetables or plants.

Mannington, Norwich NR11 7LY 01263 584175 manningtongardens.co.uk   May & Sept Sun 12–5pm, Jun–Aug Wed–Fri 11–5pm

On the edge of the little village of Ringstead is the largest remaining chalk grassland in Norfolk. In summer it is a great place to see over twenty species of butterfly, as well as linnets and yellowhammers.

6 RINGSTEAD DOWNS

Meadows

6 RINGSTEAD DOWNS

On the edge of the little village of Ringstead is the largest remaining chalk grassland in Norfolk. In summer it's a great place to see over 20 species of butterfly, as well as linnets and yellowhammers. Two lovely walks are accessed from the car park. The first is through the woods to the 'loosely' gardened chalk pit, known for its bee orchids. The other takes you from the car park through the Downs' steep valley, where common rock-rose, wild thyme, and salad burnet flourish.

→ From Ringstead Village take road S twds Sedgeford. After 0.3 miles turn R down track to small car park PE36 5JL norfolkwildlifetrust.org.uk. Access is via permissive bridleway through the Downs. 52.9301,0.5377 ↴

7 GREAT WOOD AT BLICKLING HALL

In spring, head to the Great Wood at the National Trust's Blickling Hall and enjoy the glorious displays of primroses, wood anemone, wild garlic, greater stitchwort, and yellow archangel, followed later by native bluebells and campion. Thousands of bluebell bulbs were transplanted to Blickling Hall's formal gardens in the 1930s and here, protected from the deer, they have thrived.

→ Direct access: NT car park at W edge of woods, 1.2 miles SE of Itteringham NR11 6PY. Main access: Blickling Hall, Blickling NR11 6NF 01263 738030 nationaltrust.org. uk 52.8217,1.2065 ↴

8 ROYDON COMMON

A joy to visit throughout the summer, but the common is at its most stunning in late summer and early autumn when the heather is in full flower. This is the largest remaining heathland in the area and a great place for butterfly watching. Bog myrtle, the carnivorous sundew plant, harebells, and the fantastical minotaur beetle can be all be seen here. As night falls, listen for the mystical churring of nightjars.

→ Car park 1.4 miles W of Roydon. Lynn Road, Roydon PE32 1AS norfolkwildlifetrust. org.uk 52.7776,0.4892 ↴

Accommodation

9 THE WOODSHED NARBOROUGH HALL

The lovely gardens of Narborough Hall are rarely open, but there is a June NGS day. Stay in their well-appointed woodshed, set in the wildlife-rich Nar valley. Inside, the simple wood-panelled interior has a cosy woodburning stove and a comfortable bedroom. B&B or self-catering is available. There are also wildflower walks to enjoy along Narborough's Railway Line NNR (see Norfolk Wildlife Trust for details).

→ Narborough Hall, Narborough, PE32 1TE, 01760 338827 narboroughhallgardens.com

9 THE WOODSHED

10 LING'S MEADOW CAMPING

If I were to run a campsite, I would try my hardest to recreate the halcyon meadow camping at Stanton Road farm. At Ling's four-acre natural meadow site, there are no cars (wheelbarrows provided), but you can light campfires and enjoy some serious stargazing – pure unadulterated fun. Over the last ten years, the meadows have been managed to increase the biodiversity, and meandering paths cut through the long grasses to each pitch. You can either erect your own tent or relax in one of the blanket-strewn bell tents. The sustainable facilities – compost loos and warm showers – are the smartest I've seen.

→ Stanton Road Farm, North Common, Hepworth, Diss, IP22 2PR 01359 250594 lingsmeadow.co.uk 🏠 ⚡

11 COURTYARD FARM

Hidden down a quiet lane, this peaceful corner of Norfolk is a wonderful place to camp simply, or you can stay in the bunkhouse barn. The organic farm is the home of Lord Melchett, former Greenpeace campaigner and Soil Association policy director, and it illustrates – quite beautifully – how responsible farming practices can ensure nature and crops thrive. The wild flowers that grow along the lanes and the butterflies (we saw several common blues) that flit around the arable fields conjure up a bucolic image that seems to belong in another era. There are footpaths and permissive paths throughout the estate where you can enjoy nature's glorious displays. Details of walks and wildlife can be found on the website.

→ N off Docking Road, Ringstead, Hunstanton PE36 5LQ 01485 525251 courtyardfarm.co.uk
🏠 ⚡

10 LING'S MEADOW

11 COURTYARD FARM

Food

12 COCOES CAFÉ & DELI

Strattons boutique hotel and CoCoes fantastic deli offer a quiet, green haven in the centre of busy Swaffham. The café/deli, which is deservedly popular, serves first class, Brecklands-sourced food in its bijou hideaway, either at shared tables or outside in the courtyard. This is exactly the kind of place where it would be easy to while away a whole day – reading the papers and meeting friends for breakfast, lunch, and then cake.

→ 4 Ash Close, Swaffham, Norfolk PE37 7NH 01760 723845 strattonshotel.com
⏰ Mon 9–3pm, Tue–Thu 9–5pm, Fri 9–6pm, Sat 8–6pm 🍴 🏠

13 VICTORIA INN

Forming part of the Holkham estate, the Victoria Inn is perfectly placed between the sea and the grand house with its acres of parkland. Food is locally sourced and much of it comes from the Holkham estate, including venison, beef and game.

There is even a special 'fifteen mile' menu. Cromer crab is often available, but we decided on steak and chips – just what we needed after a morning spent wandering around Holkham's fantastic walled gardens, followed by swimming at the beach. The restaurant is spacious, often busy, and child-friendly. Bedrooms are available.

→ Park Rd, Holkham, Wells-next-the-Sea NR23 1RG 01328 711008 holkham.co.uk
⏰ daily 8am–9pm (Sun 12–10.30pm) 🍴 🏠

The wild flowers that grow along the lanes and the butterflies that flit around the arable fields conjure up a bucolic image

12 COCOES CAFÉ & DELI

13 VICTORIA INN

14 SARACEN'S HEAD INN

Enjoy a delicious meal at this charming and award-winning country inn, a Norfolk local food hero prize-winner. The summer menu was not only packed with good, honest food that celebrated the first-class ingredients used, it even displayed the number of food miles. The lovely courtyard garden is a real draw when the sun shines. In cooler months, head inside and sit by the fire and then retreat upstairs to bed where even the soap is locally made. Nearby is Mannington Hall Gardens.

Wall Road, Wolterton, Near Erpingham, Norfolk NR11 7LZ 01263 768909 saracenshead-norfolk.co.uk closed Mondays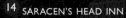

Northants & Cambridge

The flat fenlands and fields of Cambridgeshire and Northamptonshire are teeming with rare wild flowers and inspirational gardens.

Northants & Cambridgeshire

The highlights

›› Treat your taste buds to one of Kathy Brown's delicous floral creations (1)

›› Explore the verdant lunar landscape at Barnack Hills and Holes and see the rare pasque flower (6)

›› Be amazed by the wild and wondrous birdlife and kunekunes at Coton Manor (3)

›› Experience a meadow filled with local wildflower species at the home of Faith Raven (2)

Best for ancient woods, ponds and meadows

Best for a wild garden

Best for native flora

Best for a creative wild garden

There is something very special about being welcomed into the garden of a private house. Four of my favourite gardens in this area are not only the work of their gardener-owners, but also testament to their passion for and love of nature. And each garden appeals to us in a way we can see, feel, touch, and sometimes even taste.

Kathy Brown's intimate and creative garden in Stevington is a humorous horticultural theatre that is both accessible and inspiring. Her cakes, made from the flowers in her garden, are divine. Coton Manor offers thoughtful planting, strange birds and other delightful surprises as well as an excellent tea room and plant nursery. Hemingford Grey might just be the perfect garden: happy chickens, grand cottage borders, witty topiary, and a natural meadow. Here, free-flowing form and colour, rich with the buzz of insect life, is perfectly balanced by controlled, formal planting. I visited in late summer and I cannot imagine when it would look finer. Open all year and always with something to see is beautiful Docwra's Manor, where Faith Raven, mother of Sarah Raven, has created a stylish and romantic home for the wild local flora. Within the structure created by walls and large trees, plants have been encouraged to self-seed in borders that feel uncontrived and look glorious. Take a closer look at the meadow and marvel at the sheer number of native species that flourish there.

For the best natural meadows in the area, seek out some of the last surviving limestone grasslands. At

Barnack Hills and Holes nature reserve, the wondrous landscape features rolling humps and bumps created by medieval lime quarrying, and the flora and fauna are stunning. Glow-worms, rare butterflies – including chalkhill blue and green hairstreaks – thrive in the flower-rich meadows. It's a great place to see rare flowers such as the spring pasque flower (*Pulsatilla*), followed by orchids, purple milk-vetch and mountain everlasting in summer, then clustered bellflower and autumn gentian. For yet more stunning biodiversity, visit nearby Castor Hanglands reserve near Peterborough. It is surely an entomologist's dream, and there are a staggering 450 species of plant to discover.

Gardens

1 KATHY BROWN'S GARDEN

One of my favourite gardens in the area, The Manor at Stevington is the creation of the owners, Simon and Kathy Brown. On their four and a half acres, the couple have manifested a number of inspiring, sometimes even theatrical, naturalistic gardens. Each with its own ideology and beauty. Taken as a whole, the garden space is intimate and with the kind of attention to detail that will make you smile again and again. Although this is a private garden and home, you feel very much welcomed. On Tuesday and some Sunday afternoons in summer, the garden is open for visits and at 2pm Kathy will guide you round her garden, relate its fascinating 20-year story and introduce you to the plants. Afterwards, tea and cakes are served on the lawn, or inside if wet. But these are no ordinary cakes. They are very special cakes, all made by Kathy using edible flowers from the garden and based on mouth watering recipes from her cookbook *Edible Flowers*.
→ Manor House, Church Rd, Stevington, Nr Bedford MK43 7QB 01234 822064 kathybrownsgarden.homestead.com
⌚ May–Sept, Tue 1–5pm (& some Sundays)
🍵 🌱 🍴

1 KATHY BROWN'S GARDEN

1 KATHY BROWN'S GARDEN

2 DOCWRA'S MANOR

Set around a very handsome Queen Anne-faced farmhouse, the gardens of Faith Raven are delightful. Their ebullience must be partly due to the naturalistic philosophy that holds sway. Here, self-seeding and wild flowers are encouraged and, in the walled garden, even allowed to dictate the palettes and design of the borders. Faith's passion for native flora can be seen to great effect in the wild garden. In spring, cow parsley creates a stunning display under the blossoming apple trees, while across the road, an idyllic-looking meadow blooms with colourful local flora and creates fantastic forage for a host of creatures. There is a small orchard and many 'rooms' to discover, as well as a selection of plants for sale, all raised in the garden. For tea, the nearby Wimpole Estate and its kitchen gardens are 5 miles away.
→ Meldreth Rd, Shepreth, Royston, Herts SG8 6PS 01763 260677 docwrasmanorgarden.co.uk ⌚ Wed & Fri 10–4pm & 1st Sun of the month 2–4pm
🍵 🌱 🌸

3 COTON MANOR

Incredible bluebells, wildflower meadow, great café, and the most surprising birds (I won't spoil it for you) make Coton unmissable. The species-rich wildflower meadow is a particular success story and its May to July display shows what can be achieved in ten years with some good management and two kilos of yellow-rattle seed. May's highlight is the five-acre bluebell walk from the end of the garden, but a visit is worthwhile in any month. In August, roses were still blooming in the orchard, where tress with red-flushed fruit provided shade for the sun-drowsy kunekune pigs. Follow the sound of water from a natural spring to find the water garden and its relaxed woodland plantings. Besides pigs and birds, there are long-horned cattle and wonderful vistas to the hills beyond, while the tea room and extensive nursery are destinations in themselves. Bring your children or your grandchildren – this is not your average garden.
→ Coton Rd, Coton, Northants NN6 8RQ 01604 740219 cotonmanor.co.uk
⌚ Apr–Sep, Tue–Sat 12–5.30pm & BH and some snowdrop days 🍵 🌱 🌸 🍴

4 KELMARSH HALL

In this triangular walled kitchen garden, there is a charming gardener's cottage backed by a glasshouse. The 18th-century walls are ornamented with fruit trees and, in August, they were heavy with plums and pears. Artichokes, sunflowers and sweet peas all provided an earthy contrast to the theatrical dahlia displays. Vegetables grown here supply the house and café and the freshly picked overspill is sold from a little cart. Here you can also purchase stunning cut flowers grown in the kitchen garden. There is a tea room in the converted stables and lots of seating outside where you can relax and enjoy your cake with a view of the extensive gardens.
→ Harborough Rd, Kelmarsh, Northants NN6 9LY 01604 686543 kelmarsh.com
⌚ Apr–Sept Tue–Thur & Sun & BH 11–5pm
🍵 🍴 🌸

3 COTON MANOR

4 KELMARSH HALL

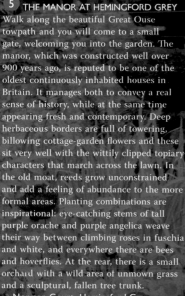

5 THE MANOR AT HEMINGFORD GREY

Walk along the beautiful Great Ouse towpath and you will come to a small gate, welcoming you into the garden. The manor, which was constructed well over 900 years ago, is reputed to be one of the oldest continuously inhabited houses in Britain. It manages both to convey a real sense of history, while at the same time appearing fresh and contemporary. Deep herbaceous borders are full of towering, billowing cottage-garden flowers and these sit very well with the wittily clipped topiary characters that march across the lawn. In the old moat, reeds grow unconstrained and add a feeling of abundance to the more formal areas. Planting combinations are inspirational: eye-catching stems of tall purple orache and purple angelica weave their way between climbing roses in fuschia and white, and everywhere there are bees and hoverflies. At the rear, there is a small orchard with a wild area of unmown grass and a sculptural, fallen tree trunk.

Norman Court, Hemingford Grey, Huntingdon PE28 9BN 01480 463134 greenknowe.co.uk

daily 11–5pm (dusk in winter)

Swathes of wild flowers
and butterflies carpet
the bizarre undulating
hillocks that were created
by medieval quarrying
for limestone.

8 RUMMERS LANE ORCHARD

Meadows

6 BARNACK HILLS AND HOLES NNR

Swathes of wild flowers carpet this incredible, undulating landscape, which is criss-crossed by paths. The topography of this National Nature Reserve was created in medieval times when the site was quarried for limestone, and the whole effect is rather playful. The site is also designated a Special Area for Conservation for its rare limestone grassland and is home to 300 species of wild plants including the pasque flower, blooming in April and May, and the rare man orchid. The main display is in June and July when you might also see glow-worms, then in the autumn, cattle graze the grassland. There is a lovely 30-minute circular marked walk around the site.

→ Information and car park Wittering Road, Barnack, Nr Stamford, Peterborough PE9 3EY 01780 444704 gov.uk 52.6286,-0.4121 ⤵

7 CASTOR HANGLANDS NNR

The ancient woods, ponds, and limestone grasslands provide an oasis of diversity in this area of intensively farmed land. The 90-acre reserve awakens in March with the noisy mating of 2,000 toads in the main pond. In the scrubland, you'll hear nightingales and in the woods there are carpets of yellow archangel, primroses, and then bluebells. Cowslips and violets also inject colour and nectar into the landscape. With the onset of summer, butterflies flit in the wooded glades, while hundreds of orchids (southern marsh and common spotted) colonise the marshy lowlands.

→ Two waymarked walks; Heath Walk & woodland Hanglands Walk, approx 1 hr each from car park. 3.6 miles SE on Marholme Rd from Barnack. Southey Wood Forestry Commission car park, Langley Bush Rd, Nr Peterborough PE6 7BF 01780 444704 gov.uk 52.6078-0.3618 ⤵

8 RUMMERS LANE ORCHARD

If, like me, you find old fruit trees heaving with rosy red apples appeal to your inner romantic, then you will love the walks around Rummers Lane Orchard. The waymarked permissive paths take you around the 22-acre site, which is run as part of the Countryside Stewardship Scheme. Sheep graze underneath the gnarled trees, many of which were planted in the early 1900s and many are the traditional fenland varieties, not often found elsewhere.

→ Park in layby opposite bridge over drain and start of circular walk. 0.4 miles SE of High Rd on Rummers Ln, Wisbech St. Mary PE13 4UB orchardnetwork.org.uk 52.6451,0.0896 ⤵

8 RUMMERS LANE ORCHARD

Accommodation

9 THE COACH HOUSE B&B

On sunny mornings there is nothing nicer than throwing open the windows and letting the sun stream in while you laze in bed. In the Coach House's twin room, floor-to-ceiling windows open out right on to the garden. Here you can enjoy a delicious breakfast cooked by owner, Sarah, on the terrace overlooking her lovely gardens. There are three very comfortable rooms and Coton Manor garden and nursery is nearby.

→ Duncote, Towcester, Northants NN12 8AQ
01327 352855 thecoachhouseduncote.co.uk

10 KARMA FARM CAMPING

Enjoy back-to-nature camping on a working fenland organic farm in a landscape rich with birds, butterflies, and wild flowers. Take a slow walk along the River Lark to the nearby village of Isleham or explore the farmland, where you'll find a bird hide. The site offers solar-powered showers and is run with respect to the enviroment. Campfires are encouraged and accommodation is either in the yurt, tipis, or your own tent. There is a separate one-acre field away from the main site that would be perfect for a camping party.

→ 8 Fen Bank, Isleham, Ely, Cambridgeshire CB7 5SL 01638 780701 (Fork L at sign for Marina) karmafarm.co.uk

10 KARMA FARM CAMPING

9 THE COACH HOUSE B&B

Food

11 THE GARDEN CAFÉ

Within walking distance of the centre of busy Cambridge, the University Botanic Garden has been on this site since 1846. Home to many national collections, including species tulips, it is a tranquil space with lots to see, even in winter. The garden's modern café with big glass windows is a great place to relax with a coffee, soup, salad, or delicious falafel. There is also a dedicated kids' menu.

→ 1 Brookside, Cambridge CB2 1JE 01223 763425 thegardencafecambridge.co.uk
⏰ daily 10–6pm (until 5pm Feb, Mar & Oct and until 4pm Jan, Nov, Dec)

12 THE WILLOW TREE

Although this pub does not grow its own vegetables, it does have a very sweet garden, dominated of course by a willow tree. There is also a big top and several deckchairs. The food is first class and atmosphere lively. We visited on one of their magical theatre nights and enjoyed delicious fresh pea soup, fish, and good local ales , while watching an eccentric candlelit production of Alice in Wonderland. The menu changes according to the season and food is sourced from local suppliers. Do check their website to see listings of their themed supper club events and music dining.

→ 29 High Street, Bourn, Cambridgeshire CB23 2SQ 01954 719775 thewillowtreebourn.com
⏰ daily food served 12–3pm, 5.30–9.30pm (12–8pm on sundays)

We visited on one of their magical theatre nights, and ate delicious fresh pea soup while watching an eccentric candlelit Alice in Wonderland.

12 THE WILLOW TREE

12 THE WILLOW TREE

4 KELMARSH HALL

VEDDW

The Usk & The Wye

From the beautiful valleys of the Usk and the Wye, through the picturesque Golden and Monnow river landscapes to the Brecons, the truly stunning scenery is a continuing inspiration for poets, painters and gardeners alike.

The Usk & The Wye

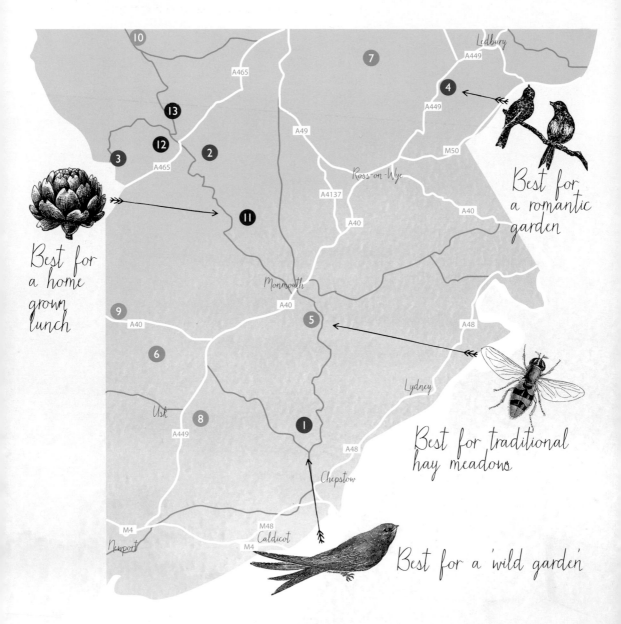

Best for a home grown lunch

Best for a romantic garden

Best for traditional hay meadows

Best for a 'wild garden'

The highlights

>> 'Capture the castle' then gorge on home-grown food fresh from the kitchen garden (11)

>> Wander through a flowering hay meadow that has remained unimproved over centuries (5)

>> Lose yourself in the romance and deep floral borders at Kentchurch Court (2)

>> Discover Anne Wareham's unique, confident, and conscious gardening style (1)

In this dramatic landscape, beyond its ruined castles and behind the severe grey stones of house and farmstead lies a strong, artistic and food-focused culture. Much of the area is classified as an Area of Outstanding Natural Beauty and the Wye was the first river in Britain to be designated a Site of Special Scientific Interest along its entire length.

There are some serious gardening gems here, both old and new. For medieval romance, visit the house and gardens of Hellens in Much Marcle, or the charming and floriferous plantings at Kentchurch Court. Both are surrounded by some very special parkland and woodland walks rich with wildlife, so bring your walking boots and make a day of it.

Veddw, the garden designed by the author of *The Bad Tempered Gardener*, Anne Wareham and her photographer husband Charles Hawes, is one of the gardens that has most excited me and given me the most inspiration for my garden at home. It is also an exquisite and intimate 'wild garden' with enhanced native meadows and an intrinsic understanding of its natural landscape. You can't visit but you

can stay at Allt-y-Bela, the gorgeous medieval farmstead and home of Arne Maynard. The gardens he has helped to design feature heavily in this book and are full of trademark tumbling roses, cottage gardens gone wild, and topiary that sits among meadows. I hope one day to treat myself to one of his courses.

What all the gardens in this area share is their essential and constant connection to the hills and landscape, which exert a strong and determined influence. The grandeur of this backdrop may account for why even the flower-strewn hay meadows, such as those at Pentwyn Farm, Joan's Hill, and High Valley Yurts, look so stunning.

Gardens

I VEDDW

The sign on the gate reads, 'If weeds upset you, you may be best to save your hard earned money: we garden to enhance the natural, not to conquer it'. I don't remember seeing any weeds, what I do remember is an incredibly bold garden that seems to have a feisty disregard for any rules. Some of Anne Wareham's trademark waved hedging I personally found austere, unnecessary – too much like hard work. I like meadows and towering tresses of flowers buzzing with insects but those are here, too. That's the beauty of this garden; it has it all, although I've never seen it done quite like this before. The harsh hedges work because they link with and echo the landscape. Restraint in plant choice is inspirational and the deliberate repetition of just a few specimens like the blue bellflower (*Campanula lactiflora*), adds a modern and severe beauty. Wild flowers are clearly much revered and bullies like rosebay willow herb can be seen in many incarnations throughout the garden. The meadow garden is a triumph, not only for its range of species, but because it shows the garden in its raw, untended state. Like the rest of the space it's been shaken up and enhanced, and is more beautiful for it.

 Off Devauden Rd between St. Arvans and Devauden follow sign for 'The Fedw'. 1st on R. Devauden, Monmouthshire NP16 6PH 01291 650836 veddw.com
⏰ Open Jun–Aug, Sundays 2–5pm 🫖 🌿🌱

① VEDDW

① VEDDW

2 KENTCHURCH COURT

The Lucas-Scudamore family have lived in Kentchurch Court for nearly 1,000 years. It's a glorious site, set under Garway Hill in the lovely Monnow Valley. The gardens have the air of an intimate family space, not the grounds of a grand house, and are not too manicured and sometimes even irreverent. At the entrance of the garden you are immediately hit by an incredible feast of colour. Plants romp in and over the old bones of the derelict greenhouse in joyous abandon and swallows swoop. The smell of lilies in the long show borders is just on the right side of overwhelming. A gardener's cottage stands proud, guarding the vegetable patch. In the orchard, a shepherd's hut is framed by the hills beyond. The walled garden was a colourful wonderland of the deepest, tallest herbaceous perennial borders spilling over onto the narrow, grass paths. The deer park extends out from the main lawn to wildflower-edged meadows and up to an arc of woodland containing some of the largest field maples in England.
➜ From Pontrilas off the A465 follow B4347 S to Kentchurch. At Gatehouse follow sign to Garway, turning L opposite Church Pontrilas, Hereford, Herefordshire HR2 0DB 01981 240228 kentchurchcourt. co.uk ⏰ Easter–Sep Tue–Sun 11–5pm 🫖 🌿🌱

3 MONNOW VALLEY ARTS

Having visited so many abundant gardens filled with dense planting, it was refreshing to come to the sculpture gardens of Monnow Valley Arts Centre. Here, you are confronted with an open space where the landscape does the talking. It is known as 'The Garden of the Wind' and the plantings are simple and en masse. The upper garden slope, for example, is covered solely with a tall purple veronica. With the constant movement of the wind, the space feels alive and gentle. At the arts centre, the memory gardens display sculpture and lettering as well as the Memorial Arts Charity's permanent collection. As part of the 'Quiet Garden Movement', the space is reserved as a place of stillness and contemplation on certain days. Carved lettering, standing stones and quiet fountains hold the space but still the beautiful valley beyond sings loudest. From the mown grass the land simply flows into damp meadow, then grazed field, then into hills and mountains. At the back of the house there is a lovely cottage garden-style vegetable plot with more stunning views.
Middle Hunt House, Walterstone, Hereford HR2 0DY 01873 860529 monnowvalleyarts. org ⏰ Apr–Oct Thu–Fri 11–5pm, Sat & Sun 2–5pm 🫖

2 KENTCHURCH COURT

3 MONNOW VALLEY ARTS

4 HELLENS

Bathed in its unique Jacobean romance the garden seems lost in a world of its own. Huge modern sculptures in organic forms hang from the tall trees or are dotted through the parkland savannah. Near the house, urns spill with velvety pelargoniums, lilies fill the ponds, and roses, lavender and clipped box trick you into thinking that this is a traditional garden gone a little wild. Keep wandering and you will find anomalies such as clipped hornbeam underplanted with wild flowers or crisply edged parterres filled with an effusion of unruly cottage-garden plants. Beyond the wavy yew, the rolling parkland has a unique Herefordshire softness. Meadows here remain unmown well into late summer and big tree trunks lie slowly rotting in the grass. The vegetable garden is a riot of colour and unkempt productivity within formal lines.

Signed off B4024 Monk's Walk, Much Marcle, Herefordshire HR8 2LY 01531 660504 hellensmanor.com ● Easter Sun–Sept Wed, Thu, Sun 2–5pm & BH

Spring starts with
thousands of cowslips
and early purple orchids
followed by oxeye
daisies, scented greater
butterfly orchids and
knapweeds.

7 JOAN'S HILL FARM

Meadows

5 PENTWYN FARM

Step back in time and enjoy a circular walk (40 mins) around the old-farm nature reserve on the Trellech Ridge. The meadows, which have remained unchanged for centuries, are managed to preserve the flora and fauna, so hay is cut at the end of summer. Spring starts with thousands of cowslips and early purple orchids, followed by scented greater butterfly orchids and knapweed.

→ Park by modern barn next to The Inn at Penallt. Follow path through orchard or green lane to medieval barn (with disabled parking). Pentwyn, Penallt, Monmouth NP25 4SA 01600 740600 gwentwildlife.org 51.7810,-2.6925

6 COED-Y-BWNYDD

For a glorious spring, head to the high wooded paths around Coed-y-Bwnydd – the beautifully preserved Monmouthshire hill fort and the largest in the county – to see carpets of primroses, bluebells, campions, and orchids. Paths take you through open glades and old beech and oak woodland. A four-hour walk via Clytha castle can be downloaded at nationaltrust.org.uk and Cosy Clytha Arms is 2 miles N.

→ No official parking. Narrow layby near NT foot path access gate from NP15 1JS (1m NE on road from Bettws Newydd). 01874 625515 nationaltrust.org.uk 51.7563,-2.9188

7 JOAN'S HILL FARM

At Joan's Hill Farm, 46 acres of land offer a glimpse of the Herefordshire landscape before agricultural improvements. Now a Plantlife reserve, the farm meadows in the Wye Valley AONB are at their best from May until mid-July. Among the rich array of insects that feed on the cowslips, meadow buttercup, self-heal, knapweed and dyer's greenweed that proliferate in its gently sloping fields are 50 species of moths and 17 species of butterfly.

→ 15 min walk N on main woodland ride. At x roads straight downhill. L at T-junction for 200m to entrance. Haugh Wood car park btwn Woolhope & Mordiford, Hereford HR1 4QX coronationmeadows.org.uk 52.0256,-2.5957

Accommodation

8 ALLT-Y-BELA B&B

This beautiful, Grade II listed Elizabethan farmhouse is the home of renowned garden designer Arne Maynard. The location is idyllic and the house, with its antiques and fine linens, is decorated simply. In the gardens, the mix of wild flowers, topiary, romantic rambling roses, fruit and vegetables is perfectly in tune with both house and landscape. From here, Maynard offers a range of gardening courses.

→ Llangwm Ucha, Usk, Monmouthshire NP15 1EZ 07892 403103 alltybela.co.uk

8 ALLT-Y-BELA

9 PENPERGWM LODGE B&B

At Penpergwm the rooms are large and the hearty, traditional breakfasts will set you up for a walk around the lovely garden. Fairytale brick follies smothered in roses offer great viewing platforms over the thoughtfully designed gardens. I loved the newly laid out kitchen garden and its beautiful loggia – perfect for a glass of wine as the sun goes down. Amid the formality of structure the abundant planting is very loose and free. There is the added bonus of a plant nursery on site – although this seems to be winding down.

➜ Penpergwm, Abergavenny, Monmouthshire NP7 9AS 01873 840208 sawdays.co.uk 🏠 🍵 🌻

10 WELLBROOK MANOR GARDEN STUDIO

Since 2009, lovely Wellbrook Manor has been looked after by Vivat, the historic building preservation trust. The grounds have been restored and there is a kitchen garden, crisp topiary, roses and wildflower walks. If you rent the exquisitely renovated Garden Studio, with its wood beams whitewashed walls, and first-floor studio space, you can wander freely in the garden. It's a perfect hideaway for two (or for three if you bring the dog).

➜ Off the B4348, Watery Lane, Peterchurch, Herefordshire HR2 0SS 01981 550753 vivat-trust.org 🏠 🍵 🐾

9 PENPERGWM LODGE

Food

11 THE BELL AT SKENFRITH

Enjoying views of ruined Skenfrith castle and the pretty river Monnow, the pub has its own extensive kitchen gardens, polytunnels, and rooting pigs. It's a great place to enjoy home-grown, local produce in lovely rural surroundings. Everything from tomatoes and chillies to asparagus and berries is grown in the organic gardens and they are open for you to wander through. Dishes are inspired by the super-fresh ingredients in season and the food is delicious. There are 11 lovely rooms if you want to stay for breakfast.

➜ Off the B4521 at Skenfrith, Monmouthshire NP7 8UH 01600 750235 skenfrith.co.uk ⌚ daily 10–11pm 🍷 🍴 🏠

12 ROWLESTONE COURT

Enjoy award-winning, home-made ice-cream among the old tractors, willow dens and wildflower meadows of Rowlestone Court. The café does light lunches as well as ice-cream and there is camping in summer. For the last eight years, Mary and Mark have been developing the seven acres of wildflower meadows that put on a fine display in summer. In spring, head into the ancient woods to see bluebells, ramsons and orchids blossoming under the small-leaved limes and coppiced ash. Very child-friendly.

➜ Signed off A465 at Pontrillas. Rowlestone, Hereford, HR2 0DW 01981 240322 rowlestonecourt.co.uk ⌚ mid Apr–Sept Wed–Fri 11–4pm, weekends & BH 11–5pm 🍴 🐾 🏠

10 WELLBROOK MANOR

12 ROWLESTONE COURT

13 ABBEY DORE

13 ABBEY DORE THE STABLES TEA ROOM

13 ABBEY DORE COURT GARDENS

This is a lovely old-world garden, family home, and tea room. Matriarch, Charis Ward, looks after the garden and plant sales, daughter Sarah the tea room, and Charis's granddaughter takes care of the house, which can be rented by large groups. I've often been disappointed by garden tea rooms but the Stables tearoom at Abbey Dore is a real find. Sarah serves delicious organic, and sometimes even raw-food, homemade pâtés, salads, soups and cakes. In the sunny courtyard, we enjoyed a memorable feast of apple, beetroot, and horseradish salad alongside smoked salmon and cream cheese, served with still-warm bread rolls. The garden has wonderful peonies and geraniums and is worth a visit for the atmosphere alone.

Signposted off B4347 in Abbey Dore village HR2 0AD, 01981 240279
abbeydorecourt.co.uk   mid-Apr–Sep
Tue, Thu, Sat, Sun 11–5pm

RHODDS FARM

Hereford- shire North

Follow the dingles and orchards north of the River Wye to the slopes of the Hergest Ridge, across the thriving market town of Leominster, past hill forts to the Malvern Hills.

Herefordshire North

The highlights

>> Discover highbrow garden artistry and a love of wildlife combined near Presteigne (1)

>> Take a flower filled walk through Herefordshire's largest area of unimproved grassland (7)

>> Stay in the lovely hop pickers' house set in the charming gardens of Brook Farm (10)

>> Eat Michelin pub food in unpretentious, cosy surroundings (12)

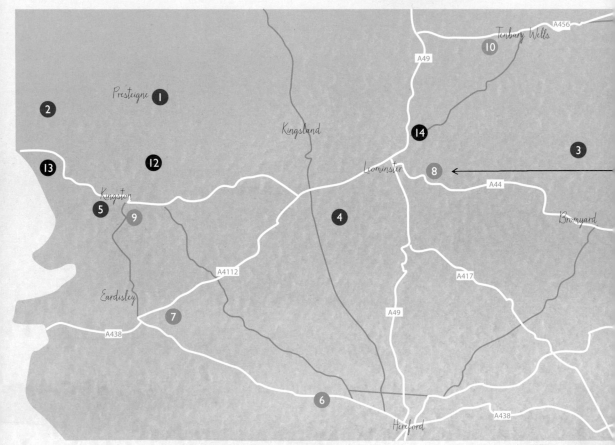

Buy wild flowers and native hedging

Best for irises

Great Malvern

A449 Welland

There must be some special ingredient in the soil here, beyond its fertility. Like iron filings to a magnet, the Herefordshire landscape seems to have attracted an amazing concentration of incredible wild gardens. It is a land of plenty, renowned for its cider, Hereford beef, and fruit production.

At Hampton Court Castle and Garden you will find an ornamental, organic kitchen plot and through the NGS you can visit the lovely gardens of Grantsfield, Upper Tan House, and the mouth-watering Brockhampton Cottage. As for nurseries, you are spoilt for choice both in terms of variety and plant stock. Whimble, Aulden Farm, Plant Wild and Ivycroft all come packaged with the most creative and inspiring 'wild' gardens. The three, very different B&Bs recommended also come with the most exquisite garden attached, and for a day or two it is yours to dream in.

We loved our spring time visit to Hergest Croft gardens and you can combine your visit with a stay in their Haywood Cabin, a converted old workshop with views of the Black Mountains and a cosy woodburner.

I cannot speak highly enough of beautiful Bryan's Ground near Presteigne. It is an inspirational space that merges exquisite design skills and plant knowledge with a deep appreciation of the local landscape and its wildlife.

If you are looking for meadows and wildflowers, head to the The Weir (National Trust) or The Sturts nature

reserves. And if fundraising targets are reached, Birches Farm SSSI will soon be open for visits. Herefordshire Nature Trust is working hard to save the old farm's 60 acres of species-rich grassland, and ensure the harebells, orchids and hares that call it home continue to flourish.

To learn more about the area's green spaces, 'Gardens in the Wild' is a fantastic Herefordshire garden and landscape festival held in June with a crop of top speakers, stalls and walks through meadows. Find out more at gardensinthewild.org.

Gardens

1 BRYAN'S GROUND

You won't find a more innovative or thoughtful garden than the one created by David Wheeler and Simon Dorrell, the prolific partners behind the gardening journal, *Hortus*. Every inch is perfect, from the hawthorn topiary – a fantastic idea – to the theatrical follies, reclaimed corrugated-iron walls, and orchards underplanted with thousands of Iris sibirica. It really is wild-garden bliss. When I visited for the first time in May, the garden was already a fantasia of colour and form and each area was a delight – intimate and a masterpiece of gloriously artistic planting. The two seem to have taken from every garden throughout history, raw ones, cottage gardens through to the most formal ones, creamed off the top and then added their own spice. Rusty bicycles hang from trees, and planters are filled with the garlicky weed *Alliaria petiolata*. Yet nothing feels too forced or too quaint. Clumps of native teasel, which form communities on the nearby river embankments feature prominently in the front terrace. 'For the goldfinches', remarked David. Quite clearly I loved it, and so will you. Teas are available in the loggia.
→ Stapleton, Nr Presteigne, Herefordshire LD8 2LP 01544 260001 bryansground.co.uk
⏰ Apr–mid-Aug, Sun & Mon 2–5pm 🍵 🍴

1 BRYAN'S GROUND

1 BRYAN'S GROUND

2 WHIMBLE GARDEN & NURSERY

Also near Presteigne is modest Whimble nursery and its glorious wild gardens that look out on to the Radnorshire hills. Here among the parterres filled with herbaceous perennials, grasses, and unusual annuals, lie acres of meadow walks. At the end of the gardens sits a wooden toposcope for viewing the surrounding nature reserve and wildlife pools. You can buy plants raised in organic and peat-free compost, or enjoy tea and cakes on the terrace. It's a delightfully fun and relaxing collection of garden spaces, each displaying its own distinctive collection of reclaimed slate, steel, or weathered oak for fencing, edging, and arches. There are rustic loggias and several seats where you can read the newspapers, or borrow or buy a book from the mini-library.
→ Park Road, Kinnerton, Presteigne LD8 2PD 01574 560413 whimblegardens.co.uk
⏰ Easter–Sep Mon, Thu, Fri, Sun 10.30–5.30pm 🍵 🌿 🍴 🌸

3 MOORS MEADOW

Eclectic and tranquil, the gardens of Moors Meadow are open only by appointment, although the sign on the lane often reads OPEN in summer. Do check for opening times before you visit. The old smallholding and market garden, the life's work of Rosie and Ros – mother and daughter – is now a wondrous space where ornamental plants dance among the long grasses, wild flowers, and old orchard trees. The location couldn't be more halcyon: no roar of traffic, no shouts or calls; just the sound of birds, cows and insects. The sloping site where naturalised perennials mix with self-seeded annuals, shrubs, and grasses, is enhanced by the upcycled pieces of old farm machinery that Ros has placed artfully around. Wildlife is ever-present: a cacophony of birdsong and buzzing added magic to an already very special place. I hope Ros can find a way to keep the garden open to the public.
→ Collington, Bromyard, Hereford, HR7 4LZ 01885 410318 moorsmeadow.co.uk
⏰ phone for opening times 🍵 🌸

4 AULDEN FARM

Aulden Farm is the delightfully intimate seat of the national collection of siberian irises and it's also a beautiful representation of a wild garden at home. In less than 10 years Alun and Jill Whitehead have gently cultivated the three acres of land around their old farm into a glorious wild garden analogy. On classic Herefordshire clay soil they have dug ponds, planted hedges and green tunnels and made a beautiful home for the iris collections and the wild flowers that proliferate in the area. Near the house, the farm outbuildings are in the perfect state of dishevelment and offer a charming context to the needlework effect of primulas and May spring-seeded flowers that thrive in the gravel. An artist's eye is ever present with relaxed positionings of weathered wooden posts, painted chairs and metal finds. The birdsong is glorious.
→ 3 miles S of Leominster. Aulden, Leominster HR6 0JT 01568 720129 auldenfarm.co.uk
⏰ phone for opening times 🍵 🌸

4 AULDEN FARM

3 MOORS MEADOW

5 HERGEST CROFT

In the heart of the Welsh Marches, the gardens of Hergest Croft, home of the Banks family, have an air of bygone glory. Early family members were deeply inspired by the writings of William Robinson, the pioneer of 'wild gardening' and the planting reflects his influence. The gardens and their miles of woodland labyrinths offer sanctuary to native spring flowers and ferns, as well as exotic trees planted in the late 19th century. Here you will find the national collections of maples and birches, while the ancient oak-filled Park Wood, Maple Grove, and the Azalea Garden accomplish stunning displays throughout the season. We visited in spring when bluebells and ferns were unfurling, the trees were coming into leaf, the Azalea Garden was beginning to perform, and Park Wood was a cathedral-like celebration of spring. The kitchen garden was a riot of playful colour and I have never seen dandelion heads looking so good. If you want to stay awhile, rent cosy Haywood Cabin with its views of the Black Mountains.

Ridgebourne Road, Kington, Herefordshire HR5 3EG 01544 230160 hergest.co.uk
Apr–Oct daily 12–5.30pm

Enjoy lovely riverside walks along the Wye through paths thickly fringed with spring bulbs and summer woodland flowers.

7 THE STURTS

Meadows

6 THE WEIR

Enjoy lovely riverside walks along the Wye through paths thickly fringed with spring bulbs and summer woodland flowers. There are only slight hints that the flora is being managed and the paths have been made by footsteps alone. Magnificent specimens of beech and oak hang their long limbs over the terraces, adding sculpture to the already glorious scene. There is seating along the way or you can bring a picnic and bask in the sunshine in the open glades. Adjacent to the entrance kiosk is the well-stocked walled garden, with beehives.

→ Access off the A438 W of Swainshill, Hereford HR4 7QF 01981 590509 nationaltrust.org.uk 52.0761,-2.8015

7 THE STURTS NATURE RESERVE

Lying in the flood plain of the river Wye, The Sturts meadows offer a rare opportunity to see some of the largest areas of unimproved grassland in Herefordshire. Their undulating fields are host to a rich array of wild flowers and fungi, and birds thrive in the hedgerows, ponds, old orchards and meadows. When we visited in May the delicate cuckoo flower dotted the new grass. Summer sees an explosion of meadow flora, and in autumn flocks of fieldfares feast on the windfall fruit.

→ Off A4112 0.8 miles S of Kinnersley. Car park signed off Ailey Lane, Hereford HR3 6NY 01432 356872 herefordshirewt.org 52.1309,-2.9698

8 PLANT WILD

This specialist native plant and wildflower nursery is run by Keith Arrowsmith and Suzanne Noble, whose passion is to recreate wild habitat. Located in the hills east of Leominster, the nursery sells native wildflower seeds and plugs, as well as shrubs and trees. Meadow seed is collected from the remaining hay meadows of the Marches.

→ A44 E from Leominster. 2nd L along Tick Bridge Ln. Straight over x road. Then R. Strawberry Cottage, Hennor, Leominster HR6 0RH ☼ Apr–Sep Tue 9.30–4.30pm 52.2194,-2.6852

Accommodation

9 RHODDS FARM

The luxurious, converted threshing-barn has its own garden and views of the Malvern Hills and Black Mountains. You are free to roam the gardens, bluebell-filled woodlands, pond, meadows, and parterres – all skillfully planted over the last ten years. Sculptures and a dovecote add artistry to the old arable fields now bursting with colour and texture. Garden open by appt. and first Friday in month. May–Oct, 11–5pm.

→ W off Jack's Ditch Lane, Lyonshall, Kington, Herefordshire HR5 3LW 01544 340120 rhoddsfarm.co.uk

9 RHODDS FARM

10 BROOK FARM

Brook Farm and the Heartfelt Garden ooze with love and lusciousness. Outside is a sanctuary of hammocks, campion-fringed babbling brooks, blossom-crammed courtyards, meadows, and vegetable gardens. Everywhere is a picture. They call it chaos; we thought it was perfection. Accommodation is in the old farmhouse or you can rent the converted Hop Pickers' House or the old Hen House where Sarah's eye for detail adds to the charm. Life here is wholesome and we cannot think of nicer hosts, or a better place to stay. Garden open Easter–Sept, Fri–Sun noon–dusk.
→ Hayes Lane, Berrington, Tenbury Wells, Worcestershire WR15 8TJ, 01584 819868 brookfarmberrington.org 🏠 🗝 🍴 🦆

11 OLD COUNTRY FARM

We stumbled upon the enchanting Old Country Farm when we were exploring the borders of the Malvern Hills and hunting for old orchards. Everything is delightfully rustic and redolent of a bygone era. Two old brick oast houses welcome you into the wild cottage garden that cradles the 600-year-old house. Ella and family manage the whole 220-acre farm for the benefit of wildlife and all feels fruitful. Inside, the terracotta kitchen and snug are cosy and charming. There is an Aga, vases of flowers, and a large inglenook. The sun was shining and bees bumbled around the blossom in the surrounding orchards. As well as the three B&B rooms, self-catering is available in the green-oak Lighthouse hidden in the orchards. Nearby is Coddington Vineyard.
→ Mathon, Malvern, Worcestershire WR13 5PS 01886 880867 oldcountryhouse.co.uk 🏠

10 BROOK FARM

11 OLD COUNTRY FARM

Food

12 THE STAGG INN

The Stagg Inn was the first pub to be awarded a Michelin star, which it has retained owing to a winning combination of an informal atmosphere and exquisite local food. It is a busy, well-loved place so do book in advance and enjoy an innovative, perfectly cooked, yet unpretentious selection of Hereford beef, foraged greens, and the best artisan cheeses. There are three rooms should you wish to stay or head to their sister pub, the Vicarage, for more accommodation.
→ Off the B4355. Titley, Kington, Herefordshire HR5 3RL 01544 230221 thestagg.co.uk ⏱ Wed–Sun food served 12–2pm, 6.30–9pm 🍴 🏠 🗝

13 THE HARP INN

Enjoy local ales and well-hung Welsh Black steaks in the ancient longhouse, or sit outside in the wild garden with its incredible views of the surrounding Radnor valley. The cosy dining rooms and bedrooms are filled with vases of fresh flowers and the whole atmosphere is relaxed and very comfortable. Following a delicious lunch, we spent a long rainy afternoon reading newspapers by the fire.
→ Old Radnor, Presteigne, Powys, LD8 2RH 01544 350655 harpinnradnor.co.uk ⏱ Wed & Thu 6–11pm and Fri, Sat, Sun noon–3pm, 6–11pm 🍴 🏠 🗝

We stumbled on the enchanting Old Country Farm while exploring the borders of the Malvern Hills, hunting for old orchards.

10 BROOK FARM

11 OLD COUNTRY FARM

14 STOCKTON BURY GARDENS

This four-acre space is the official garden of the popular magazine, *The English Garden*. Plantsmen Raymond Treasure and Gordon Fenn have cleverly created a flowing network of luscious garden rooms around the handsome wisteria-clad house. In the old farm buildings there is a museum displaying well-oiled garden instruments, while outside, allées of espaliers traverse the kitchen garden to the ponds and past perfectly planted troughs. The muted tithe barn in the orchard is the setting for the lovely restaurant where you can indulge in a seasonal menu of creative salads, soups, and casseroles all made with fresh garden produce. Access to the restaurant is free.

Kimbolton, Leominster, Hereford HR6 0HB 07946 318887 stocktonbury.co.uk Apr–Sep Wed–Sun & BH 12–5pm

South Wales

From the industrial ports of Port Talbot and Swansea to the wilds of the Brecon Beacons, the Black Mountains and the southern Cambrian mountains and west to the sublime peninsula of the Pembrokeshire coast; each area brimming with magic.

South Wales

The highlights

›› Discover beds of grasses and feasting goldfinches at the wild and wonderful garden at Dyffryn Fernant (1)

›› Explore miles of awesome Pembrokeshire coastline rich with wildflowers (5)

›› Stay on your own private nature reserve (10)

›› Enjoy the sight of thousands of common spotted and heath orchids growing wild at Cors y Llyn (6)

Best for a truly wild garden

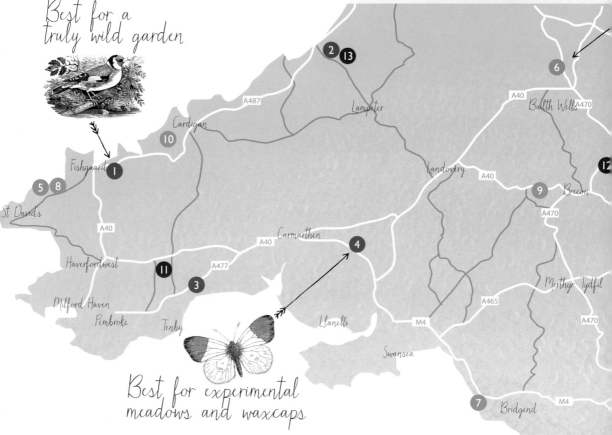

Best for experimental meadows and waxcaps

Best for wild orchids

Best for a local produce lunch

A465

Newport
M4

Cardiff

Pembrokeshire used to be known as Gwlad Hud a Lledrith, 'Land of Mystery and Enchantment'. Its rugged coastline, dotted with golden beaches, is stunning and the Wales Coast Path, which opened in May 2012, follows its entire length. The route has enabled access to a whole new world of coastal wild flowers, picturesque cliffs and glorious sea views. A perfect walk between Porthgain and Abereiddy carries you across the spongy coastal path, carpeted in sea thrift and trefoil, and past the fantastic white sands of Traeth Llyfn beach.

Near Fishguard I was to discover one of the most enchanting wild gardens I have ever seen. Dyffryn Fernant is a spectacular and magical new garden, carved out of the boggy and rocky wilderness at the foot of the Preseli uplands. Here, there are no rules and there are no discernible influences in either planting or design style, which is rare indeed. The result is truly beautiful and reflects the powerful and rugged landcape it inhabits. I can think of few places that manage to create such an artistically fine and yet still fun wildlife rich garden.

I would also recommend the National Botanic Garden near Carmarthen. The dome, the largest single-spanned glasshouse in the world designed by renowned architect, Lord Foster, was definitely a draw but the gardens have so much more to offer. There are acres of rich wildflower meadows and delightful new experimental meadows that incorporate perennials and blur the line between ornamental garden and meadow. Nearby is fantastic Dinefwr Castle (National Trust), the only National Nature Reserve parkland in Wales, great for traditional hay meadows and ancient trees.

Gardens

1 DYFFRYN FERNANT

This is without doubt one of my favourite wild gardens. In less than ten years, Christina and David have created a biodiverse garden wonderland from the wild terrain surrounding their pink house. The garden feels experimental, joyful, and life-affirming. Expectantly, I pushed flower, grass, and leaf out of the way to emerge, surprised and happy, into another new space. And I found myself constantly checking the lovely hand-drawn map to confirm that this was indeed the path. Each area is intimate, thoughtful, playful and respectful of its glorious mountain setting. Clinging to the house, the exotics huddle for warmth and protection. This is a garden where the line between the wild and the cultivated is so blurred in places that you can easily be fooled. If in doubt, stay a little longer and rent the garden bothy, Y Bwthyn Bach, or head to the garden library and get down to some serious research with a cup of tea. Christina holds a number of informal courses on 'garden making' and runs a garden consultancy.

→ A487 btwn Dinas Cross and Fishguard, follow sign S to Llanychaer, after 600m L down lane. Dinas, Fishguard, SA65 9SP 01348 811282 dyffrynfernant.co.uk
⏰ Apr–Sep daily 12–6pm 🍵 🐾 ❀ 🏠

1 DYFFRYN FERNANT

1 DYFFRYN FERNANT

2 LLANERCHAERON

Llanerchaeron is working farm where time seems to have stood still. Geese patrol the farmyard, there were longhorn cattle in the yard, and swallows and swifts swooped and darted. The secluded walled garden was bursting with produce, and we bought plentiful supplies for our supper from the shop. A great way to see the estate is to rent bicycles, or you can just enjoy strolling

Visiting in summer I discovered meadows teeming with rare butterfly orchids and experimental meadows spot-planted with surprising perennials

around the farmland and gardens. The hay meadow to the south-west of the house hasn't been ploughed since it was dug for victory in World War II and is now a great example of a species-rich hay meadow. There is a lovely little café near the river.

→ Ciliau Aeron, near Aberaeron, Ceredigion, SA48 8DG, 01545 570200 nationaltrust.org.uk
⏰ Jan–mid Mar & Nov–Dec Sat, Sun 11.30–3.30pm, mid Mar–Oct daily 10.30–5.30pm, Nov–Dec daily 11.30–3.30pm 🍵 🐾 🍴

3 COLBY WOODLAND GARDEN

Put on your comfortable shoes and take a walk along the many paths that flow through Colby Woodland garden (National Trust). Statues and urns, which come as something of a surprise, indicate that this is a garden landscape and not just a beautiful wooded river valley with open pasture. Spring starts with crocus and camellias, then bluebells; wild meadow flowers are at their peak in summer; and in autumn acers planted among native woodland trees blaze with stunning colour. Cross bridges over streams, build dens in the wood (and lots of great activities for the kids), or simply enjoy a fantastic lunch. We had an amazing selection of local cheeses with home-made apple chutney and oven-fresh bread, that we still continue to rave about. The café is fully licensed and there is a good selection of wines and local ciders.

→ Stepaside, Amroth, Pembrokeshire SA67 8PP, 01834 811885 nationaltrust.org.uk
⏰ daily 10–5pm 🍵 🐾 🍴

4 LLANERCHAERON

3 COLBY WOODLAND GARDEN

4 THE NATIONAL BOTANIC GARDENS OF WALES

The 568 acres of gardens and reserve, feature so much more than the amazing Lord Foster designed glass biome that seems to peep out over the hill. Supporting over 1,000 species the Botanic Gardens have worked hard to get to where they are today. As well as various themed garden areas and plant collections including thalictrums and witch hazels, there are acres of incredible meadows, woodland, and a home farm with a herd of rare-breed Welsh black cattle. The animals are integral to the careful management of the adjoining Waun Las reserve grasslands and are well suited to the conditions, as well as able to digest the rough forage that it offers. Visiting in summer, I discovered meadows teeming with rare butterfly orchids and experimental grasslands spot-planted with surprising perennials. This place demands a day and if you live close or visit often, then a season pass will give you a whole year of discovery. In the autumn, waxcap fungi abound in the Waun Las reserve. The botanic garden, which is committed to sustainability, is also spearheading a grow-your-own initiative across the whole of Wales.

Cycle Route 47, Llanarthne, Camarthenshire SA32 8HN, 01558 667149 gardenofwales.org.uk
daily 10–6pm (4.30pm Oct-Mar)

The Pembrokeshire coastline is Britain's only coastal National Park and its stunning coast path offers miles of wildflowers set against the sparkling backdrop of the turquoise sea.

6 CORS Y LLYN

Meadows

5 PEMBROKESHIRE COASTLINE

The breathtaking coastline of Pembrokeshire is Britain's only coastal national park and the coast path offers the best opportunity to see colourful tapestries of spring and summer wild flowers set against the sparkling backdrop of the turquoise sea. For a really wild walk head to Strumble Head, or enjoy an easy family walk from Abereiddy stopping for a swim at Traeth Llyfn beach before heading to the excellent Shed Bistro in Porthgain for a fresh fish supper.

→ Start at Abereiddi beach (parking charge) SA62 6DT NE on coast path to Porthgain. pembrokeshirecoast.org.uk 51.9363,-5.2054 🦅

6 CORS Y LLYN NATURE RESERVE

At Cors y Llyn SSSI you can gaze on fields of orchids and the carnivorous round-leaved sundew. Within a few steps of the car park thousands of heath and common spotted orchids bloom in late June. This rich, boggy enclosure escaped land draining after World War II and is now a truly diverse habitat. Access is superb and a wheelchair or pushchair can, with a little effort, be manoeuvred through. A boardwalk allows visitors to penetrate the wet bogland areas.

→ From Newbridge on Wye S on A470. Cross River Ithon continue 800m. R onto narrow road, past farmyard to reserve car park. Builth Wells, Powys LD2 3RU 0845 1306229 ccgc.gov.uk 52.1905,-3.4404 🦅

7 KENFIG DUNES NATURE RESERVE

Beyond the belching chimneys of Port Talbot and conveniently accessed off the M4, you'll find Kenfig NNR, one of the most important nature reserves in Europe. The vast landscape of green hillocks descends to pretty Kenfig pond and to the sea beyond. It is the principal habitat of the rare fen orchid (*Liparis loeselii*), which I didn't see, but the southern marsh and fragrant orchids were thriving.

→ M4 junction 37. Visitor centre at Ton Kenfig, Bridgend, Mid Glamorgan CF33 4PT 01656 743386 ccgc.gov.uk 51.5153,-3.7287 🦅

Accommodation

8 TRELLYN WOODLAND CAMPING

Trellyn campsite is a lovely quiet site in a wooded valley, sheltered from the sea winds and yet right on the coast path. It offers simple camping facilities and stargazing and campfires are de rigeur. If you don't have your own tent you can rent their hippy tipi, a yurt or the geo-eco dome. There are bread ovens, wood stores, and private access to the beach and village below. If you want a pitch, book the Meadow site in advance – it's popular and well-loved for a reason.

→ Abercastle, Haverfordwest, Pembrokeshire SA62 5HJ 01348 837762 trellyn.co.uk 🏠 🦅

7 KENFIG DUNES

9 PENPONT

The setting is a glorious Grade I large country house deep in the Usk Valley above Brecon. The estate has been in the same family since 1666, and although recently restored it retains its mellow charm and atmosphere. You can camp in the Old Rose Garden or near the river and spend days wandering through the gardens, meadows and woods and out to the countryside beyond. Self-catering accommodation is offered in the Courtyard Wing – perfect for a large party. The onsite, organic farm shop sells vegetables and fruit from the walled gardens, as well as local meats and eggs.

→ Signposted off A4, 5 miles W of Brecon. Penpont, Brecon, Powys LD3 8EU 01874 636202 penpont.com

10 TY GLAS

Set in 40 acres of meadows and wildlife reserve, Ty Glas cottage and its sister Little Barn must be the most idyllic, low-impact accommodation in the country. Both buildings have one room, and each sleeps two people. Perfectly rustic and yet luxurious, both cottage and barn have fires, plump pillows, period furniture, and the most incredible views of Carningli (Angels) mountain. Meadows full of orchids in spring roll out from your window, while horses peep over the open fences. The landscaping here provides true inspiration for wild gardening, and the whole place is in every way a little piece of holiday heaven.

→ Crymych, Pembrokeshire SA41 3XJ 0844 5005101 underthethatch.co.uk

10 TY GLAS

9 PENPONT

Food

11 THE GROVE

If you are looking for a luxurious, secluded country getaway head to The Grove, an award-winning restaurant that has been recommended to me time and time again. The small hotel and self-catering cottage are set within wildflower meadows, woods and lawns. It offers the best of Welsh cuisine, with produce sourced as locally as possible, and the lovely, organic kitchen garden is continually expanding. The only disadvantage is the hotel's inland location in an area with such a fantastic coastline. Its position does, however, offer easy access to the coast and lively Narberth town where there are excellent independent food shops.

→ Signposted off A478. Molleston, Narberth, Pembrokeshire SA67 8BX 01834 860915 thegrove-narberth.co.uk daily breakfast, lunch, dinner

12 FELIN FACH GRIFFIN

This is the sister pub of the Gurnard's Head near Penzance, one of our all-time favourite pubs with rooms. The same relaxed, arty ambience pervades Felin Fach. Food is a celebration of Welsh and Borders produce, combined with vegetables and fruit from the organic kitchen garden out back – do take time to wander around it. It is unfortunate that the busy A470 is right on the doorstep but bad weather isn't an issue. When the rains come, there are fires and cosy rooms to retreat to and indulge in a long lunch or candlelit dinner. It's an incredibly relaxed and welcoming place where children and excellent food happily combine.

→ Brecon, Powys, LD3 0UB, 01874 620111 eatdrinksleep.ltd.uk Easter–September

Nearby is TyGlyn, a walled garden hidden in the woods alongside the river Aeron. Their kitchen-garden produce is often for sale.

12   FELIN FACH GRIFFIN

13   BLAENCAMEL ORGANIC FARM

chilli sauce
Sweet for dipping, or hot, or £3.00
with coriander

Chutneys £4

Jams + jellies £4 (large)
small jars £2.75

Hot Chilli sauce
Add a Kick to
your cooking, or
use as condiment
if you dare!

Sweet Chilli
sauce
Great with
fishcakes/cheese
stir-fry

13   BLAENCAMEL ORGANIC FARM

This family-run farm has been proudly organic for over 30 years, and its aim is to balance sustainable crop production with the preservation of its landscape and wild habitat. After you have filled your bags with flowers and fruits, stroll round the greenhouses or take a walk along the special woodland trails. In spring, wild daffodils, anemones, and bluebells carpet the woods and in summer butterflies and birds feast on the wild flowers that are encouraged to thrive. Nearby is Ty Glyn (Ciliau Aeron, Ceredigion, SA48 8DE), a walled garden hidden in the woods alongside the river Aeron. Leave a donation and buy some of the kitchen-garden produce that's often for sale. All profits go to the Davis Trust for special-needs children.

Ciliau Aeron, Lampeter, Ceredigion SA48 8DE 01570 470529 blaencamel.com

PLAS BRONDANW

North Wales

Through the wild Cambrian landscapes to Anglesey
and the unspoilt Llyn peninsula, flowering plants thrive,
while imaginative gardens flourish in sheltered valleys.

North Wales

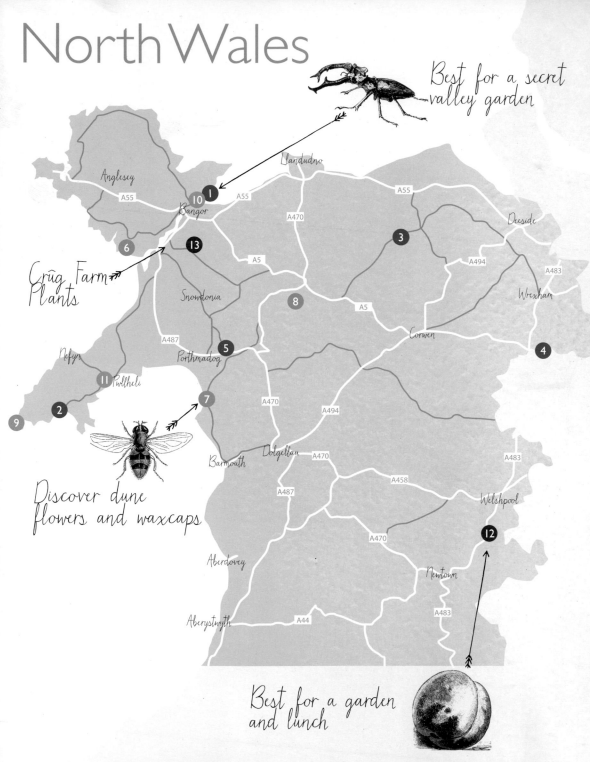

Best for a secret valley garden

Crûg Farm Plants

Discover dune flowers and waxcaps

Best for a garden and lunch

Anglesey

A55

Llandudno

Bangor

10 1

A55

A55

Deeside

A470

3

A494

A483

Wrexham

6

13

A5

Snowdonia

8

A5

Corwen

4

Nefyn

A487

Porthmadog

5

11 Pwllheli

2

7

A470

A494

9

A470

A483

Barmouth

Dolgellau

A470

A458

A487

Welshpool

Aberdovey

A470

12

Newtown

Aberystwyth

A44

A483

The highlights

›› Enjoy swims and strolls along the Llyn peninsula or Anglesey's wildflower-studded coast (6)

›› Discover Clough Williams-Ellis's garden nestled in the Welsh mountains (5)

›› Stay in the abundant Cadnant valley and explore jungle gardens and wildlife-rich meadows (1 & 10)

›› Combine a garden visit with a delicious jazz supper under the stars at Glansevern Hall (12)

Continuing north along the Cambrian mountains to the tip of the Isle of Anglesey, this vast area is one of eye-watering beauty. Foxgloves abound in the wild mountainous – and what George Monbiot would call a 'sheepwrecked' – landscape. In the old Kingdom of Gwynedd, the Welsh national and cultural identity continues, resilient and strong.

When it comes to gardens the landscape and climate, which are often harsh, dictate what grows. And yet, in protected valleys and on southern hill slopes, strange microclimates allow a surprising collection of delicate plants to thrive. At Plas yn Rhiw on the Llyn, at Bodnant, and in the reclaimed valley garden of Plas Cadnant on Anglesey, you can find tender plants such as tree ferns thriving in their wet cwms. If you are looking for hardy plants, head to Crûg Farm Plants where virtuoso plant-hunters Bleddyn and Sue Wynn-Jones have an inspiring show garden and nursery filled with glorious species that flourish in damp and fierce weather.

For garden artistry, seek out eccentric Clough William-Ellis' home at Plas Brondanw. Away from the pomp of Portmeirion, he created a garden that, although formal, plays with the wild landscape in which it resides. The woods around the estate and wider area are thronged with cuckoos, foxgloves, ferns, and tumbling waterfalls. There are miles of picturesque walks to enjoy. From late spring, when the bluebells still stand above the bracken, through to end of summer take your map and get walking; you won't be disappointed.

If you want beaches, the 'lost world' of the Llyn Peninsula is one of my favourite places to explore and see wild flowers in summer. Its tiny quiet lanes are perfect for cycling along and its stunning coastline and ancient earthworks are alive with flowers and butterflies. To see more, head to the unique sand-dune systems of Newborough Warren and Morfa Harlech where you can delight in huge stands of orchids, as well as fungi and delicate stunted flowering plants that act as generous hosts for the foraging wildlife.

Gardens

1 PLAS CADNANT

In the beautiful Cadnant valley on Anglesey, the biodiverse Cadnant estate and its gardens are being restored and reinvigorated. The Valley Garden is a magical interpretation of a picturesque landscape with ponds and waterfalls tumbling over mossy rocks. The ferns, tree-ferns, foxgloves and large trees covered in climbers give it a wonderful jungle atmosphere and it is also full of birdsong. The estate has been given SSSI status for its bluebells, ferns and mosses; and its chemical-free regime celebrates this status and allows these valued species to take centre stage. In autumn, you can enjoy fungi forays around the estate with expert mycologists. Over 20 acres of chemical-free, uncultivated meadows surround the gardens and the insect and bird life was tangibly present on our summer visit. There is a good tea room and accommodation (see listing).
➜ Cadnant Road, Menai Bridge, Isle of Anglesey LL59 5NH 01248 717174 plascadnant.co.uk ✿ Feb Sun; Apr Sun, Wed, Thu; May–Sep Sun, Tue–Thu & BH; Oct Sun, Wed 12–5pm (4pm Feb) ☕ 🍴 🌿 ❀ 🏠

2 PLAS YN RHIW

Nestled in the woods overlooking Cardigan Bay on the Llyn Peninsula is the small rustic manor house of Plas yn Rhiw. It was rescued by the Keating sisters, friends of Clough Williams-Ellis, who began restoring the historic small estate in the 1940s. Keen conservationists, their long-term aim was to leave the estate to the National Trust and it was always tended for the benefit of wildlife. The garden is still chemical-free and a haven for nature. Today, the rare and specialist plants that they collected and the wild flowers they loved are still nurtured. The effect is of a romantic cottage garden with packed borders and narrow paths that meander down the sloping terrain. It is a quiet place and the views are stunning. Simple camping is at nearby Treheli Farm.
➜ Rhiw, Pwllehli, Gwynedd, LL53 8AB 01758 780219 nationaltrust.org.uk ✿ opening days vary check website 12–5pm ☕ 🌿 🏠

1 PLAS CADNANT

3 GWAENYNOG HALL

Deep in rural Denbighshire are lovely Gwaenynog Hall Gardens. Beatrix Potter would come to visit her uncle here and her wanderings in his kitchen garden inspired the *Tale of the Flopsy Bunnies*. We saw one of them lolloping around the garden despite the polite sign on the gate. Today it is still

> *"It is very productive but not tidy, the prettiest kind of garden where old fashioned flowers grow amongst the currant bushes*
>
> Beatrix Potter's diary May 1895

a lovely working traditional cottage garden, although not a large garden open to the public. Owing to its history, however, Janie Smith is very happy for visitors to come and discover the charm of this delightfully old-fashioned and very much lived-in garden. We arrived in May and despite the incessant rain were enchanted by the beautiful floral show that very much reflected the illustrations in the story that I now read to my daughter. Self-seeded violas clustered in the gravel by the mossy birdbath and everywhere hungry bumble bees clung to the comfrey and borage waiting for the rain to cease. Please call for an appointment.
➜ 1½ mile W of Denbigh on A543, L at drive with Lodge. ½ mile, under stone arch. Iron garden gate past cottages on R. Pentrefoelas Road, Denbigh LL16 5NU 01745 812066 ☕

4 THE GARDEN HOUSE

The garden house is a beautiful 5-acre garden created from farmland 22 years ago. Picturesquely situated overlooking the river Dee, its design was 'drawn on the back of a fag packet'. The result is a delightful combination of wild ponds, clipped box parterres and rowan walks. Each garden 'idea' is perfectly executed and repeated. Beds are generous, filled often with just one or two species, topiary is large and everything feels abundant and happy in its place. When we visited in the summer of 2014, there was no gardener, teas had been stopped, and the future of the garden was unknown. The garden holds over 250 species and cultivars of hydrangea and many are for sale. Apart from the lovely topiary and the profusion of thrushes, the highlight was the stunning pond with its simple arched bridge and such a colourful matrix of wild and cultivated flowers that it looked like an Impressionist painting. It is a formal garden gone wild and for me it was at its peak.
➜ RHS free Thursdays. Erbistock, Wrexham, LL13 0DL 01978 781149 simonwingett.com ✿ May–Sep Thu & Fri 10–5pm ☕ 🌿

4 THE GARDEN HOUSE

3 GWAENYNOG HALL

5 PLAS BRONDANW

Not far from the famous Italianate village of Portmeirion, is the architect's home, Plas Brondanw. Clough Williams-Ellis was handed control of the old family estate, nestled in a beautiful valley in the Snowdonia National Park, in 1902. From the end of World War I until his death at the venerable age of 95, he devoted himself to developing the gardens, bringing to them the same passionate artistry as he did to Portmerion. He worked tirelessly, spending all his income, to extend the gardens out into the fields and woods, where they merged into the wild mountains. The true beauty of this garden is that it is designed to celebrate its divine landscape. Every vista, avenue, ornamental gate and folly is placed carefully in order to maximise the mountain views. It is not the most accomplished of gardens. Planting in the borders could be more effusive but its bones are so fine that all is forgiven. The topiary peaks effortlessly follow the contours of the mountains and sit perfectly against the rolling backdrop of mature trees. Its terraces and balustrades, although grand, maintain a sense of humour and invite the visitor to explore further and further. Outside the main gardens woodland walks continue to the faux ruins and fern-filled quarry gardens.

→ Llanfrothen, Gwynedd LL48 6SW 01766 772772 plasbrondanw.com
☼ Easter–Sep 10–5pm

I enjoyed a quiet hour
of dune exploration while
my family played on
the beach

6 NEWBOROUGH WARREN

Meadows

6 NEWBOROUGH WARREN

The forested warren in the Ynys Llanddwyn NNR is one of the best coastal sand-dune systems in Britain and a haven for wildflowers from spring to autumn. Vast colonies of marsh helleborines thrive in summer when the rain filled hollows dry out, while dune pansy, early marsh, northern marsh and spotted orchids add to the beautiful display. The pretty white flowers of grass of Parnassus (*Parnassia palustris*) are at their peak in August. The whole reserve of dune and forest is criss-crossed by a network of paths leading down to the Menai Strait and to the island of Llanddwyn (cut off at high tide).

→ From Newborough Village follow Church Street SE towards Traeth beach cark park (fee charged), Isle of Anglesey LL61 6SG
. ccw.gov.uk 53.1442,-4.3856 ⤵

7 MORFA HARLECH

Beneath Harlech Castle in the unique dune 'slacks' (flat ground), between views of Snowdonia and the sea, the accreting and constantly shifting dune system harbours rare sand lizards, colonies of various orchids, wild pansies and Portland spurge. Skylarks and butterflies add to the richness of the landscape, while autumn fungi, including waxcaps and puffballs, grow in the sandy hillocks. Explore with care.

→ Car park and FP to beach at Ffordd Glan Mor, Harlech, Gwynedd LL46 2UG. 01766 770274 ccgc.gov.uk 52.8633,-4.1193 ⤵

8 TY MAWR WYBRNANT

In the heart of the Conwy valley sits the farm of Bishop William Morgan, the first man to translate the Bible into Welsh. You can walk for miles across rich, traditionally managed upland farmland and through woods. Bluebells, foxgloves, ferns, meadow flowers and bog myrtle (its sweet resinous scent helps to deter midges) all flourish here. Download walks from NT website.

→ W on Glasgwm Road forking R to follow NT signs. Penmachno, Betws-y-Coed LL25 0HJ 01690 760213 nationaltrust.org.uk
⌚ Farmhouse; Apr–Oct Thu–Sun 12–5pm 53.0547,-3.8365 ⤵

Accommodation

9 MYNYDD MAWR CAMPSITE

On the western-most point of the Llyn peninsula with views of Bardsey Island, is the simple campsite of Mynydd Mawr. Walk straight out onto the wildflower-fringed coastal path and explore the many sandy beaches that dot the coastline. From nearby Aberdaron take a boat trip to Bardsey, where thrift and orchids, including the lovely autumn lady's tresses, thrive. The area is a renowned marine conservation zone.

→ Llanllawen Fawr, Aberdaron, Pwllheli, North Wales, LL53 8BY 01758 760223 aberdaroncaravanandcampingsite.co.uk 🏠 ⤵

9 LLYN COASTLINE

10 PLAS CADNANT

There are five gorgeously decorated self-catering cottages to rent on the beautiful Cadnant estate. It's a great way to discover the beautiful gardens out of hours (see garden listing) and explore the biodiverse rolling parkland and secret waterfalls. Each cottage has its own character and you can choose from from the large, airy Coach House accommodating twelve, to the cosy Brewhouse for two people. Our favourite is the Garden Cottage where your door and windows open straight out onto the lovely long borders in the walled garden. The town of Menai, which has independent shops and boutiques, is very close.
→ Cadnant Road, Menai Bridge, Isle of Anglesey LL59 5NH 01248 717007 plascadnant.co.uk

11 PLAS BODEGROES

Plas Bodegroes (Rosehip Hall) is a romantic wisteria-covered Georgian manor with ten chic but very relaxed rooms and charming gardens. Welsh paintings and fresh flowers fill the house, which is quiet, elegant and informal. There are lots of places to sit outside under the roses and enjoy an aperitif before you sit down to a first-class lunch or supper using the freshest Welsh fare. If you seek luxury on the Llyn Peninsula, this is the place.
→ Signed off the A497 1.5 miles NW of Pwllheli. Nefyn Road, Pwllheli, Gwynedd LL53 5TH 01758 612363 bodegroes.co.uk

11 PLAS BODEGROES

Food

12 THE POTTING SHED AT GLANSEVERN HALL

The gardens here are a delightful mix of styles. Chubby stone angels hide behind the cow parsley in the wild garden and throughout the meadow to the bird hide. Sweeps of naturalised camassias blend into the buttercup-scattered fields beyond. A beautiful, huge bronze hare sits lazily in the long grass. Boundaries blur here and that is what makes the space work. The walk around the lake and across to its island is delightful and a whole tour of the garden is a great excuse to indulge yourself in the excellent Potting Shed café in the courtyard. Enjoy flower-strewn salads, seasonal soups, and delicious home-made cakes. On Friday evenings, you can listen to jazz, drink wine and eat gourmet pizzas.
→ Signed off the A483. Berriew, Welshpool, Powys, SY21 8AH, 01686 640644 glansevern.co.uk
🕑 Tue–Sat & BH 10.30–5pm

13 CABAN CAFÉ

We love this little café at the foot of Snowdon. It is at the heart of a social enterprise scheme to bring rural, economic development to this wild area of Wales. There are studios and workshops and all profits from the café go to the hub. The food is delicious: excellent local cheeses and meats are on offer with as much produce as possible harvested from the 40 raised beds in the kitchen garden. There is a huge range of vegetables and fruits, as well as honey, and almost everything on your plate has been freshly harvested and cooked in the kitchen. Other produce is either foraged, locally sourced, or fairtrade. The café is fully licensed and they do excellent breakfasts.
→ Yr Hen Ysgol, Brynrefail, nr Llanberis LL55 3NR 01286 685462 caban-cyf.org
🕑 daily 9–4pm

10 PLAS CADNANT

12   GLANSEVERN HALL

12   GLANSEVERN HALL

12   THE POTTING SHED CAFE

WALCOT HALL

Shropshire & Cheshire

Visit the birthplace of the Industrial Revolution, eat delicious fare in one of Britain's foodie capitals, and feast your eyes on historic hay meadows and contemporary gardens.

Shropshire & Cheshire

The highlights

›› Welcome the year with magic carpets of snowdrops and crocuses (3)

›› Enjoy a fantastic lunch in my favourite tea room filled with lions and tigers (2)

›› Experience over two hundred plant species in some of Britain's best lowland hay meadows (7)

›› Stay in the Dipping Shed, a showman's caravan, a country house wing or a cosy yurt on the glorious Walcot estate (10)

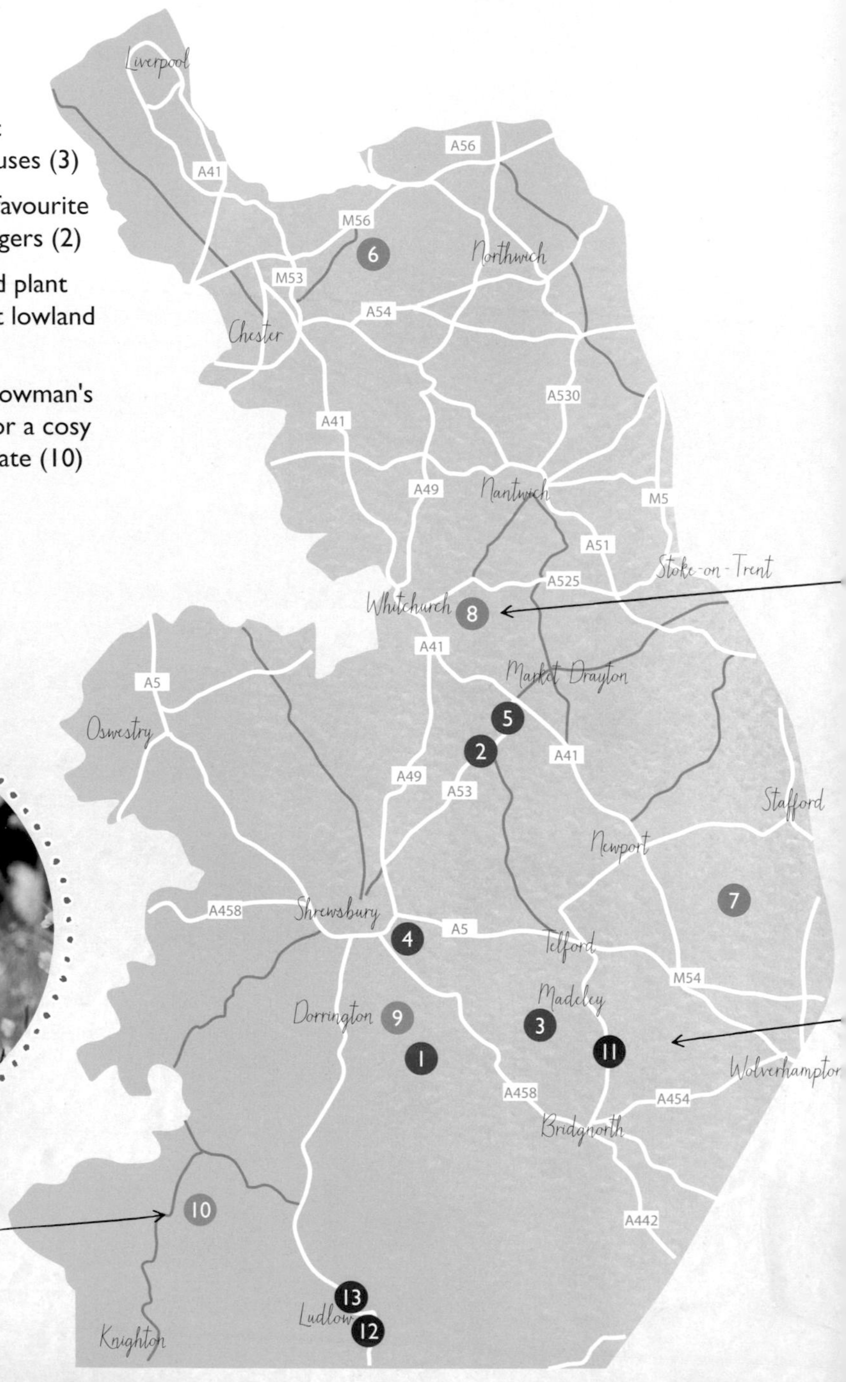

Liverpool

A41

M56

M53

A56

Northwich

6

Chester

A54

A41

A530

A49

Nantwich

M5

A51

A525

Stoke-on-Trent

Whitchurch · 8

A41

Market Drayton

A5

5

Oswestry

2

A41

A49

Stafford

A53

Newport

A458

Shrewsbury

A5

7

4

Telford

M54

Dorrington

9

Madeley

3

1

11

Wolverhampton

A458

A454

Bridgnorth

A442

Best for a magical place to stay

10

Knighton

Ludlow

13

12

1

5

Best for butterflies and moths

Best for a local produce lunch

This beautiful area tells two very different stories. To the north are the Shropshire and Cheshire plains - flat, fertile lands that are perfectly suited to the big agriculture that they support. It's hard to believe this was the pounding heart of the Industrial Revolution, which was to change our world and landscape forever. Today, the birthplace of that revolution, Ironbridge Gorge, is a quiet, wooded river valley dotted with picturesque villages. As a UNESCO World Heritage site, its history has been preserved.

To the south, 'batches' (valleys, in local dialect) cut through rivers and woods creating a rolling landscape more suited to pastoral farming. Life here is peacefully rural, and some parts, such as the Clun Forest, are really quite wild.

On the border south west of Whitchurch is Bettisfield Mosses NNR. One of Britain's most important boglands, it is home to the carnivorous round-leaved sundew, bog rosemary, and a staggering 670 different species of moth! If you like moths, head to Melverley meadows where you can find the delightfully named shoulder-striped wainscot, (*Leucania comma*) and green pug (*Pasiphila rectangulata*). Indeed the entire farm is a place steeped in history as well as ephemeral beauty.

With such rich pockets of biodiversity I was surprised and saddened to discover that Shropshire's Coronation Meadow is the tiny one-acre Hayton meadow near Ludlow. Great things do come in small packages, however, and Hayton abounds with the the rare pasque flower (*Pulsatilla vulgaris*).

To experience some stunning 'wild' gardens, visit the resurrected meadow at Jessamine Cottage, the romantic Benthall, or Hodnet Hall gardens, where you can spend a happy hour in one of my all-time-favourite garden tea rooms.

2

Gardens

1 JESSAMINE COTTAGE

At Jessamine cottage, a lovely wildflower garden has been unleashed from a field that has never been ploughed. Previously the tightly mown grass was used for a caravan park, but Pam and Lee Wheeler simply decided to leave it to grow. Up sprang common spotted orchids – multiplying year on year – sprawls of meadow buttercups, and a rich diversity of grasses, without any rye at all. Behind the pond is a pretty, shaded brook walk where ferns and foxgloves glowed in the low light of late May. At the front of the garden, near the tea room groaning with home-made jams, there are flowing borders, specimen trees, and columns of tumbling roses. Looking out to the hills beyond, the sight of clipped hornbeams towering over a rolling sea of yellow buttercups really was a work of art. To see what can become of a boring green field in less than 15 years is very exciting.
5 miles SW of Much Wenlock. Kenley, Shrewsbury, Shropshire SY5 6NS 01694 771279 ⏰ May–Aug Thu–Sun & BH 2–6pm & NGS days 🍵 🌿 🍴

2 HODNET HALL

The gardens here are a sylvan paradise and within them is one of my most esteemed garden tea rooms. Our welcome came courtesy of an army of froglets that pounced from our feet, residents, no doubt, of the many ponds and lakes that punctuate the estate. April kicks off with swarms of daffodils, camellias and rhododendrons followed by the sweeping mists of bluebells in May. There are meadows with mown paths to wander in summer, a working kitchen garden where apparent chaos is skilfully orchestrated and as autumn

1 JESSAMINE COTTAGE

unfolds, fiery birches and acers in the gloaming. Housed in the large, light-filled old stables, on every wall of the fantastic tea room is an eccentric and delightful display of the taxidermist's art. As well as a divine cake selection, food is restaurant-quality: fresh salads and soups, or local sausage cassoulets served with artisan bread.
→ Hodnet, Market Drayton, Shropshire TF9 3NN, 01630 685786 hodnethallgardens.org ⏰ Apr–Sept Sun & BH 12-5pm 🍵 🌿 🍴

3 BENTHALL HALL

Down a wooded lane above the river Severn, you'll find pretty St Bartholomew's church with its unusual built-in apiary, and 16th-century Benthall Hall. The present garden dates from 1860, when geologist and botanist George Maw took on the tenancy and filled the garden with his horticultural finds. Maw was a collector of crocuses and many of the species he planted survive. Later, Robert Bateman, the Victorian romantic painter and sculptor, was to put his stamp on the garden. Son of the infamous horticulturalist James Bateman, his rockeries, terraces, and topiary were clearly influenced by his father's monumental creations at Biddulph Grange. Despite all this history, Benthall remains a quiet, unassuming small estate. Its gardens are incontrovertibly naturalistic and rich with unusual plants – a collection that belies its size. Spring starts with snowdrops and Benthall's famous crocuses.

→ Off the B4375 Benthall Lane. The Avenue, Broseley, Shropshire, TF12 5RX 01952 882159 nationaltrust.org.uk ⏰ Feb Sat & Sun 1–4.30pm, Mar–Oct Tue, Wed, Sat, Sun & BH 1–5.30pm 🍵 🌿 🍴 🌸

4 ATTINGHAM PARK

Attingham's story is one of rise and ruin, and the house and its garden are part of an extensive, ongoing restoration project. In its acres of parkland, where deer roam, are ancient woods that are carpeted with snowdrops and bluebells in spring. Make sure you pay a visit to the fantastical 650-year-old Repton oak. From the historic Bee House with its traditional straw skeps, to the incredible walled kitchen garden, the estate is a haven for fungi, woodpeckers and barn owls. In the walled kitchen garden there is a bothy where the unmarried gardeners would have led their monastic lives. Mushroom-growing sheds, stove-rooms and glasshouses have been succcessfully resurrected. I loved the relaxed nutwalk borders and the meadow with its magnificent trees. After a good walk head to the main house and Lady Berwick's tea room where you can enjoy seasonal produce brought over by gardener's bicycle from the garden that very day.
→ Atcham, Shrewsbury, Shropshire SY4 4TP 01743 708123 nationaltrust.org.uk ⏰ Jan–Mar and Nov–Dec 9–5pm, Apr–Jun and Sep 8–6pm, Jul–Aug 8–7pm, Oct 9–6pm 🍵 🍴

2 HODNET HALL

2 BENTHALL

3 ATTINGHAM PARK

5 WOLLERTON OLD HALL

To my eyes, Wollerton is like a beautiful and flamboyant peacock. Set around a muted old timber hall, the garden is a glorious, chaotic mix. At one end, there is a vegetable garden that reflects Charles Dowding's no-dig philosophy and, at the other The Croft is a wild celebration of informality. Sandwiched in the middle, through allées, parterres, long borders and clipped shrubs is a jaw-dropping assault of colour and careful landscape design. I loved the overtly relaxed kitchen garden, especially the way it contrasted with the classic English designs of the formal enclosures. The garden is seriously romantic and its colour combinations range from toning shades of soft muted lilac to passionate affairs of bold blue and raging orange. Inside the hollyhock-festooned tea room you can enjoy a proper lunch with salads from the garden. There's lots of seating, both indoors and out and many visitors come for the food alone. The adjoining nursery sells plants propagated at Wollerton. Specialities are salvias, iris and phlox – all which can be seen at their best in the garden. Pay a vist and bring your credit card.

Wollerton, Market Drayton, Shropshire TF9 3NA 01630 685760
wollertonoldhallgarden.com
Easter–Aug Fri, Sun, BH & Fri in Sep
12–5pm

Wheeldon Copse was the target of Landlife's soil inversion projects - where deep ploughing turns soil upside down exposing the low-fertility sub-soils and creating the perfect medium for wild flowers.

7 MOTTEY MEADOWS

Meadows

6 WHEELDON COPSE

The Woodland Trust's Wheeldon Copse was the target of Landlife's soil-inversion projects – deep ploughing turns soil upside down, exposing the low-fertility sub-soils and creating the perfect medium for wild flowers. Nearly ten years later, much of the wildflower landscapes have been taken over by the growing woodland, which is all part of the plan. Hopefully these woods will become havens for bluebells, foxgloves, red campion and wood avens. Under the canopy of an unfortunately sited overhead power line are long walks where you will see stunning wild flowers smothered in insects that buzz louder than the cables above.

→ 1/2 mile N of Manley. Park in layby on Manley Road next to entrance gate. Frodsham, Cheshire WA6 9EH woodlandtrust.org.uk 53.2571,-2.7294

7 MOTTEY MEADOWS NNR

The rich floodplains of Mottey are some of the UK's best lowland hay meadows.

Over 240 species of traditional hay meadow plants – including great burnet, ragged robin, meadow rue, and knapweed – put on a summer display. At this Special Area for Conservation, the permissive paths are open between June and August, although hay is often cut at the end of July. Late April is the time see the most northerly, wild snake's head fritillary colony on guided walks led by Natural England.

→ Park in Wheaton Aston, walk 0.6 miles along Broadholes Lane (bridleway) to info sign/gate on R into Weate's Meadow. Follow permissive path along fence line on R. Staffs ST19 9NS 01952 812111 naturalengland.org.uk 52.7177,-2.2369

8 MELVERLEY MEADOWS

The flower-rich hay meadows of Melverley farm are amazingly well preserved. They were farmed in the traditional way from the mid-16th century until just ten years ago, when the Wildlife Trust purchased the land. And the farm even remained in the hands of a single family. The patterns we still see under the grass were made by the 19th-century horse drawn ploughs and the fields are small and irregular – the result of the original clearance of dense woodland. Between its native mixed hedges moths, butterflies, and meadow flowers thrive. In a sea of intensely farmed arable fields, Melverley is a floriferous treasure island. It's best to visit in spring and summer.

→ From Ash Magna N along Church Lane, past church, 1st R onto no-through road. Small car park on L. Whitchurch, Shropshire SY13 4EA 01743 2844280 shropshirewildlifetrust.org.uk 52.9599,-2.6252

8 GREEN PUG MOTH

Accommodation

9 ACTON PIGOT B&B

In the hamlet of Acton Pigot, near picturesque English Heritage's Langley Chapel and Langley Manor, is a rose fest of house and garden. John has lived and farmed here all his life and his wife, Hildegard, has created the glorious gardens with their profusion of foxgloves, ferns and roses. From May to midsummer, the wisteria covering the traditional red brick farmhouse morphs into a deep cape of pink-apricot roses that drape lazily across the front door. Inside, it's warm and comfortable with deep sofas and roaring fires. Ample breakfasts include eggs from the chickens and kitchen-garden produce.
➜ Acton Pigot, Acton Burnell, Shropshire SY5 7PH, 01694 731209 actonpigot.co.uk 🍵 🏠

10 WALCOT HALL

Walcot Hall is a real find, a world away from the mundane materiality of life. Down the magnificent beech-lined drive there is a cornucopia of imaginative accommodation choices. Near the entrance is the camping field, with its converted tram, where you can pitch your tent and check-in at the nearby pub. Up past the horses and old carts, near the flowery ponds and beehives are two separate, cosy yurts with incredible views and a whole oak-studded field in which to run wild. The divine Dipping Shed, converted from an old hunting lodge, is a glorious secret retreat. Other options include numerous flats in the stables courtyard, wings in the main house, and renovated caravans and shepherd's huts – choose one and explore the estate.
➜ Signed off the B4385 Brampton Road, Lydbury North, Shropshire SY7 8AZ, 01588 680570 walcothall.com 🍵 🏠

10 WALCOT HALL

9 ACTON PIGOT

Food

11 THE HUNDRED HOUSE HOTEL

Enjoy plates of juicy local fare enhanced by one or more of the 50 different varieties of herbs that grow in the grounds. Summer, when you can take a drink from the bar and wander through the apple trees, vegetable plots and flower gardens is the ideal time to visit. Either eat at the bar or in the restaurant – a cosy, colourful affair with roaring fires in cold weather, and great food. Chef and patron Stuart Philips holds a calendar of cookery classes celebrating foraged food and local producers. There are also rather bizzarely decorated bedrooms.
➜ Bridgnorth Road, Norton, Telford, Shropshire TF11 9EE, 01952 580240 hundredhouse.co.uk 🕙 daily 🍵 🍴

12 THE GREEN CAFÉ

On the banks of the river Terne in a converted mill is the honourable Green Café. It consistently and justifiably gets fantastic reviews for the honest, heartfelt nourishment that it cooks up under the arches of Dinham Bridge. It's an unassuming place with simple seating inside in the mill, or outside on the green where you can watch the river. There are only two lunch sittings a day and it's best to call and book a table. We'd heard the hype, been recommended numerous times, and it lived up to all the rave reviews. Our food was, quite simply, delicious.
➜ Under the Dinham Bridge W side of Ludlow. Mill on the Green, Linney, Ludlow SY8 1EG, 01584 879872 thegreencafe.co.uk 🕙 lunch sittings 12-ish and 1.30pm 🍴

The divine Dipping Shed is a glorious lost world secret retreat, renovated from an old hunting lodge.

10   WALCOT HALL

13   THE LUDLOW FOOD KITCHEN

13   THE LUDLOW FOOD KITCHEN

If you want to fill your basket and stock up your cupboards, the Ludlow Food Centre is the place to do it. With its deli and kitchen (and the Ludlow pantry in town), this is a serious farm shop. All the beef, Gloucester old spot pork and lamb comes from the Oakly Park estate, as well as seasonal fruit and vegetables from Lady Windsor's private walled garden. Artisan producers and growers who work nearby also supply the shop and ensure that the 'fresh, local, seasonal' philosophy really is adhered to. In the airy café we breakfasted on delicious tomatoes, spinach and eggs from the gardens, honey from the estate's hives, and excellent coffee.

Bromfield Rd, Bromfield, Shropshire SY8 2JR, 01584 856020
ludlowkitchen.co.uk
daily 9–5pm (Sun 10–4pm)

Heart of England

Teeming with people and wildlife, our 'middle-lands'
from Kidderminster to Derby are also blessed with
a rich heritage of deeply romantic gardens and
precious nature reserves.

Heart of England

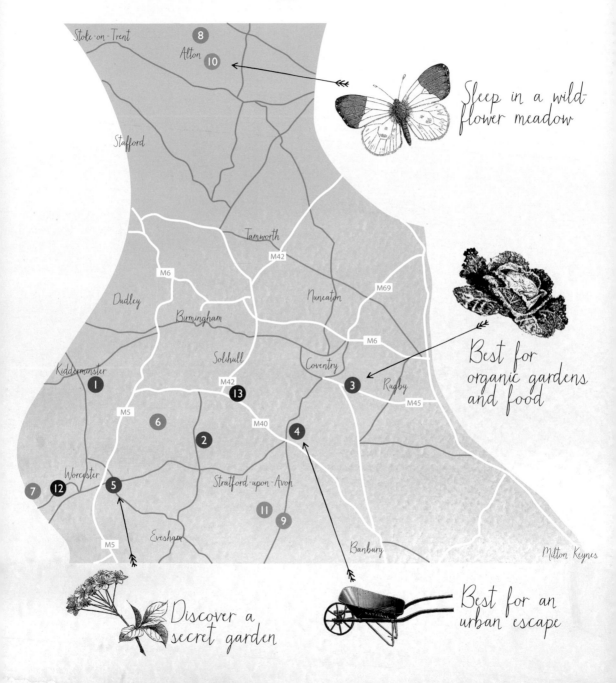

Stoke-on-Trent

8

Alton

10

Sleep in a wild-
flower meadow

Stafford

Tamworth

M42

M6

Nuneaton

M69

Dudley

Birmingham

M6

Solihull

Coventry

Kidderminster

1

M42

13

Rugby

3

M45

Best for
organic gardens
and food

M5

6

M40

2

4

Worcester

7   12   5

Stratford-upon-Avon

11

9

Evesham

Banbury

Milton Keynes

M5

Discover a
secret garden

NATIONAL

Best for an
urban escape

The highlights

›› Enter the lost world of romantic Spetchley Park (5)

›› Climb fairytale towers and visit Louisa Arbuthnott's special plant nursery (1)

›› Run free through acres of incredible hay meadows (6)

›› Sleep in a wildflower meadow and enjoy a woodland sauna at the idyllic Farm on the Hill (10)

The metropolitan county of the West Midlands and the cities that border it, represent the third most populous area in Britain. But even here, swathes of non-urbanised green retain their rural character and provide much-needed corridors for wildlife.

Sutton Park National Nature Reserve and Site of Special Scientific Interest is one of the largest urban parks in Europe. Its ancient woodlands, lakes, and acres of heath and wetlands cover a massive 970 hectares. To the north, Cannock Chase, designated an Area of Outstanding Natural Beauty, is rich with rare lowland heath, woodland and agricultural land.

South of Birmingham, you will discover a shining arc of gardens to visit. From the fairytale folly garden and special-plants nursery of the Stone House Cottage near Kidderminster, head east to Garden Organic near Coventry. At Hill Close Victorian Leisure Gardens in Warwick, the lovely collection of individual productive gardens has a fascinating history. The garden that stole my heart, however, was within the walls of Spetchley Park, home of the Berkeley family. It shows the influence of the extravagant and fierce 19th-century plantswoman Ellen Willmott. In a stunning and tranquil setting, this hidden English country shangri-la of a garden is packed solid with a luscious palate of rare plants. I cannot imagine it looking any better than it did in June, but I look forward to testing my theory and returning to walk its enchanting paths in a different month.

I am waiting patiently to find out when the historic Croome Walled Garden, with its focus on sustainable and healthy living, will open again to the public. There have been a few open days during the painstaking restoration period and considering the attention given to detail, it should prove to be a beautiful place. Do keep an eye out for news.

Gardens

1 STONE HOUSE COTTAGE NURSERY

The cottage garden is a dreamy treasure chest of rare herbaceous plants, shrubs, and climbers, many of which can be found in the nursery. Appearing so much bigger than its one-acre plot, the garden is a labyrinth of small rooms, each showcasing Louisa Arbuthnott's clever eye for plant pairings. Everywhere you look Rumplestiltskin-like red-brick gazebos and towers, built by husband James, keep watch and tempt you up their rickety steps. From these towers, you can really see the garden and get your head around its cunning layout. I also found it hard to believe that this antique, fairytale garden with its impressive plant collection was a field until just 40 years ago. The wild garden in June was a watercolour work of art, bright with the pink of ragged robbin, buttercup yellow, the purple of orchids, and white splashes of ox-eye daisies. Hot pink spires of *Gladiolus illyricus* made me wonder whether it was wild or wanton. What I really like about this garden is that the native wild flowers and trees are considered of equal rank to the more exotic species. If you are looking for inspiration and special plants, this is the place.
→ Stone, Kidderminster, Worcs, DY10 4BG 07817 921146 shcn.co.uk ⏰ end Mar–early Sept Wed–Sat 10–5pm 🍵 ⚘ 🌱

1 STONE HOUSE COTTAGE NURSERY

2 COUGHTON COURT

2 COUGHTON COURT

Whether you want theatre or meadows, you'll find both here. On the one hand, there are standard wisterias in clipped-box rings and on the other, swathes of foxgloves and wild lake walks. Taken together, the ornamental gardens, orchards, kitchen garden and lake surrounding the imposing Tudor House are more than enough to fill a relaxing day out. We had missed the blossom in the orchard but the walled garden looked like a giant bowl filled with fresh greenery, all bejewelled by May's rain. Alliums, foxgloves and fountains of roses spilled over each other. Large hawthorn trees smothered in flower added informality to what could have so easily been a show of frivolity and extravagance. It was a pastel love poem intensified by the refracted light. After a tart of home-grown vegetables in the Stableyard café, we headed out across the meadow, crossing the river to Timm's Grove, the bluebell wood. There is a great kids play area.
→ Alcester, Warwickshire B49 5JA 01789 400777 nationaltrust.org.uk
⏰ Mar & Oct Thu–Sun, Apr–Sep Wed–Sun & BH 11–5pm 🍵 ⚘ 🍴 🌱

3 GARDEN ORGANIC, RYTON

Garden Organic, the UK's leading organic gardening charity has its headquarters at Ryton, near Coventry. There are ten acres of different gardens to explore from the small and lively Cuban *organoponico* (kitchen garden) plot, to the quiet meadows of the orchards. Everywhere you will find long grass and innovative plantings that are bright, alive, and inspiring. Entry is free on Sundays and the organisation works hard to make organic gardening as accessible as possible. Its 4m x 6m garden shows just how much you can do with a small patch of land. The onsite café, Fresh Rootz, won one of the the BBC regional street food awards. They they fill hearts and stomachs, serving tasty world food from their own garden produce.
→ Wolston Lane, Ryton-on-Dunsmore, Coventry CV8 3LG 02476 303517 rytongardens.co.uk
⏰ daily 10–4pm 🍵 🍴

4 HILL CLOSE GARDENS

On the edge of old Warwick, lost in a maze of houses, the Victorian gardens of Hill Close have survived modern development. The precious collection of gardens remains the pride and joy of a community that works tirelessly to keep them productive and open for our enjoyment. They started life in Victorian times as leisure gardens, offered for rent to artisans and shopkeepers who lived above their workplaces and had no outside space. Here they grew vegetables and flowers, and also kept pigs and poultry. They built sheds and spent evenings and free days tending their plots. The gardens are fiercely protected by the community group that tends them but you are very welcome to walk around, hear the stories, and visit the nursery. There is a lovely modern airy café that's open at weekends.
→ Next to Warwick racecourse. Pay & display car park and entry off Bread and Meat Close, Warwick CV34 6HF 01926 493339 hillclosegardens.com ⏰ Apr–Oct daily 11–5pm, Nov–Mar Mon–Fri 11–4pm 🍵 🍴 🌱

4 HILL CLOSE GARDENS

3 GARDEN ORGANIC, RYTON

5 SPETCHLEY PARK

I fell head over heels in love with the gardens
of Spetchley Park. I was not expecting
to find such an abundance of beauty and
romance here. Shame on me. The gardens
are the joyous result of 400 years' care by
generations of one family alone. Now they
are perfectly ripe, mellowed and bursting
with mouth-watering plant temptations. One
person was particularly influential in their
creation: the great Edwardian gardener and
plantswoman Ellen Willmott, who helped
her sister Rose Berkeley plant and design
many of the garden spaces. The inimitable
collection of plant varieties and the setting
are compelling enough reasons to visit, but
so is the air of magical intimacy that seems
to pervade the gardens. Exploring in June
felt like trespassing into a secret garden.
We met the sister of the great estate owner
wandering in the garden, deadheading as she
went. This does not feel like a formal garden,
although there are many formal elements.
Mostly it is a glorious mixture of packed
borders and beautiful specimen trees, such
as the cork oak near the 19th-century root
house. My favourite place was the secretive
Fountain Garden, where the ghost of Ellen
may still linger. A lovely tea room serves
light lunches and cream teas.
→ Spetchley, Worcester WR5 1RS, 01905
345106 spetchleygardens.co.uk
⟳ Apr–Sep Wed–Sun & BH 11–6pm

Eades meadow has neither been treated with pesticides or herbicides, nor ploughed for the last 100 years and in June the display was breathtaking.

6 EADES MEADOW

Meadows

6 EADES MEADOW

Part of the Fosters Green Meadows, Eades meadow was discovered by Fred Fincher, Worcestershire's great naturalist. Back in the 1950s, it must have been a sight to behold. Today, such flower-rich hay meadows are even rarer and on our visit in June the display was breathtaking. The best time to visit is from early May through to July, when yellow cowslips give way to pink ragged robin, then to green winged orchids. The meadow has neither been treated with pesticides or herbicides, nor ploughed for the last 100 years, and its rich diversity is the result of its annual hay cut, followed by regrowth and then cattle grazing. Please stick to the mown paths.
→ No parking. I mile S of Lower Bentley. Access and information off Woodgate road Lower Bentley, Bromsgrove B60 4HX worcswildlifetrust.co.uk 52.2813,-2.0281 ↴

7 THE KNAPP AND PAPERMILL

From the information centre, you make your way through the delightful old orchard, where the fruit tree trunks are covered in lichens. From here, follow the nature trail down to Brook Walk, past Big Meadow, which is full of cowslips, green winged orchids, knapweeds and butterflies. It's also fun to search for the 25 insect species that forage in Papermill Meadow.
→ Car park and cafe at Stocks Road Bridges Stone, Nr Alfrick WR6 5HR, 01905 754919 worcswildlifetrust.co.uk 52.1671,-2.3667 ↴

8 SIDE FARM MEADOWS

These unimproved small meadows bloom with bluebells, scabious, and knapweeds. Each is edged by old stone walls covered in 50 species of lichen – vertical gardens in their own right. Meadow flowers peak in June, but the meadows are a delight from April through to the end of July. It is steep, can be muddy, and there are no formal paths. One mile south, see spring flowers at Cotton Dell Woods NR (with parking).
→ Follow Blakeley Lane off A52,1st L, then fork R. Entrance on L after 0.9 miles. Oakamoor, Staffs, ST10 3DU 01889 880100 staffs-wildlife.org.uk 53.0161,-1.9147 ↴

Accommodation

9 THE OLD MANOR, HALFORD

On the edge of the Cotswolds, 7 miles from Stratford-upon-Avon is the timber-framed Old Manor House. Sleep in cosy, beamed bedrooms and wander through the rose-filled gardens down to the pretty river Stour. The views of the thatched cottage and the gardens are picture perfect. Jane is a cordon bleu cook, so you can look forward to a really good breakfast.
→ Halford, Shipston-on-Stour, Warwickshire CV36 5BT 01789 740264 sawdays.co.uk 🏠 ↴

9 THE OLD MANOR

10 FARM ON THE HILL

Enjoy secluded camping on a family farm between woodland and wildflower meadows. There is space for just five tents, so it's a perfect place for a weekend gathering with friends. Children can count butterflies in the meadow or find twigs for the evening campfire. The view down the valley is divine, especially from the loo. Facilities are, however, basic with no hot water or showers. If you don't have your own tent there is bell-tent hire available, or you can rent cosy Keepers Cottage. Comfortable B&B is also offered at the farmhouse. Keepers Cottage, which belonged to the owner's grandfather, has a woodburner and wonderful views over the hills. On summer weekends, the rustic tea shop in the barn is open. Onsite cycle hire also offers a chance to explore the the Churnet valley

→ Manor House Farm, Quixhill Lane, Prestwood, Staffs, ST14 5DD 01889 590410 farmonthehill.co.uk 🐾 🏠 🍽

11 TALTON LODGE

Stay in a fun selection of yurts, tipis, and wagons in the red-brick, walled kitchen garden of the lovely smallholding surrounding pretty Talton Lodge. Vegetables, chickens, and fruit trees share the kitchen garden and there is lots of grass to run around in. It's a great place to go with children, with bike hire available as well as good canoeing and swimming in the nearby river Stour. Delicious home-raised pork is also for sale. The famous gardens of Kiftsgate and Hidcote are just 8 miles away. You can also rent the barn, lodge, and house for larger parties.

→ Newbold-on-Stour, Stratford-upon-Avon CV37 8UB 07962 273417 taltonlodge.co.uk

10 FARM ON THE HILL

Food

12 THE FOLD CAFÉ

You'll find the café at heart of the The Fold, a community hub that includes an organic farm, designer/maker studios, and a natural therapy centre. Set in a 17th-century threshing barn, the café serves delicious, organic, home-grown slow food. The menu changes weekly depending on what's available and the organic Sunday roasts are deservedly popular, so do book ahead (exciting vegetable alternatives to roasts are offered). The café is fully licensed and there are always lots of events and courses going on, including philosophy evenings with supper. You can buy farm produce on site and there's a food market every 4th Sunday of the month 11–2pm.

→ New House Farm, Bransford WR6 5JB 01886 833633 thefold.org.uk
⏰ daily 9–4pm (Sun 10am) 🍽

13 KITCHEN GARDEN AT PACKWOOD

Packwood is famous for its stupendous yew garden and the wondrous, eccentric collections of exotica that fill the Tudor house. You cannot fail to be amazed by the 350 clipped beasts that romp across the great lawn, but I also loved the adjacent orchard, which was blanketed with wild flowers. From here you, can enjoy a lovely walk around the lake. The organic kitchen garden has been restored and its produce is served in the new barn café, a fresh take on the traditional garden tea room. I had a delicious goat's cheese, pearl barley and beetroot salad. Plenty of outdoor seating.

→ Signposted off B4439 Packwood Lane, Lapworth, Warwickshire B94 6AT 01564 782024 nationaltrust.org.uk
⏰ daily 9–5pm (shorter hours in winter)
🍷 🍽 🌼

Children can count butterflies or collect twigs for the evening campfire.

11 TALTON LODGE

11 TALTON LODGE

13 PACKWOOD

13 PACKWOOD

EASTON WALLED GARDENS

Lincolnshire & East

Beyond the mega-fields of agriculture hide rich pockets of traditional hay meadows, ancient woodland, orchards and bountiful kitchen gardens.

Lincolnshire & East

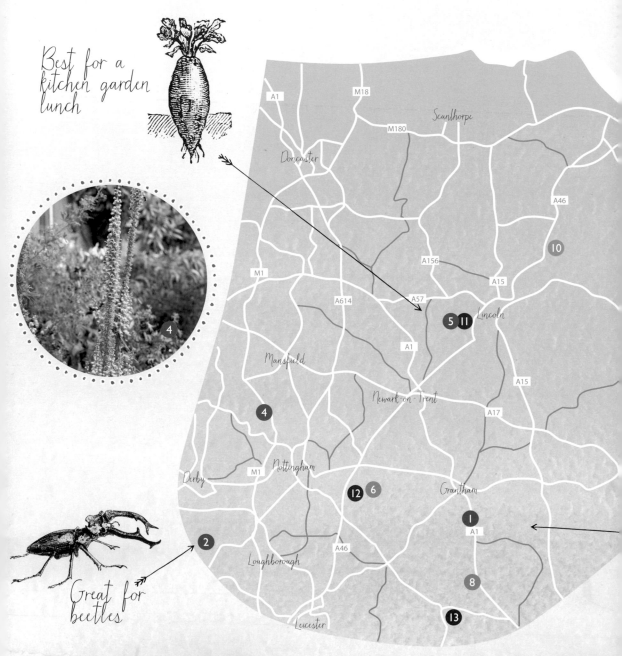

Best for a
kitchen garden
lunch

Great for
beetles

4

A1
M18
Scunthorpe
M180
Doncaster
A46
10
A156
A15
M1
A614
A57
5 11 Lincoln
A1
Mansfield
A15
Newark-on-Trent
A17
4
M1 Nottingham
Derby
12 6 Grantham
1
A1
Loughborough
A46
8
Leicester
13

The highlights

›› Be serenaded by birdsong as you wander the meadows, orchards and gardens of Easton (1)

›› Visit Doddington Hall's bountiful kitchen gardens and enjoy a garden fresh lunch (5 & 11)

›› Discover forty acres of wildflowers and buy seeds for your garden at Naturescape (6)

›› Go on a mini-beast safari in a flower-strewn traditional hay meadow at Calke Park (2)

Best for a wildlife filled garden

The Lincolnshire Wolds are an undulating landscape of chalkland and rich 'drift' soil. Once covered in species-rich, flower-strewn chalk downland, the landscape today is dominated by intensive agriculture and mono-cropping, and the chalk streams and aquifers are running short of water. Only a creative search of the landscape will uncover its pockets of rich diversity. Here, maybe more than in other regions, places such as roadside verges offer vital wildlife corridors through the mega-fields of cereal crops, vegetables and flower bulbs.

Often, many of the flower-rich hay meadows are small fragments that have been saved by one person's love of the flora and fauna. Merry's Meadows in north-east Rutland is a great example. It is the result of one man's conscious decision to preserve the flower-filled pasture.

For meadows and wildlife on a grand scale head for the estate lands of Calke Park NNR and SSSI. Vast meadowlands surround the majestic yet semi-derelict house, and its eccentric museum of natural-history relics. In the woods and open wood pasture orchids, bluebells, and insects – particularly beetles – flourish.

Easton Walled Garden is another example of a beautiful wild garden that marries a love of wildlife with stunning ornamental planting. The incredible birdsong we heard there was achingly beautiful and more resonant than in many other gardens I have visited.

Gardens

1 EASTON WALLED GARDENS

Dotted around the site of the ruined foundations of Easton Hall, wildlife and walled gardens flourish on the poor limestone soils. Reclaimed after years of neglect by Ursula Cholmeley and her team of gardeners, the 'lost' gardens are noticeably abundant with birds, bees and butterflies. Meadows are alive with insects, there are bird hides, and otters have been seen in the river. Easton is a great example of how to include long-grass meadows in both formal and informal ways. I loved the innovative yet unfussy criss-cross and circular mowing patterns. These created structure as well as pathways around the folly-lined orchard and on the grand slope up to what was the big house. The gardeners are lucky to have such a wonderful setting in which to 'go wild'. In the orchard, roses literally crawled among the long grass in July, while the avenue of ancient yew offered both shelter and vistas. In the vegetable and cutting gardens, mulch and manure have created fertile fenced spaces bursting with colour and edible produce. We saw shrews running across the paths, and an incredible diversity of birds delighted us with their intoxicating song. Everywhere there is a spirit of play and informality. A small tea room serves light lunches and cream teas.
➜ Don't follow sat nav. Exit A1 Easton on B6403. L after 1 mile. Planting Road, Easton, Grantham, NG33 5AP, 01476 530063 eastonwalledgardens.co.uk ✆ Mar–Oct Wed–Fri & Sun & BH 11–4pm 🚰 ❧ 🍽 ❦

2 CALKE ABBEY & CALKE PARK NNR

A wonderful mix of wildlife and history, Calke Abbey and Park is a place of ancient trees, orchids, ruined grottos, abandoned kitchen garden buildings and eccentric taxidermy collections. The gardens are lovely to wander through and I particularly loved the deserted gardener's bothy, left untouched, still full of old tools, and offering insights into an 18th-century gardener's life. But the nature reserve is definitely the location's greatest treasure. Far away from any roads or development,

1 EASTON WALLED GARDENS

Calke Park is home to some of the oldest trees in Europe, with vast seas of bluebells blooming beneath them in spring. A one-mile walk takes you through the open parkland to the 'Old Man of Calke' an ancient oak over 1,000 years old. For wildflowers, embark on the circular three-mile walk from Calke Park through the Ticknall Limeyards SSSI. Passing through flower-filled grasslands and rare wood pasture, you'll reach the old limekilns and their 're-wilded' spoil heaps where thousands of common spotted orchids and lime-loving twayblade bloom in midsummer. Detailed walks are available from visitor information.
➜ Signed off A514 at Ticknall, Derby, Derbyshire DE73 7LE 01332 863822 nationaltrust.org.uk ✆ times vary for gardens and reserve 🚰 ❧ 🍽

3 GUNBY HALL

Not far from Tennyson's home at Somersby, the Gunby Estate, which was landscaped by Capability Brown, sits on the edge of Lincolnshire Wolds. Tennyson called it a 'haunt of ancient peace' and this description still rings true. The planting style is cottage-garden but with the volume turned up. Under grizzled pear and apple trees, head-high flowers billowed. Around the pigeon house, there is a pleasant petalled pandemonium of roses, yarrow and iris. In the orchard, the beehives hummed with life and you can buy the honey in the shop. In spring head out from the walled gardens to St Peter's church and enjoy a wildflower walk back to the front of the house. There are apple stores, glasshouses, and a lovely carp pond to explore. The tea room is located in the sunny stables courtyard. Here you can buy freshly picked produce from the organic vegetable gardens.
➜ Signed off A158 Gunby, Nr Spilsby, Lincs PE23 5SS 01754 890102 nationaltrust.org.uk ✆ end Feb–Oct daily 11–5pm 🚰 ❧ 🍽

4 FELLEY PRIORY

Some elements of the 12th-century priory remain, but this is now a family home and a perfect setting for the plants sold in the adjacent nursery. The lightly terraced gardens roll out into the hills of Nottingham's 'Hidden Valley', the yew hedges and topiary echoing the contours of the landscape. In spring, the orchard is carpeted in spring bulbs and the grass is left to grow long and wild throughout the summer. On the wall of the house, an ancient Jargonelle pear maintains its vigour after more than 400 years. Looking out over the hills, a large naturalistic pond is thick with reeds and flag irises. The Farmhouse Tea room serves pies and quiches; you can eat inside or outside in the orchard garden.
➜ M1 Junction 27, signed off A608 W. Underwood, Notts NG16 5FJ 01773 810230 felleypriory.co.uk ✆ Tue–Fri 9–4pm and 1st, 3rd Sun of month Feb–Sep 10–4pm 🚰 🍽 ❦

4 FELLEY PRIORY

2 CALKE ABBEY

5 DODDINGTON HALL

Splendid Doddington Hall is a lovely food
and garden destination. The renovated
walled kitchen garden was a hive of
production in dry mid-July when we visited.
Tomatoes filled the greenhouses and onions
hung in the rafters drying. Entry to the
kitchen garden is free and it is open most
days, as are the adjacent shops. As well as
growing seasonal produce for the café and
shop, the kitchen garden is also where florist
Rachel Petheram grows and sells her English
seasonal flowers. She also offers a range
of floristry and willow-weaving courses.
The large Elizabethan dipping pool is now
managed for wildlife and meadow flowers
fill the empty beds. The main gardens
surrounding the Elizabethan house are open
fairly infrequently, but offer a stunning array
of heritage daffodils, fritillaries, and bearded
irises. The Wild Garden is a delight in spring
and there is a one-mile nature trail that
takes you from just beyond the Temple of
the Winds through woods, open parkland,
and a flowering wetland meadow.

→ Cycle route 64. Main Street, Doddington,
Lincolnshire LN6 4RU 01522 694308
doddingtonhall.com

mid-Feb–Easter and Oct 11–4pm, Easter–
Sep & BH Wed, Sun 11–5pm

The 40-acre wildflower farm has been growing native wild flowers for seed since 1978

6 NATURESCAPE

Meadows

6 NATURESCAPE

If you want to guarantee seeing acre upon acre of wild flowers stretching into the distance, then head to Naturescape nursery. The 40-acre wildflower farm has been growing native species for seed since 1978. For the last 15 years, visitors have been able follow walks through the meadows, wetland meadow, and the spinney to the wildlife ponds. The nursery sells everything from bare-root native hedging to plug plants and seeds, and there is a tea room selling cakes and ice-creams.

→ Maple Farm, Coach Gap Lane, Nottingham NG13 9HP 01949 860592 naturescape.co.uk
⏰ Apr–Sep daily 11–5.30pm

7 RED HILL NATURE RESERVE

Once a barley field, Red Hill is now Lincolnshire's Coronation Meadow. A stunning fragment of ancient 'sheep walk', it is now considered one of the best chalk downland meadows in Lincolnshire. The 4 acres cover a steep escarpment where, between April and August you can find the elusive bee orchid, pyramidal orchids, felwort, basil thyme and yellow-wort. Common lizards thrive here and you may spot a grass snake. Over the lane nearly 60 acres of arable land are being reclaimed using donor seed. No dogs.

→ Parking and info board off Asterby Lane, Asterby LN11 9UE 01507 526667 lincstrust.org.uk 53.3078,-0.1028

8 MERRY'S MEADOW SSSI

In a sea of intensive farmland, the survival of Merry's Meadow is a testament to the work of farmer George Merry, who preserved its 30 acres, and the Rutland naturalists who ensured it remained protected. Awash with traditional hay-meadow flowers from April to July, it is one of the most diverse grassland sites in the area. Newts and moths abound and there are waxcaps in autumn.

→ Park off Great Lane / Thistleton Lane junction, Oakham, Rutland LE15 7RJ, 01162 629968 lrwt.org.uk. Follow track on R NE for 400m to entrance 52.7304,-0.6165

Accommodation

9 ORCHARD COTTAGE, GUNBY HALL

Stay in the bright, newly renovated gardener's cottage at Gunby Hall. Doors open straight out into your own orchard garden and you have free access to the Hall's eight acres of gardens. You can also enjoy the miles of parkland that surround the hall after the gates have closed to the public. It's lovely and airy in summer and in winter you can cosy up by the open fire. Dusk is also a great time to watch the rich diversity of bats that call Gunby home.

→ Off A158 Gunby, Nr Spilsby PE23 5SS, 0844 800 2070 nationaltrustcottages.co.uk

9 ORCHARD COTTAGE

The restaurant uses produce fresh from the kitchen garden and the estate's honey and red Lincoln beef. Other food is sourced locally and you can stock up on a wide range of artisan breads and cheeses

11 DODDINGTON HALL

10 EAST FARM B&B

Enjoy traditional farmhouse B&B in a classic 18th-century Lincolnshire red-brick farmhouse at the foot of the Lincolnshire Wolds. Your rooms overlook the little lake, pretty gardens, and 400 acres of arable farmland that has won an award for conservation work. Peace reigns here, broken only by birdsong and the clucking of chickens who will lay your breakfast eggs. Local sausages and bacon come from the local farm shop and bread is baked daily by Gill. It's only four miles to Market Rasen or head out on the Viking Way for a walk or a cycle along the area's hidden lanes.
➔ Mill Lane, Middle Rasen, Lincolnshire LN3 5AQ 01673 842283 eastfarmholidaycottage.co.uk/bed–breakfast ⌂

10 EAST FARM B&B

Food

11 DODDINGTON HALL

After wandering the gardens at Doddington Hall, reward yourself with a scrumptious lunch at the café or in the old coach-house restaurant. The café is a light, gardening-themed room and there is plenty of outside seating in the red-brick walled garden. The restaurant is a much cosier affair, serving delicious and unfussy lunches and dinners. Both use produce fresh from the kitchen garden and their own red Lincoln beef. Other food is sourced locally and you can stock up on a wide range of artisan bread and fresh produce, including meats, cheeses, and Doddington estate honey from the deli.
➔ Main Street, Doddington, Lincs LN6 4RU 01522 694308 doddingtonhall.com ⌚ daily 9–4.45pm (Sat 4.30pm and Sun 10–4.30pm) 🍺 🍴 🍷

12 THE MARTIN'S ARMS

Only two miles west of Naturescape is the swish country pub, the Martin's Arms. Winner of many awards, it serves good food and still retains a real-ale, country pub feel.

In winter, there's a roaring fire in the bar; in summer, the large garden is full of people eating outside. With a creeper-covered facade and pretty views of the church spire, this is the quintessential English inn. Food is fancy pub fare and you must try the famous Colston Bassett stilton from the village's dairy farm.
➔ School Lane, Colston Bassett, Notts NG12 3FD 01949 81361 themartinsarms.co.uk ⌚ daily, no food Sun pm 🍴

13 THE FINCH'S ARMS

The Finch's Arms is a lovely, if a little rakish, village pub set on the island that juts out into Rutland Water. Roaring fires warm the flagstone and wood-beam interiors and outside, lavender-scented terraced gardens offer enviable views over the beautiful reservoir. Food is sourced from the surrounding farms and producers. A good walk takes you from here to the Rutland Water nature reserve.
➔ 2.5 miles E of Oakham. Oakham Rd, Hambleton, Leicestershire LE15 8TL 01572 756575 finchsarms.co.uk ⌚ daily lunch and dinner (food served all day Sunday) 🍴

12 THE MARTIN'S ARMS

11 DODDINGTON HALL

Kitchen Garden
Custard White
Summer Squash
95p each

11 DODDINGTON HALL

SWALEDALE

Peaks & Dales

From the limestone grasslands of the White Peak to the moors of the Dark Peak, through to the rolling Dales of Yorkshire and Derbyshire; discover grand kitchen gardens, medieval rose gardens and picture-book hay meadows.

Peaks and Dales

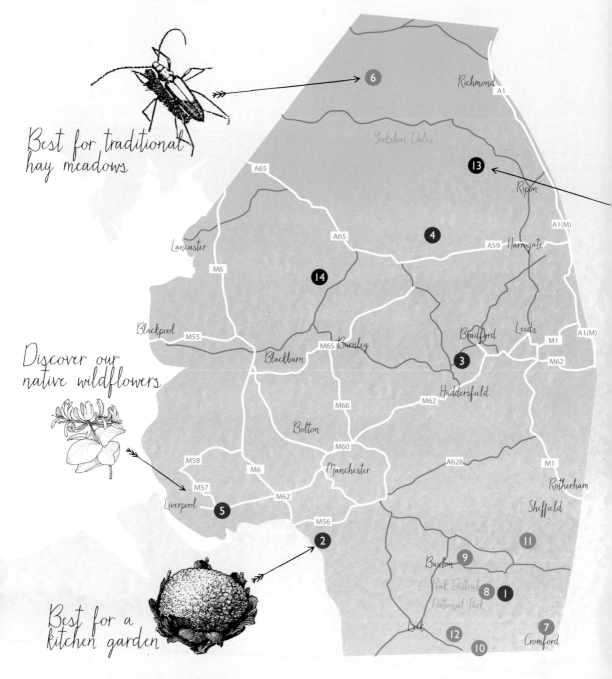

Best for traditional
hay meadows

Discover our
native wildflowers

Best for a
kitchen garden

Richmond
A1

Yorkshire Dales

A65

13

Ripon

A1(M)

A65

4

A59 Harrogate

Lancaster

M6

14

A1(M)

Blackpool

M55

Bradford

Leeds

M1

Blackburn

M65 Burnley

3

M62

Huddersfield

M66

M62

Bolton

M60

A628

M1

M58

Manchester

Rotherham

M6

Sheffield

M57

M62

Liverpool

5

M56

2

11

Buxton

9

Peak District

8

1

National Park

Leek

12

7

10

Cromford

The highlights

›› Discover native flora and romantic planting at ancient Haddon Hall (1)

›› Eat and stay at the refreshingly contemporary Bivouac café, shop, and shack (13)

›› Walk through Swaledale's incredible hay meadows – among the best in Britain (6)

›› Visit really wild 'show' gardens and learn all about our native wild flowers (5)

Best for a garden fresh lunch

Limestone rock links the Yorkshire Dales and the southern White Peak, and wild flowers flourish in these thin, alkaline soils. In contrast, the northern Dark Peak is covered in vast sweeps of moorland, fit only for heather and rough sheep pasture. The Derbyshire Dales NNR lies in the heart of the Peak District national park and brings together five rich limestone valleys. One of them, Lathkill Dale, is strewn with wild flowers from April right through to August. The area is also studded with old lead mines and now mossy saxifrage and spring sandwort thrive on its tainted soils. Cressbrook Dale, an enchanting wooded valley, is one of the few wild places filled with the intoxicating, sweet scent of lily of the valley in spring. A little further south, the Monsal trail follows the Wye Valley, one of the richest ecological sites in the park and home to a staggering eleven nature reserves. Yet even in the urban centres there are wonderful meadows to explore. At Landlife, the national wildflower centre just outside Liverpool, you can experience the vast spectrum of native flora and learn about their starring role within our ecosystems. The centre works with a huge number of private-and public-sector partners, and you can even visit one of their

sites. Nearby Woolfall Heath meadow at North Huyton, Knowsley, is at the centre of a housing project and offers an inspirational and colourful summer habitat for residents and visitors. As for the region's gardens, I was swept off my feet by the romance of Haddon Hall, its terraces overflowing

with roses, herbs and cottage-garden blooms. My only regret is that I haven't yet made it to designer Arabella Lennox-Boyd's garden at Gresgarth Hall, which is open for just one day a month.

Gardens

1 HADDON HALL

The renovated gardens surrounding the castellated Hall, parts of which date from medieval times, are incredibly romantic. The meadows, too, offer a wonderful array of wildflower species typical of the area. Gardening here in the Wye Valley is not easy. In this region, the limestone of the White Peak joins the gritstone of the Dark Peak and only the addition of tons of mulch have enabled the garden to flourish. The borders are filled with a blowsy, deeply naturalistic 'high cottage' flowers and herbs that harmonise perfectly with the weathered stone and timber of the Tudor facades. Ferns and stonecrop sprouted from the old walls and roses, clematis and everlasting pea (*Lathyrus latifolius*) tumbled over each other; they provided welcome colour on a very grey, overcast day. In July, yarrow, mullein, hollyhocks, tansy and dill spilled onto the wide gravel paths. Even the topiary and the knot garden seemed to have been liberated by the fresh and whimsical plantings of designer Arne Maynard. There is no separate entry to the garden so enjoy the house tours – it will certainly enhance the experience.

→ A6 Haddon Rd, Bakewell, Derbyshire DE45 ILA, 01629 812855 haddonhall.co.uk
🕐 May–Sep daily 12–5pm, Easter–Apr & Oct Sat, Sun, Mon 12–5pm 🍴 🌱 🍴

2 TATTON PARK

2 TATTON PARK KITCHEN GARDEN

Tatton Park is a huge – almost overwhelmingly large – National Trust estate, but once you've homed in on the best areas to visit, you are in for a treat.

1 HADDON HALL

Tatton is the location of one of the Trust's most treasured kitchen gardens. Behind its red-brick walls lie orchards, giant beds containing long rows of lovely vegetables, and multiple glasshouses and hothouses for growing everything from pineapples, grapes, and peaches, to tomatoes and aubergines. The abundant vegetables are for sale on the produce stall in the main courtyard, or you can head to the gardener's cottage for lunch or high tea. One word of warning – there is a parking fee, regardless of membership. Cycle if you can; it's the best way to discover the estate.

→ Ashley Road, Rostherne Drive, Knutsford, Cheshire, WA16 6QN, 01625 374400 tattonpark.org.uk 🕐 Apr–Oct daily 10–6pm, Nov–Mar Tue–Sun & BH 10–4pm 🍴 🌱 🍴 🌱

3 DOVE COTTAGE

I have lost count of the number of times the tiny garden at Dove Cottage nursery has been recommended to me. In just one-third of an acre on a northerly slope, Stephen, Kim and Katie Rogers have created an exciting showcase for their much-loved grasses and late-flowering perennials. If you seek some naturalistic, late-season colour and winter structure, this is the place to come for inspiration. Every autumn, after the garden closes for the year, the family set off on their plant-hunting adventures, searching out more new and wondrous specimens to add to their already enviable collection. Grass here means anything but

lawn, and the sense of movement from the plants and the pollinators that dance among them is quite enchanting. It's a highly effective show garden so you'll need to bring a large dose of self discipline along with your credit card.

→ Shibden Hall Road, Halifax, West Yorkshire HX3 9XA 01422 203533 dovecottagenursery.co.uk
🕐 Jun Wed–Sun, Jul–Sep Wed–Sat 10–5pm. Nursery open from March 🍴 🌱

4 PARCEVALL HALL

Hidden in the heart of rugged Wharfedale, the gardens of Parcevall Hall cling to the steep, rocky slopes of the Dales. Its woodland gardens and wide terraces were carved out of the hillside in the 1930s by visionary plantsman and devout Catholic, William Milner. Featuring formal terraces and woodland areas, the gardens have an abundance of native and regional plants as well as specimens collected from all around the world. There is much to discover, but even with such plant bounty I often found it hard to keep my gaze from wandering to the hills. The light here is literally heavenly, constantly changing, and allowing each plant a chance to take its turn in the sun's ever-moving spotlight. No doubt none of this was lost on Milner.

→ Skyreholme, Skipton, North Yorkshire BD23 6DE 01756 720311 rhs.org.uk
🕐 Apr–Oct daily 10–6pm 🍴 🌱

2   TATTON PARK KITCHEN GARDEN

3   DOVE COTTAGE

5   NATIONAL WILDFLOWER CENTRE

Located just outside Liverpool, the Landlife National Wildflower Centre has stunning gardens, a café, and an educational centre. Its aim is to promote the importance of wildflower landscapes, both as vital habitat for wildlife as well as spaces for people to enjoy. From large areas of industrial scrubland to nature reserves and small domestic gardens, the centre demonstrates 'creative conservation' and encourages everyone to plant wild flowers. We found the centre a buzz of vibrant activity and particularly welcoming to children. The airy café served us a big breakfast before we headed out into the collage of 'really wild' show gardens. What really stood out was the diversity of colour and form that can be achieved using only a wildflower palette. The insect life was audible and I had hoped to see one of the many hawkmoths spotted that day, but they remained elusive to me. There's lots of information on no-dig methods, composting, soil health, and the history and culture of our native wild flowers.

Signed off A5080 Roby Road. Court Hey Park, Roby Road, Liverpool, Merseyside L16 3NA 0151 nwc.org.uk

Apr–Sep daily 10–5pm

At Lathkill Dale nature reserve witness the dramatic limestone geology studded with wildflowers in July and August.

6 MUKER HAY MEADOW

Meadows

6 SWALEDALE & MUKER HAY MEADOW

In Swaledale, the most northerly of the Yorkshire Dales, are some of the best traditional hay meadows in Britain. It's a stunningly picturesque valley where traditional hay-farming methods have been maintained – partly on account of the terrain and partly owing to practical considerations. Locally bred Swaledale sheep leave the meadows in May and return after the grass has been cut in July. This annual regime preserves the golden tapestry of meadow buttercups, threaded with orchids, melancholy thistles and pignut.

➜ Follow public FP N through meadows parallel to river. Off B6270 Muker Village, Swaledale, Yorkshire DL11 6QH natureinthedales.org.uk 54.3772,-2.1397

7 ROSE END MEADOWS SSSI

The 16 small fields, which have never been sprayed, abound with native wildflowers and a spring or summer walk across the reserve will bring joy to even the most

sullen teenager. The meadows show just how diverse the flora of these predominantly limestone meadows was in the past. From spring through to autumn see celandines, cowslips and bluebells followed by harebells, orchids and betony.

➜ Walk up FP R of 86 Cromford Hill (park on street), take FP NE across meadow to Alabaster Lane. Cromford, Derbyshire DE4 3QU, 01773 881188 derbyshirewildlifetrust.org.uk 53.1052,-1.5650

8 LATHKILL DALE NATURE RESERVE

At Lathkill, witness the dramatic limestone geology of the southern White Peak. In May, cowslips bloom, followed by early purple orchids, then common spotted orchids in June. In July there is a good chance of seeing Jacob's Ladder, Derbyshire's regional flower. July and August are the peak flower months.

➜ For a fantastic 5 mile walk start at Over Haddon walking down Lathkill W towards Monyash. Buses run between the villages. Car Park on Main St, Over Haddon, Bakewell, Derbyshire DE45 1HZ naturalengland.org.uk 53.1921,-1.6983

9 PRIESTCLIFFE LEES SSSI

Perched on steep, limestone slopes above the river Wye at Miller's Dale, Priestcliffe Lees is renowned for its summer wildflower displays. The area was once mined for lead and spring sandwort (known as leadwort) thrives there. We also heard of sightings of native columbine growing in late spring.

➜ For a thigh-burning walk join Monsal Trail at Millers Dale dir E then FP SW opp Ravenstor to top of valley. Weaker knees can start from Broadway Lane, Priestcliffe village. Monsal Trail at Millers Dale Station (car park) Buxton, Derbyshire SK17 9TN 01773 881188 derbyshirewildlifetrust.org.uk 53.2557,-1.7938

8 JACOB'S LADDER LATHKILL

Accommodation

10 NEW HOUSE ORGANIC FARM

New House Farm is a wonderful location for simple, no-frills camping. The site has no electricity, no fixed pitches, and no hot water but there are lovely compost loos. Children will revel in the farmyard which has goats, a pony and rabbits. Conservation is the farm's guiding principle and there are wildflower meadows, traditional pasture, a pond, and ancient barrows to discover. At the organic farm shop you will find home-reared and locally slaughtered beef and lamb, a selection of duck, goose or rare-breed Derbyshire redcap hen eggs, plus salads and fruits when in season. What more could you want?

→ Leave the B5035 at Kniveton along Longrose Lane. 3rd exit at Junction up lane, farmhouse on R. Kniveton, Ashbourne, Derbyshire, DE6 1JL 01335 342429 newhousefarm.co.uk 🏠 🛖

11 HORSELEY GATE HALL

Resting at the bottom of a verdant valley on the eastern edge of the Peak District national park is Horsleygate Hall. The ivy-clad outbuildings and lovely gardens make this the perfect bolthole from nearby Sheffield. Although just 10 minutes distant, it feels more like a hundred miles. The holiday apartment, which is in the house, has its own sun terrace with views over the main gardens. The kitchen garden is being restored to its former productive capacity and Mel is happy to sell you some garden fare and eggs for your kitchen table.

→ Horsleygate Lane, Holmesfield, Derbyshire S18 7WD 01142 890333 horsleygatehall.co.uk 🏠

12 CASTERNE HALL B&B

For a touch of living history, stay at the imposing but charming Casterne Hall, which offers near-perfect country-house B&B. With magnificent views over the Manifold valley, the gardens also give access to miles of wonderful walks. Casterne has been in the Hurt family for 500 years and house tours are also available. Horses can be stabled, bicycles housed, and rooms are large and comfortable. Breakfast, including home-made marmalade, is a feast and you can pre-book supper – fresh vegetables from the kitchen garden and good local produce.

→ From Ilam N on Lodge Lane, 1st lane on L, over cattle grid Ashbourne, Derby, DE6 2BA 01335 310489 casterne.co.uk 🏠 🍵 🛖

3 DOVE COTTAGE

Food

13 THE BIVOUAC

On the edge of the Yorkshire Dales, five miles from Masham sits High Knowle Farm, location of the fantastic Bivouac. It's the most stylish bunkhouse, yurt, shack, café and shop eco-complex around and we just loved its mix of reed beds, biomass boiler, reclaimed wood, and design. The fantastic café is open to residents and visitors and serves simple, great local produce in the stunning barn. Views from inside the café are incredible or you can wander through

10 NEW HOUSE ORGANIC FARM

the family den into the walled kitchen garden. Breakfast starts at 8.30 and dinner is served until 8pm daily.

→ 5 miles W of Masham on Fearby Rd. Pass Fearby take 1st L onto Rigg Bank then 1st R onto Knowle Ln. High Knowle Farm, Knowle Lane, Masham, Ripon, North Yorkshire HG4 4JZ 01765 535020 thebivouac.co.uk ⏰ 8.30–8pm 🏠 🍽️

14 THE GARDEN KITCHEN

Down the dry-stone walled lanes of the Ribble valley in the hamlet of Holden Clough is the popular nursery and Garden Kitchen cafe. Food includes the usual coffees and cakes, soups and quiches, but here you can also indulge in hearty breakfasts or lunches of locally sourced roasted duck breast or braised pork belly with mustard mash. The nursery specialises in alpines and heathers, as well as crocosmias, and runs a range of gardening courses throughout the year.

→ Barrett Hill Brow, Holden, Bolton-by-Bowland, Lancashire BB7 4PF 01200 447447 holdencloughnursery.com ⏰ daily 9–5pm 🍽️ 🌱

14 HOLDEN CLOUGH NURSERY

12 CASTERNE HALL

13 THE BIVOUAC

HELMSLEY WALLED GARDEN

York & North York Moors

Beyond the industrial cities and heavily-farmed arable land, there are forests, meadows, flowery cliff paths and healing gardens to discover.

York & North York Moors

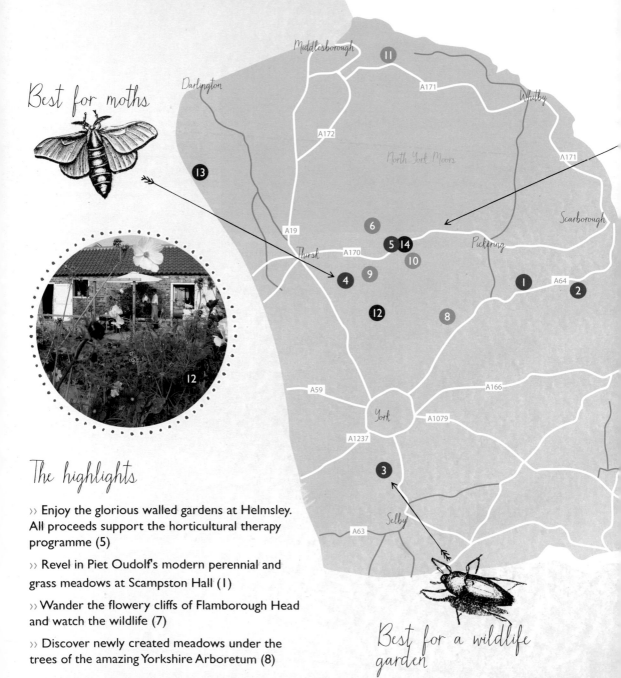

Best for moths

Best for a wildlife garden

Middlesborough

Darlington

A171

Whitby

A172

North York Moors

A171

13

Scarborough

A19

6

Pickering

Thrsk

A170

5 14

10

4 9

A64

1

2

12

8

York

A59

A166

A1079

A1237

3

A63

Selby

The highlights

›› Enjoy the glorious walled gardens at Helmsley. All proceeds support the horticultural therapy programme (5)

›› Revel in Piet Oudolf's modern perennial and grass meadows at Scampston Hall (1)

›› Wander the flowery cliffs of Flamborough Head and watch the wildlife (7)

›› Discover newly created meadows under the trees of the amazing Yorkshire Arboretum (8)

Best for a kitchen garden lunch

The North York Moors is one of England's most forested national parks. Although small, this area contains many ancient and champion trees and offers glorious woodland walks through stunning countryside. Practical conservation programmes include the north-east Yorkshire Cornfield Flowers Project, which works with farmers to reintroduce native flora – some of them rare – including corn buttercups and corn marigolds, red hemp-nettle, shepherd's needle, and prickly poppies into the fields and margins of arable farmland. Many seeds have gone to the Millennium Seed Bank for protection and the rest sown in the hope they will bring colour and life back to the region's intensely farmed fields.

Yorkshire Arboretum is transforming the vast grasslands under its living 'tree museum' to encourage even more biodiversity. Previously mown almost to perfection, the aim now is to create a matrix of species-rich wildflower and grass meadows. For still more incredible biodiversity you can join in a moth count at Shandy Hall.

The Stillingfleet Gardens feature regularly on the Yorkshire Wildlife Trust's calendar of events and mini-beast experts and wildlife groups often visit to analyse the resident garden population. There is an organic kitchen garden here and at the lovely little café you can enjoy home-made cakes surrounded by a changing backdrop of local artists' work.

And finally, don't miss out on the opportunity to see the fantastic horticultural therapy gardens of Helmsley, followed by a first class lunch in the converted glasshouse.

Bridlington

A165

Best for coastal flora

Hull

For meadows, the area has every kind you could imagine from the contemporary perennial meadow creations at Scampston Hall to the wildflower meadows of Rievaulx Terrace. There are maritime meadows, too, at the thrift-covered cliffs of Flamborough Head.

Gardens

1 SCAMPSTON HALL

I was welcomingly surprised by my visit to Scampston. I had seen the photos of the 'stunning, contemporary' walled garden, read reviews and heard trusted accounts of its geometric modern perennial meadow plantings. I had expected it to be beautiful, effective and impressive but I didn't expect it to be so much fun. What I experienced one July afternoon was a surprisingly intimate and energetic space. The word 'naturalistic' did not go far enough - Piet Oudoulf's schemes felt even more relaxed than I have seen elsewhere, more delicate, a true illustration of plant pointillism. Living corridors of green led me into a maze of grass and perennial play. Dead end after blocked path I was forced to review the scape from yet another angle and another, the light now from the west or the south impacting the visual display. It was more than I hoped for. I loved the pyramid mound that was covered with peacock butterflies gorging on the devil's bit scabious beds. From here you can look over into the glass fronted Garden Restaurant where they serve Scampston estate venison burgers and soups and salads from the kitchen garden.

→ Malton, North Yorkshire YO17 8NG 01944 759111 scampston.co.uk ⏰ Easter–Oct Tue–Sun & BH 10–5pm 🍵 🌱

1 SCAMPSTON HALL

2 JACKSON'S WOLD

2 JACKSON'S WOLD

High on the chalky Yorkshire Wolds in the midst of farm land, you'll come upon the stylish cottage gardens designed and planted over the last 30 years by owners Sarah and Richard. The small nursery sells unusual, alkaline-loving plants – mostly herbaceous perennials – that they have propagated. Vistas through doorways and glimpses of the Pickering Valley far below are used to great effect, while pigs and garden fowl add to the bucolic atmosphere. The garden is open only in the summer months, and then just for one afternoon a week plus NGS days. It's definitely worth the adventure. Teas with delicious home-made cakes and scones are served at old school desks in the Chalk Barn.

→ Sat Nav wrong. A64 Sherburn traffic lights S. After 100yds fork R for 1 mile. L on farm track, 1st L. Sherburn, Malton, YO17 8QJ 01944 710335 jacksonswoldgarden.com ⏰ May–Jul Tue 1–5pm plus NGS 🍵 🌱 🍴

3 STILLINGFLEET LODGE & NURSERY

The gardens here are wildlife heaven, the three organically managed acres beautifully displaying the nursery's selection of plants. The nursery specialises in unusual perennials and has one of the UK's most extensive offerings of hardy geraniums, and shade-loving brunneras and pulmonarias – all adored by our pollinators and stalwarts of any wild-garden scheme. The garden rooms are planted according to a sort of cottage-garden philosophy – pack in as much as you can and let the plants fight it out. It reduces the maintenance and increases the impact. My favourite area was around the meadow and the adjoining pond. A preserved fragment of ancient hay meadow, the space was full of native species, with the addition of bulbs, including narcissus and camassias, and spot-planted hardy geraniums to add interest and nectar.

→ Stewart Lane, Stillingfleet, York, YO19 6HP 01904 728506 stillingfleetlodgenurseries.co.uk ⏰ Apr–Sep Wed, Fri, 1st & 3rd weekend of month 1–5pm 🍵 🌱 🍴

4 SHANDY HALL

Here in the mid-18th century, Laurence Sterne wrote the gloriously irreverent *The Life and Opinions of Tristram Shandy, Gentleman*. The gardens are true to the period and feature an apple orchard and a walled garden leading to the wild garden beyond. In an old stone quarry a beautiful little wildlife garden begs to be discovered. In summer, mown paths lead through the meadow areas and we came across a couple sharing a romantic picnic in the sun. If you are interested in moths, then you will adore Shandy Hall's moth project. For a five years moths have been regularly trapped and photographed. So far over 330 species have been logged, and their delightful names – gold spangle, clouded magpie, Timothy tortrix, and true lover's knot – adorn pages of records.

→ Thirsk Bank, Coxwold, York, North Yorkshire YO61 4AD 01347 868465 laurencesternetrust.org.uk ⏰ May–Sep daily except Sat 11–4.30pm 🍵

3 STILLINGFLEET LODGE & NURSERY

5 HELMSLEY WALLED GARDEN

5 HELMSLEY WALLED GARDEN

This is another great story of an abandoned, derelict garden rising from the ashes to blossom once again. But Helmsley's story has a particularly interesting dimension. Alison Ticehurst, a local nurse, visited the garden for the first time in 1994. She was looking for a place where she could develop a therapeutic horticulture programme. "I went in – staggered by the huge nettles, massive space, total neglect", is how she described the moment in her diary. Fast forward to a July day 20 years later and its five acres were throbbing with colour and drama and natural delights. There are fruit orchards, wildflower hay meadows, annual meadows, jaw-dropping hot long borders, a physic garden, vegetable plots, bees, chickens. And then there is the divine ruin of the castle that peers over the walls. In 1900 this garden would have had 20 gardeners working full time to feed the 'big house'. Today, the garden is run by committed volunteers and gardeners and employs two horticultural therapists who work onsite to grow flowers that are then sold in the nursery. The views are idyllic, the food in the café delicious, and it's a very worthy cause to support.

Cleveland Way, Helmsley, N Yorkshire
YO62 5AH, 01439 771427
helmsleywalledgarden.org.uk
Apr–Oct daily 10–5pm

At the end of the walk
you step out into the
open terrace high above
the fantastical fairytale
ruin of Rievaulx Abbey

8 SATA VISTA, YORKSHIRE ARBORETUM

Meadows

6 RIEVAULX TERRACE

This is a wonderfully theatrical meadow to visit in summer if you have a National Trust membership card. From the entrance, you journey along a glorious, meandering path through verdant woodland dotted with sculpture that invites you to pause awhile. At the path's end, you step out onto the open terrace high above the fantastical, fairytale ruin of Rievaulx Abbey below. In July, the great meadow slopes were alive with bees and butterflies, and covered in harebells, betony and knapweed – all sweeping down the steep hill to the valley bottom. The views are incredible.
→ Rievaulx, N Yorkshire YO62 5LJ, 01439 748283 nationaltrust.org.uk
⏰ mid Feb–Oct 11–5pm

7 FLAMBOROUGH CLIFFS RESERVE

Above the 100-foot-high chalk cliffs along Flamborough Head are miles of cliff-edge paths decorated with bounteous displays of wild flowers. In spring and summer between Holme and Thornwick you can see pyramidal and common spotted orchids growing in the chalk grassland. The area has some of the most important breeding colonies of seabirds in Europe and you can often see basking sharks from the cliffs.
→ Cafe and visitor centre at North Marine Road, Bridlington, East Yorkshire YO15 1BJ 01904 659570 ywt.org.uk

8 YORKSHIRE ARBORETUM

Adjacent to the great mansion of Castle Howard is a 120-acre arboretum filled with such an impressive range of seed-grown, wild-origin trees that DEFRA regards it as a back-up collection for Kew. The arboretum has now turned some of its lawned areas over to wildflower meadows. Working with Buglife, the arboretum is re-seeding and managing the grass, making spring and summer visits here even more fantastic.
→ Castle Howard, York, YO60 7BY, 01653 648598 yorkshirearboretum.org
⏰ Mar–Nov daily 10–4pm (until 6pm May–Oct)

Accommodation

9 CARR HOUSE FARM

Stay in a charming farmhouse surrounded by ancient bluebell woods and orchards. This is real Herriot heartland and Anna and Jack are the perfect hosts. They serve breakfasts of local produce and offer great advice on walks, many starting outside the door. Inside, four-poster beds and timber beams add to the classic, cosy farmhouse feel. Courses ranging from photography to natural plant dyes are also held at the farm.
→ 1 mile W of Ampleforth, Jerry Carr Bank, York, North Yorkshire, YO62 4ED 01347 868526 carrhousefarm.co.uk

9 CARR HOUSE FARM

10 THE STAR INN

In the small village of Harome, on the edge of the North York Moors, is this lovely kitchen-garden pub and inn. In the garden in June, purple-podded peas were ripe for the picking and I could see the chefs choosing the freshest herbs just in time for the lunchtime feasts. The inn's Michelin star has been returned and, uncomplacent, they are continuing to serve special but grounded North Yorkshire fare that makes the most of the garden produce and locally sourced fare. Rooms are individual and quirky, there is an outdoor swimming pool, and all guests are free to wander through the gardens and see what's for supper.

→ Owmen Field Lane, Harome, Nr Helmsley, North Yorkshire YO62 5JE 01439 770397 thestaratharome.co.uk

🏠 🍽️

10 THE STAR INN

10 THE STAR INN

11 BABY MOON CAMP

For some back-to-nature nurture, head to the heartfelt hang-out of the Baby Moon yurts and circus caravans. Yurts are luxurious and their interior styles range from Frida Kahlo to pure kitsch. The circus caravans – think spangled shepherds' huts – continue the theme. There are warm showers and flushing loos, cosy hot-water bottles, and a range of treatments and courses. There is even a horse-drawn carriage. Wander through the gardens to pick your herbs and visit the Field Good farm shop, which sells everything you need from breakfast baskets with local eggs and bacon to vintage clothes. The kids will love you for it.

→ Redcar Road, Dunsdale, Guisborough, TS14 6RH 07764 928487 babymooncamp.com

🏠 🍶 🍽️ ❦

Food

12 DUTCH HOUSE

An inspiring wildlife garden, art gallery, and plant nursery, the Dutch House also has an art café offering breakfasts, light lunches, and afternoon teas. It is run by dynamic Dutch couple Sjaak, a naturalistic garden designer, and artist Cecile, and serves an array of home-grown, organic produce and Dutch specialities including my favourite – cheese pancakes with maple syrup! There is lots of summer seating outside on the sunny terrace and a really excellent selection of vegetarian and vegan food. The Dutch House runs masterclasses on wildlife gardening and sustainable living as well as offering lots of child-focused activities for all weathers.

→ Mill Green Farm, Brandsby Rd, Crayke, North Yorkshire YO61 4TT 01347 889431 dutchhouseyorkshire ⏰ Apr–Oct Wed–Sun 10–5pm, Nov–Mar Fri–Sun 10–4pm

🍶 🍽️

13 KIPLIN HALL TEA ROOM

Since 2010, the gardens, and particularly the kitchen gardens, of Kiplin Hall have been undergoing restoration to return them to the productive and beautiful gardens their romantic location so deserves. Beds for produce have been established, cart-loads of manure have been delivered by donkey, and the gardens are now providing lots of fruit and vegetables for the grand, wood-panelled tea room. Here you can enjoy cheese platters, soups, tarts, and cream teas – all made with local and garden produce. Although there is no charge for the tea room, it would be a shame to miss out on seeing the gardens, the lakeside walk, and taking the historic house tour. There is an excellent show of snowdrops in February.

→ 5 miles SW of Scorton, Richmond, North Yorkshire DL10 6AT 01748 818178 kiplinhall. co.uk ⏰ Feb–Oct Sun–Wed 10–5pm 4pm in Feb & Mar)

🍶 🍽️

13 KIPLIN HALL

14 VINE HOUSE CAFÉ

14 VINE HOUSE CAFÉ

Overlooking the Helmsley Walled Gardens (see garden listing), this lovely vegetarian café is situated in the renovated vine house. From the frangipani cake that I didn't want to share, to the fresh, garden-inspired lunches, it's a great place to come both to enjoy delicious food and support a good cause. In addition to the vegetables and fruit grown in the walled gardens, they make their own bread and pastas, and source ingredients from a range of local artisan producers. Entry to the café is free; small entrance charge for garden.

Cleveland Way, Helmsley, York YO62 5AH 01439 771427
helmsleywalledgarden.org.uk
Apr–Oct daily 10–5pm

BRANTWOOD

Lake District

One of the most popular wild-holiday destinations, this is a region of fells and deep waters that are dramatically illuminated by the ever-changing light.

Lake District

The highlights

›› Be inspired by John Ruskin's wild garden, overlooking Coniston (1)

›› Enjoy superb, garden-fresh food in the converted stables of Askham Hall (10 & 11)

›› Walk the ancient flora-filled limestone pavement of Whitbarrow Scar (8)

›› Experience the romance of Dalemain's beautiful gardens (2)

Best for a home grown lunch

Best for a wild garden

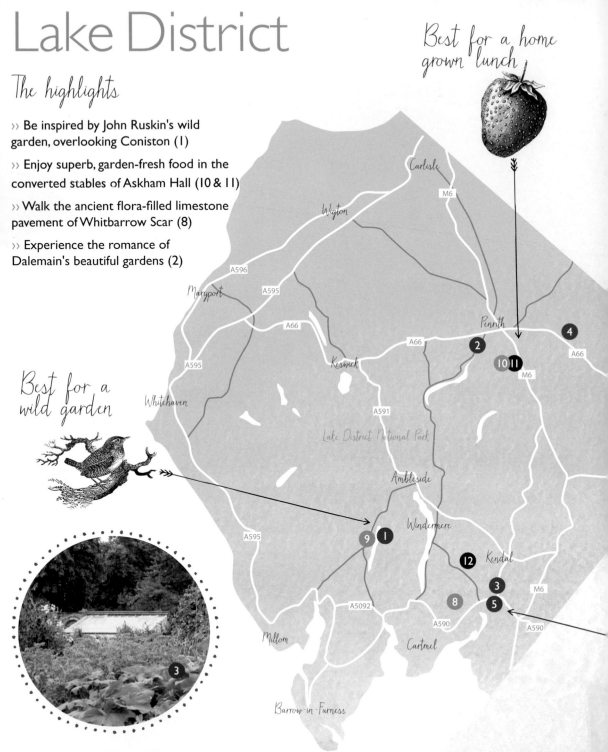

This is the land of Wainwright's walks, Wordsworth's daffodils, and Ruskin's wild gardens. The Lake District is the largest national park in England and its deeply romantic vistas have ensured its ongoing popularity.

When the heather is in bloom, the mountain slopes are painted in bruised purple shades, while in the pastoral valleys life continues at a slower pace. But here, as everywhere else, the majority of species-rich wood- and grasslands have suffered from development. Over the last ten years, hundreds of acres of hay meadow have been restored by Cumbria Wildlife Trust, together with like-minded farmers and landowners. Most stunning in June and July, the meadows are dotted with 'field houses'. These stone barns, which nestle into the field boundaries, are used for over-wintering cattle and to store hay, and enhance the picture-perfect scenes. Stunning limestone pavements, such as Whitbarrow Scar, offer specialised wildflower 'gardens' for those willing to climb their steep slopes.

Say the name 'Eden Valley' and it conjures up images of verdant grassland and clear streams bountiful with wildlife. And that is exactly what it offers, although the area is often overlooked by visitors heading straight for the national park.

All around Ravenstonedale and Askham there are fantastic meadows, gardens, places to stay, and food destinations to discover. In April, the Lyth and Winster valley orchards are decorated with the purest white damson blossom. Cumbria tourism can suggest trails around the orchards and places where you can sample the juicy, tart fruit.

At Brantwood, overlooking Coniston, you can visit the home of radical thinker, John Ruskin. In his iconic garden he worked with the natural character of the land, enhancing it with the use of indigenous wild flowers. You can also discover his ideas about 'marginal' gardening – both for growing food and uplifting the spirit.

Best for hay meadows

A685

Kirkby Stephen

Best ornamental kitchen garden

Gardens

1 BRANTWOOD

On the edge of Coniston, with superb lake views, are the home and 'wild gardens' of writer, artist, social reformer, and lover of nature, John Ruskin. The Brantwood estate covers over 250 acres and offers miles of magical trails through its ancient woodland, moor and meadow. Surrounding Ruskin's house on west-facing slopes are a collection of gardens, each reflecting Ruskin's belief in enhancing, not controlling, the natural landscape. They include some designed by Ruskin's cousin, Joan Severn. There is a moorland garden, an enclosed native herb garden, orchards, the bizarre Zig-Zaggy, and a wild daffodil field. In high summer, the fern garden, with over 250 different types of native fern, offered a verdant hideaway from the midday sun. The ten acres of gently undulating meadow edging the lake are currently being maintained biodynamically as hay meadows. Dawn scythings (open to all) offer meditation and a chance to discover the meadows hands on – and the flora is visibly returning. The whole estate is managed on organic principles under the directorship of inspirational head gardener, Sally Beamish.

→ Coniston, Cumbria, LA21 8AD 01539 441396 brantwood.org.uk

⏰ mid Mar–mid Nov daily 10.30–5pm, winter Wed–Sun 10.30–4pm 🍷 ♿ 🍽 🏠

1 BRANTWOOD

2 DALEMAIN

2 DALEMAIN

Dalemain is understated, romantic, and overflowing with the charm of a bygone era. The gardens surrounding the 14th-century manor with its Georgian facade were bursting with colour and scent when we visited in July – the roses were still in bloom and the white garden was particularly enchanting. White foxgloves, pineapple flower (*Eucomis*), chamomile, and tobacco plants (*Nicotiana*) looked serene under the huge silver Greek fir (*Abies cephalonica*). The views from the terrace to the rising hills beyond the oak parkland are simply stunning. From the knot garden, the path led to the Rose Walk and on through old varieties of apple trees, covered thickly in moss and threaded with clematis. At the end of the garden through a door in the wall is the Stumpery and secret Lob's Wood – full of Himalayan blue poppies (*Meconopsis dalemain*) in early summer. There is a lovely tea room in the Medieval Hall.

→ Dalemain, Penrith, CA11 0HB 017684 86450 dalemain.com ⏰ Apr–Oct Sun–Thu 10.30–5pm (Nov & Dec 11–3pm) 🍷 🍽 ▮

3 SIZERGH CASTLE

Owned by the Strickland family for over 700 years, Sizergh possesses a sense of intimacy and continuity. The garden holds the national collection of hardy ferns, which range from feathery to leathery, and all looked divine with their surfaces polished by rain. The organic walled kitchen garden is a relaxed affair with no-dig beds, pyramids of sweet peas, and an orchard underplanted with bulbs. Bees have been kept at Sizergh for six years and their hives were piled high with an extraordinary number of supers. I had come specially to see its celebrated limestone rock garden. Planted in the 1920s with ferns, conifers and acers, it is now handsomely mature. The wider estate encompasses historic deer parks, woodlands, fell and grassland, and you can explore the ancient burial mounds and enjoy the wildflowers and mountain views that abound. Nearby Brigsteer Woods is rich with bluebells and wild daffodils.

→ Sizergh, near Kendal, Cumbria Nav LA8 8DZ 015395 60951 nationaltrust.org.uk

⏰ daily 10–5pm (4pm in winter) 🍷 ♿ 🍽

4 ACORN BANK

17th-century Acorn Bank is a showcase for the vast array of medicinal and culinary plants that add colour, form and nectar to our gardens. Its gardens invite us to rediscover their healing properties. From spring through to late autumn, the borders are filled with clever cottage garden-inspired combinations. Under the old orchard trees in the walled garden, large swathes of meadow grass balanced the formality of the tightly clipped yews. Outside the garden there is a lovely walk through the woods to the Crowdundle Beck where you can visit the renovated watermill and see flour being milled. There are bird hides and wild daffodils in spring.

→ 1 mile N Temple Sowerby off A66, Penrith CA10 1SP 01768 361893 nationaltrust.org.uk

⏰ mid Mar–Oct daily (not Tue) 10–5pm, Nov, Dec Sat & Sun 11–4pm 🍷 ♿

3   SIZERGH CASTLE

2   DALEMAIN

5   LEVENS HALL

Even on the most blustery, rainy day nothing could detract from the majesty of Levens Hall's gargantuan beech hedges and the humour of its topiary. The hedges, glorious old beasts, are hundreds of years old and so tall and wide that it's like looking inside the engine room of a mossy old ship. The gardens are most famous for their fantastical yew topiary – 100 beautifully clipped specimens of the oldest and finest topiary in the world – but it was the vegetable garden that really made me smile. Courgettes, beetroot, sea-kale, beans, and nasturtiums were just a few of the edibles planted in formal bedding patterns. They tumbled out of their designated spaces with aplomb and contrasted wonderfully with the strict geometry of the topiary and classic country house borders. Feathery asparagus presented a beautifully airy texture next to the hazel coppice, while teepees of climbing beans and sweet peas added soft, colourful structure. Following the avenue of courgettes through green arches, I approached the orchard. Mini-meadow squares made patchworks under the trunks and heavy mounds of clematis and roses smothered their hosts. The house is open and there are lovely river walks through the deer park.

→ Off the A6, 6 miles S of Kendal, Cumbria LA8 0PD 01539 560321 levenshall.co.uk

☼ Apr–early Oct Sun–Thu 10–5pm

The village of
Ravenstonedale is a
wonderful base from
which to see many
ancient flower-rich hay
meadows.

6 AUGILL PASTURE

Meadows

6 AUGILL PASTURE SSSI

This beautifully preserved mountain hay meadow contains a rich array of grassland plants including globeflowers, bluebells, several orchids – fragrant, common-spotted, frog, butterfly and fly – great burnet, and thick purple mists of devil's-bit scabious in autumn. Sadly, fewer than 1,000 hectares of mountain hay meadow now remain in Britain. Once a heavily industrialised area, the reserve contains the remains of the 19th-century lead-smelting mill and the pasture may have been used as grazing for pit ponies. A steep, third of a mile circular route passes the old mill.

→ Park beyond Augill Beck caravan park, enter via metal gate on L. 1.5 miles E of Brough on A66, Kirkby Stephen, Cumbria CA17 4DX 01539 816300 cumbriawildlifetrust.org.uk 54.5266,-2.2859

7 PIPER HOLE CORONATION MEADOW

The village of Ravenstonedale is a wonderful base from which to see many ancient flower-rich hay meadows. Piper Hole has been designated an SSSI, as well as being named Cumbria's Coronation Meadow, for its diverse native species including great burnet, wood crane's-bill and pignut. Under the Coronation Meadow initiative, seed from Piper Hole will be used to restore other local hay meadows. You can download Cumbria Wildlife Trust's great 'Hay Meadow Walks' leaflet from the website.

→ 0.4 miles E of Ravenstonedale CA17 4NG on Townhead Lane. Kirky Stephen, Cumbria cumbriawildlifetrust.org.uk 54.4250,-2.4217

8 WHITBARROW SCAR NATURE RESERVE

The views from the elevated limestone pavement, formed some 350 million years ago, are incredible. See orchids, including dark red helleborines, blue moor grass, and rock rose growing among the cracks.

→ 6 mile walk. Park on road R of Witherslack Hall School. FP NE past Flodder Allotment then S past Barney Crags. Drop to White Scar along to Mill Side village. Return on road 01539 816300 cumbriawildlifetrust.org.uk. 54.2659,-2.8664

Accommodation

9 HOATHWAITE CAMPING

For simple camping right on Coniston, we love this location. Clean portacabins house basic loos and showers, and the views from the site are fantastic. Although you can't camp in the field on the water's edge unless you are in a pre-booked group, it's an easy walk to the lake and a great place to launch your canoe. There is room for a few campervans but no hook-ups. Next door is 4 Winds Tipis if you prefer glamping.

→ At Torver take the A5084 SE. Take 1st L continuing 1.5 miles to end of track Coniston, Cumbria LA21 8AX nationaltrust.org.uk.

9 HOATHWAITE CAMPING

10 ASKHAM HALL

Just inside the national park and only six miles from Penrith and its train station is laid back, luxurious Askham Hall. The accommodation is first class and there is a garden, restaurant, kitchen café, a lovely swimming pool, and a range of treatments to enjoy. Here at the 'Babington House of the North', everything is done exceptionally well. The gardens leading down to the river Lowther are a glorious mix of witty topiary standing to attention in meadows of long golden grass, and a long border thick with exuberant and romantic perennials. The garden, restaurant, and kitchen garden café are open to non-residents.

→ Signed in village of Askham, Nr Penrith, Cumbria CA10 2PF, 01931 712350 askhamhall.co.uk 🏠 🍴 🍵

From the pigs snuffling under the oak trees to the bounty in the kitchen garden . . . all the signs point to delicious, fresh home-reared food and it doesn't disappoint.

11 ASKHAM HALL

12 THE PUNCH BOWL INN

Food

11 KITCHEN GARDEN CAFÉ ASKHAM

From the pigs snuffling under the oak trees to the bounty in the kitchen garden and its large stone pizza oven, all the signs at the café in the old barns at Askham Hall point to delicious, fresh, home-reared food. And it doesn't disappoint. Inside, the white-washed barns are cosy and fresh with bare wood, flowers, a woodburner, and sheepskin rugs. Food at the kitchen garden café is a relaxed affair of soups, pizzas, and salads. For gourmet three-course meals reserve a table at the restaurant in the Hall, or head to the nearby George and Dragon pub and enjoy food fresh from the Askham estate. Don't, however, miss out on a tour of the garden (small entry charge).

→ Signed in village of Askham, Nr Penrith, Cumbria CA10 2PF 01931 712348 askhamhall.co.uk
⏰ Fri–Sun 11–4pm 🍵 🍴

12 THE PUNCH BOWL INN

This Lakes hotel and inn consistently gets great reviews for its food and accommodation, and our lunch there with friends lived up to expectations. From its pretty village location in the heart of the Lyth Valley with views of the church and miles of hills to the cosy, laid-back atmosphere inside, everything was perfect. We found the service impressive and appreciated it almost as much as the excellent food. We left satisfied and happy.

→ Mill Lane, Crosthwaite, Cumbria LA8 8HR 01539 568237 the-punchbowl.co.uk
⏰ Food served daily 12–9pm (weekends no food between 4–5.30pm) 🍴 🏠

10 ASKHAM HALL

10 ASKHAM HALL

11 THE KITCHEN GARDEN AT ASKHAM HALL

HERTERTON HOUSE

Northumber-land & Borders

Northumberland is a land of vast and empty, high moorland and windswept coast, yet even in this rugged landscape gardens rich with wildlife and incredible artistry abound.

Northumberland & Borders

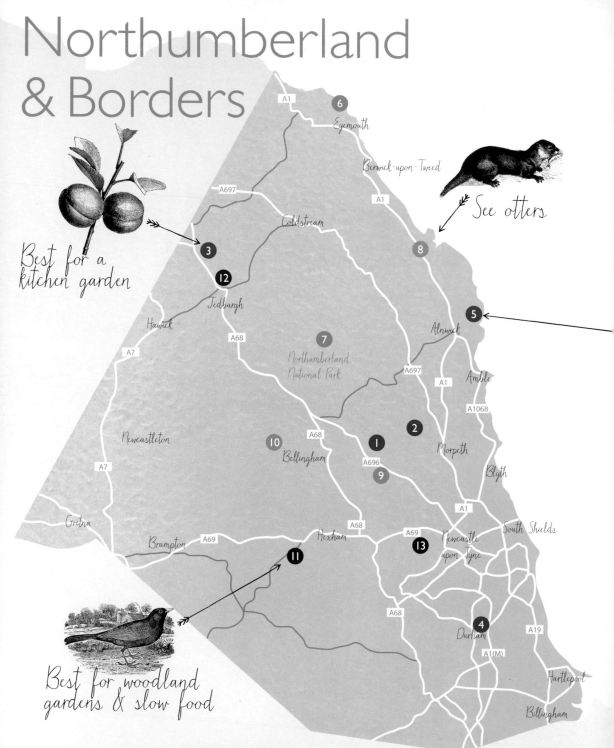

Best for a kitchen garden

See otters

Best for woodland gardens & slow food

A1

Eyemouth

6

Berwick-upon-Tweed

A1

A697

Coldstream

3

12

Jedburgh

Hawick

A68

A7

Newcastleton

A7

Gretha

Brampton

A69

8

A1

5

Alnwick

Amble

A1

A1068

7

Northumberland
National Park

A697

2

10

Bellingham

A68

1

A696

9

Morpeth

Blyth

A1

Hexham

A68

A69

11

13

Newcastle
upon Tyne

South Shields

A68

4

Durham

A1(M)

A19

Hartlepool

Billingham

The highlights

›› Explore the one-acre creative masterpiece at Herterton House (1)

›› Sleep wild in a beautifully crafted yurt or tipi strewn with sheepskin rugs (10)

›› Eat delicious home-made food in a converted Victorian railway station (11)

›› Head out for a day's walking through the stunning Coquet Valley (7)

Best for trees and a champagne afternoon tea

Over a quarter of the land mass of Northumberland is protected by its National Park status. The rugged terrain, low population density and diversity of habitat has ensured the region functions as an 'ark' for a range of fauna including otters, bryophytes, red squirrels, salmon and osprey to rare plants such as the water crowfoot.

The last one hundred remaining Chillingham wild cattle in the world continue to live in their natural habitat at Chillingham Park. Rarer even than the giant Panda, they live life on the edge. This is true border country and its castles and picturesque ruined fortifications are testament to fierce and bloody conflicts. Maybe this is why the bloody cranesbill (*Geranium sanguineum*) is the county's flower. You can see it in late summer on dry rocky outcrops or along the coast, joined by shaggy carpets of pink sea thrift and scented thyme. The flower show continues from rugged St Abb's Head north of the border to the soft grassy paths along Hadrian's Wall and I highly recommend a summer walk around Barrowburn in the awesome Coquet valley.

The region is blessed with some incredible wild gardens and there

is much to discover, from the small artistic gardens of Herterton to the grand wildlife rich estates of Howick Hall and Mertoun. Each one offers

ideas and inspiration to take back to even the smallest garden and their incredible locations offer rare insights into the dramatic landscape. I particularly love the gardens of Herterton House near Wallington where expert planting, unruliness, and playfulness are combined with great creativity in a one-acre plot. There is also a small, specialist plant nursery, where you can purchase something different for your garden.

Gardens

1 HERTERTON HOUSE

I loved Herterton. The one-acre gardens form a magical and impressive creation. Since 1976, each step in the process has been lovingly recorded by owners, Frank and Marjorie Lawley and their needlework artistry and painterly eye is clear in the interplay of pattern, texture, and colour. The threads of precision, humour, and attention to detail weave through each of the five different rooms. Ultimately, this is a plantsperson's garden and you will find rare hybrids and wild species rampaging through the perfectly clipped topiary – as though a cottage garden revolution had recently taken place. White toadflax (*Linaria lobatus*), an unusual white and pink rosebay willowherb, and delicate wild valerian added a wistful openness to the geometric and, usually, vibrantly coloured beds. It is, in Frank Lawley's words "an unlikely transition from their art to the art of the garden". I loved the tightly knit ivy trimmed around the doors and above it all, high in the little gazebo that surveys the whole garden, there were wonderful, faded photos of the garden in the making. A nursery adjoins the garden and the plants, which are grown in beds, are wrapped in newspaper for sale that day.

→ Off the B6342 2.8 miles N of Wallington, Northumberland NE61 4BN herterton.co.uk
☎ Apr–Sep Mon, Wed, Fri–Sun 1.30–5.30pm

1 HERTERTON HOUSE

2 BIDE-A-WEE

2 BIDE-A-WEE

Over the last quarter of a century, plantsman and landscape architect Mark Robson has created a delightful secret garden and nursery in and around a dramatic abandoned quarry. From its high cliff walls to its soggy base, every habitat has been exploited. North-facing woodland gardens are decorated with *Meconopsis*, while damp areas feature fern-fringed ponds and bog gardens. Owing to the huge diversity in soil and landscape combined with the winding pathways and glorious vistas, the garden feels much larger than its two acres. At the top of the garden, high above the quarry floor, clever plantings of herbaceous perennials, including the national collection of knapweed, literally flow into the hay meadow beyond. Knapweed is loved by pollinators and you can purchase the only two native species – common and greater knapweed (*Centurea nigra* and *C. scabiosa*) – as well as nearly 100 other fantastic species and cultivars.

→ Stanton, Netherwitton, Northumberland NE65 8PR 01670 772238 bideawee.co.uk
☎ mid Apr–Aug Wed, Sat 1.30–5pm

3 MERTOUN

Mertoun is a garden of surprises. From the honesty box in the woods you are led to the large manicured lawn and grand pond of new Mertoun House. Keep following the wooded path along the River Tweed and you'll see a beautiful dovecot. Dated 1567, it's considered to be one of Britain's oldest surviving examples. As you enter the walled garden and climb up through the orchard you come to pretty pink Old Mertoun House – the perfect backdrop to such a productive kitchen garden. Here in the large walled garden everything from herbs, vegetables, peaches and figs are grown in market-garden quantities. Butterflies and hoverflies clustered around the large beds of thyme, dill and marjoram, and in the heated glasshouses wooden boxes of ripe peaches were being stacked for sale.

→ Signposted off the B6404 2 miles NE of St Boswells, Melrose, Roxburghshire TD6 0EA 01835 823236
☎ Apr–Sep Fri–Mon 2–6pm

4 CROOK HALL

Crook Hall Gardens is one of the few urban wild gardens found in this guide. The Jacobean and Georgian hall is enclosed by five acres of gardens offering respite, seclusion, and romance. Just as the Hall has many facets owing to the mix of architectural styles, so does the garden. There are wildflower meadows, a fernery, and walled kitchen and secret gardens. Approached by an ivy-hung door in the wall, the Secret Garden is believed to be over 700 years old. Both Wordsworth and Ruskin are said to have walked its narrow paths and today it remains a secluded jumble of deep borders filled with knobbly old fruit trees and cottage garden plants.

→ Frankland Lane, Sidegate, Durham DH1 5SZ 01913 848028 crookhallgardens.co.uk
☎ Apr–Sep Sun–Wed 11–5pm, Oct–Mar Sun–Wed 11–3pm

3 MERTOUN

4 CROOK HALL

5 HOWICK HALL

Howick Hall is the home of Earl Grey, the man responsible for my bergamot tea addiction, and its gardens and woods are filled with richly informal planting. The bog garden was in full swing in July and my strange relationship with astilbe finally put to bed. Here mixed with the primulas, meadowsweet, ferns, and wild carrot its feathery candy-coloured plumes fitted in perfectly. Heading north towards the house, meadow grass alive with crickets and knapweeds had either replaced areas of perfect lawns or given them soft borders filled with life and movement. Lady Howick's private flower-filled garden at the front of the house is often open for charity and again here the planting is loose, cottagey, and buzzing with pollinators. They call their arboretum 'a united nations of trees and shrubs' with over 11,000 trees grown from seed collected in the wild since the 1980s. In the ethereal Silverwood, famed for its rhododendron collection started in the 1930s, marginal planting is skilful with little stands of white campanula and delicate white *Meconopsis*. The grand Earl Grey Tea room with its large oil paintings and picture windows serves light lunches and champagne afternoon teas.

Howick, Northumberland NE66 3LB
01665 577285 howickhallgardens.org
Feb–mid Nov daily 10.30–6pm (4pm in winter)

In summer cliffs are covered in the pinky purple of sea campion purple milk-vetch sea thrift and wild thyme.

6 SMALL BLUE, ST ABB'S HEAD

Meadows

6 ST ABB'S HEAD NATURE RESERVE
The dramatic cliffs and rock stacks of St Abb's on the Berwickshire coast were created by volcanic eruptions and its craggy ledges are filled with thousands of nesting kittiwakes, guillemots and razorbills. It's a great place for rock-pooling and wildflower walks along the grassy cliff paths. In summer the cliffs are covered in the pinky purple of sea campion, purple milk-vetch, sea thrift and wild thyme. The visitor centre can recommend trails including a perfect 2-hour loop north along the coastpath to Pettico Wick, returning south on the path along Mire Loch.
→ Car Park at NTS visitor centre: fork L off the B6438 600m before St Abb's Head TD14 5QF, 08444 932256 nts.org.uk ⚓

7 BARROWBURN HAY MEADOW
Above the 100-foot-high chalk cliffs along Barrowburn farm in the stunning upper Coquet valley in Northumberland's Cheviot Hills is one of the best places to see ancient hay meadows. Enjoy the area's incredible

vistas, listen to skylarks sing and you may even see an otter in the river. The farm has a bunkhouse and the tea room serves hot scones and warm lunches as well as functioning as a national park information point. Starting from Wedder Leap, enjoy a short 30-minute loop around the farm or continue on to the foot of Hazeley Law, returning on the western side of the valley for a 5-mile walk. Bring a map.
→ From Alwinton follow road up River Coquet 6 miles to Wedder Leap car park Northumberland NE65 7BP northumberlandnationalpark.org.uk ⚓

Otters play and live in the lakes and its probably one of the best chances you have of seeing one.

Accommodation

8 THE BOATHOUSE AND FOLLY
For idyllic self-catering accommodation try Middleton Hall estate, which offers secluded retreats in sumptuous and quirky setttings. The folly overlooks the Italian garden while the boathouse is a divine open-plan space that literally hangs over the lake. Otters live and play in the lakes and it's probably one of the best chances you will have of seeing them in the wild. Larger groups can rent the whole hall, which has ten bedrooms.
→ Exit A1 Belford N for 1.4 miles, L down pillared lane, Middleton, Belford, NE70 7LF 01668 219677 exploremiddletonhall.co.uk 🏠

8 THE BOATHOUSE

9 CAPHEATON HALL

From the impeccable, cosy country-house interiors to the bounteous walled kitchen gardens and glasshouses dripping with peaches and figs, Capheaton is a glorious country getaway. There are acres of parkland to discover with old ruins half hidden by ivy. Either enjoy B&B in the main house or rent the west wing for eight, where you will be welcomed with a box of seasonal delights fresh from the garden. The area is great for cycling and there is ample stabling for either your horse or your bike.

→ Capheaton, Newcastle upon Tyne, Northumberland NE19 2AB 01830 530159 capheatonhall.co.uk 🏠 ☕

9 CAPHEATON HALL

9 CAPHEATON HALL

10 WILD NORTHUMBRIAN TIPIS

For wild luxury in the heart of the Northumberland National Park, the tipis, yurts and shepherd's huts at Wild Northumbrian offer a really magical holiday experience. Everything here is done so well using local designers and craftspeople to achieve the perfect balance of rustic organic chic. The owner's love of the woods, fells, and meadows is tangible and bush craft, art and wildlife-watching events fill the calendar. Sheepskins, woodburners, candlelight, hot bush showers and an organic garden allotment where you can collect fresh eggs for your breakfast, all add to the simple cosy joys of living close to nature. It's a beautiful site, and perfect for getting into the wild.

→ Thorneyburn Old Rectory, Tarset, Northumberland, NE48 1NA 01434 240902 wildnorthumbrian.co.uk 🏠

Food

11 THE GARDEN STATION

The Garden Station is a lovely café situated in a restored Victorian railway station surrounded by beautiful woodland gardens. The atmosphere is arty and creative, and the delicious slow food is locally sourced, fairtrade, and cooked with love. Food is mostly vegetarian but there is always some carefully sourced meat for the carnivores. The gardens follow the old train line between two stone arches and its woodland borders are planted with carefully chosen woodland flowers that fit its marginal setting, including ferns, foxgloves, dog's-tooth violets (*Erythronium*) and poppies.

→ Off the B6295 Hexham, Northumberland NE47 5LA 01434 684391 thegardenstation. co.uk ⏰ daily in summer (except Tue) 10–5pm and in spring and autumn Fri–Mon 11–4pm 🍷 🍽

12 BIRDHOUSE TEA ROOM

The popular Birdhouse tea room is housed in a sweet, wooden cabin that sits in the heart of Woodside nursery's walled garden.

Home-made salads and soups using garden produce can be enjoyed inside or out. The interior is simple and quirky and the walls covered in artwork by local artists. Friday evening summer suppers are a grander affair, tempting guests with roast leg of lamb or cep risotto. The nursery specialises in bird- and pollinator-friendly plants and also sells feeders.

→ 4 miles N of Jedburgh on A68, exit onto B6400 towards Nisbet. Woodside, Ancrum, Jedburgh TD8 6TU, 01835 830315 woodsidegarden.co.uk ⏰ daily 9–5pm (10–4pm in winter) 🍷 🍽 🌸

13 THE CAFÉ AT BRADLEY GARDENS

The glasshouse café at Bradley Gardens nursery was full to bursting when we visited in July. Newly renovated with woodburners and long tables it's a great place to enjoy a delicious lunch with wine or just a coffee in the quieter vine house. There's plenty of seating outside in the sun-trap terrace with views of the nursery's walled show gardens.

→ Sled Ln, Wylam, Tyne and Wear NE41 8JH 01661 852176 bradley-gardens.co.uk ⏰ daily & BH (not Mon) 10–4.30pm 🍷 🍽 🌸

12 BIRDHOUSE TEAROOM

12 BIRDHOUSE TEAROOM

13 THE CAFÉ AT BRADLEY GARDENS

DUN ARD

Galloway to Edinburgh

From the wild Galloway coast, across ancient forests carpeted in bluebells, to the stunning Moffat Hills. Southern Scotland offers garden drama, plant hunters and incredible wild flowers.

Galloway to Edinburgh

The highlights

›› Discover 4,000 perennials collected from the wild by a modern day plant hunter at Cally Gardens (2)

›› Step into a 17th-century kitchen garden at Culross, complete with scorzonera, salsify and skirret (3)

›› Roam through ancient oak woodland, carpeted with bluebells, at Carstramon (6)

›› Visit the world's first Cryptogamic Sanctuary – home to plants that reproduce by spores (1)

Best for birds and butterflies

Best for a plant nursery

Dunbar

12   4

Edinburgh

A68

A701   A7

A703

A72

Peebles

11

A707

Selkirk

6

Rocky wild coastline; coastal plains; heath and marginal grassland; knolls wrapped in woodland; and intimate pastoral valleys – these are just a few of the terms used in the formal landscape assessment of South West Scotland.

The upland glens found in the centre of the area are termed a special 'wildland', where isolated farmsteads dot the rough pasture and moor. This diversity of geology and soil has attracted both wildlife and foresters. Along the northern Solway Firth Coastline, near Mersehead and Caerlaverock, you can hear the jungly, weird rasping calls of the natterjack toad, the UK's rarest and noisiest amphibian. The forest of Galloway is the largest of Britain's forest parks and its 300 square miles are covered with a mix of ancient woodland, moor and conifer. Its remoteness made it the UK's first Dark Sky Park and its shooting stars – and even views of the aurora borealis – are an invitation to spend some time star gazing.

At the Wood of Cree, and at Carstramon, ancient oak woodlands flaunt thick carpets of bluebells in spring. Throughout the year they offer glorious spaces for magical walks. If you want to buy plants the area is rich with nurseries that have great show gardens. I particularly loved Cally Gardens, the treasure trove of plant hunter Michael Wickenden. A passionate plantsman, he challenges Plant Breeders' Rights, believing fundamentally that nature should not be owned, particularly by big business. Forty minutes west, at Newton Stewart, you'll find Galloway

Plants and its wonderful woodland show garden Claymoddie. Dunskey Gardens, near Stranraer, feature a renovated walled garden with plant sales. On the wild side, there are incredible summer coastal flowers in June around the Mull of Galloway near Robert Stevenson's lighthouse.

The incredible botanic gardens of Dawyck house the world's first Cryptogamic Sanctuary, near Peebles, 30 miles south of Edinburgh on the River Tweed. Often sidelined by our more flashy flowering plants, the world of ferns, mosses, fungi and lichens make up the majority of our plant species. They offer a world

1

of discovery and are an essential component of the UK's biodiversity, with lichens being indicative of ecosystem health. Dawyck is the perfect place to discover more about them and also to experience some of our champion trees.

Gardens

1 DAWYCK BOTANIC GARDEN

In the deep countryside near Peebles is one of the world's most important arboretums. Dawyck's Heron Wood Reserve is the world's first Cryptogamic Sanctuary. Making up more than 80 per cent of the world's botanic diversity, these include our fungi, lichens, ferns and bryophytes (mosses and liverworts) or any plant that reproduces not with flowers or seeds but spores. Great markers of climate change, their study at Dawyck is providing ongoing research into the changes in our plant biodiversity. Dawyck is a verdant and wild garden filled with ferns, trees and shrubs from all over the world. Often, mossy urns and grass pathways are the only reminder that this is a garden as much as a woodland. From May to June the azalea terrace brings vibrant orange, pink and coral colours to the green landscape. The sedum-roofed café serves up a good selection of cakes and light lunches in its modern glass space.

➜ Stobo, near Peebles, Scottish Borders EH45 9JU 01721 760254 rbge.org.uk
🕐 Feb–Nov daily 10am–6pm (Mar & Oct to 5pm, Feb & Nov to 4pm) ☕ 🍴 🌱 🌺

2 CALLY GARDENS

Arriving on a stormy day, I ran for shelter into the vast Dutch glasshouses in the brick walled gardens of Cally Gardens, the home

1 DAWYCK

2 CALLY GARDENS

and nursery of the renowned plant hunter Michael Wickenden. The glasshouse and the garden are filled with home-propagated world treasures. The unusual perennials not only prosper in this walled haven that

shelters them from Scotland's winds but are also shown off by his expert companion planting. Most of the plants are species plants – wild plants in their native home. Thick borders are crammed with delicate gem-like geums animated by a constantly moving array of grasses. Paths have become narrowed as cushions of geraniums, veronicas, wild thymes and exotic alstroemerias spill out from the beds. Over the last 18 years, the owner's passion and his knowledge of plants have created a garden and nursery to stunning effect. The stock now includes more than 4,000 perennials. It is an absolute must for those interested in plants and history.

➜ 1 mile S of Gatehouse of Fleet, Castle Douglas, DG7 2DJ Information Line 01557 815029 callygardens.co.uk
🕐 Easter Sat–Sep Tue–Fri 2–5.30pm, Sat & Sun 10am–5pm ☕ 🌱 🌺

3 CULROSS PALACE

Behind the palace of a wealthy 17th-century merchant is a delightful reconstruction of a working garden of that period. It has high walls and is laid out in terraces on a steep slope in the cottage garden way – every inch of space is utilised to cultivate plants and herbs for food, for medicine, for dyes or other practical purposes. Rustic oak fencing separates the different areas, while crushed cockle shells have been used to make paths. In a feature typical of the time, all the beds are edged with aromatic herbs.

It's a great place to see old heritage varieties of medlars, quince and mulberry. You will also find there vegetables such as skirret, scorzonera and alexanders – names that are found increasingly on trendy restaurant menus.

➜ West Green, Culross, Fife, KY12 8JH 0844 4932189 nts.org.uk
🕐 daily 9am–sunset (palace interior open at limited times) ☕

4 INVERESK LODGE

Inveresk Lodge is a lovely little wild garden just seven miles east of Edinburgh (buses from the city stop right outside it). The garden hides behind high walls, getting wilder as it drops down to the pretty river Esk. Near the house, this typical Edwardian garden is full of hardy plants chosen specifically for these eastern climes. The restored conservatory is heavy with peaches in summer while, in the aviary, the songs of canaries and parakeets can be heard. In the untamed meadow, paths sweep down to a wildlife-filled pond. There is often a ranger on site and when we were there, children were given jars for pond-dipping. They took great delight in catching, identifying and releasing the pond's inhabitants.

➜ 24 Inveresk Village Road (A6124), Musselburgh EH21 7TE 0844 493 2126 nts.org.uk 🕐 daily 10–sunset ☕

3 CULROSS PLACE

I DAWYCK

5 DUN ARD

Dun Ard is one of the few gardens in this guide open only by appointment. That's testament to the owners' deep belief in the necessity of organic gardening, heritage edible produce and the importance of wild fauna. The garden was crafted by Niall Manning and Alastair Morton from the wild hillside pasture that rises up behind their house on Main Street. Here they have created a number of intuitive and accomplished garden rooms that are triumphant in their desire to combine nature and beauty. They were inspired by their love of historic gardens and architecture and the crafts of stone walling and carpentry. They have built terraces, a pyramid and a simple gazebo whose proportions are perfection. Vistas, avenues, hedging and a careful selection of standard trees provide structure, and work magnificently with the austere and powerful mountain views. This hard framework then allows a space in which the owners can play with the tall wispy perennials that they clearly love. Rich hay meadows, the seed always there, have been allowed to flourish under their management and add yet another link to the wilderness of the Fintry Hills. This is a private garden so please call ahead for an appointment if you'd like to visit.

Main Street, Fintry, Stirlingshire G63 0XE
01360 860369

Here at Carstramon many coppiced beech and oak have been planted for timber since the 1600s. This has created a rich woodland habitat with an enchanting blue haze of bluebells in May.

8 KITTOCHSIDE MUSEUM OF RURAL LIFE

Meadows

6 CARSTRAMON WOOD

Not far from the spectacular Cally Gardens Nursery is a beautiful woodland where most of the trees are 200 years old. Here at Carstramon, many coppiced beech and oak have been planted for timber since the 1600s. This has created a rich woodland habitat with in an enchanting blue haze of bluebells in May. Red squirrels, bats, wood sorrel, violets, honeysuckle and primroses, as well as many birds and butterflies, add to the enchanting ambience.

→ B796 N from the Gatehouse of Fleet. After 2 miles R over Water of Fleet, then R at T-junction. Limited parking in layby on L. Follow FP into the woods. DG7 2BL scottishwildlifetrust.org.uk 54.9160,-4.2025

7 WOOD OF CREE

The ancient wood is the largest old oak woodland in southern Scotland. Most of it is an RSPB reserve due to its wealth of birds including tawny owls, pied flycatchers and great spotted woodpeckers. Spring

decorates the woodland floor in wild flowers, especially bluebells. More than 20 species of butterfly, including the rare purple hairstreak, have been recorded here. The Cree Valley is rich with glorious waterfalls and water meadows, while elusive otters play in the river. It's a lovely place for a spring or summer walk.

→ 4 miles N of Newton Stewart on Millcroft Road. Parking and info on L. Cycle Route 7. Dumfries & Galloway DG8 6RJ creevalley.com 55.0057,-4.5328

8 NATIONAL MUSEUM OF RURAL LIFE

Kittochside, part of the Museum of Rural Life, is unimproved grassland and a Coronation Meadow. At the museum there's a working farm and you can get up close, feed the animals and watch the cows being milked. Enjoy tractor rides and good walks. It's an easy day out from Glasgow and the summer hay meadows and old hedgerows are rich with wildflowers.

→ Wester Kittochside, Philipshill Road, East Kilbride, G76 9HR 0300 1236789 nms.ac.uk ⏰ daily 10am–5pm 🍴

8 KITTOCHSIDE

Accommodation

9 ALTON ALBANY FARM

For a fantastic farm B&B head to Alton Albany Farm on the Stinchar River near Barr, run by Alasdair Currie and Andrea Jones. The drawing room has a log fire and plenty of games to play in the evening. Alasdair's breakfasts are famous and just what you need to start a day's walk straight from the house or perhaps in Galloway Forest Park nearby. The gardens are lovely, with a pretty burn running through them, and children and dogs have plenty of space to run around outside in the fields. Andrea is a garden photographer and much of her work can be seen at the farm.

➔ I mile S of Barr on B734. Albany Road, Barr, near Girvan, Ayrshire KA26 0TL 01465 861148 altonalbanyfarmbandb.wordpress.com 🏠

10 GLENHOLME & THE ROOKERY

Overlooking water meadows and the river Dee, and one mile from the pretty fishing port of Kirkcudbright, is lovely Glenholme Country House B&B (also offering home-cooked dinners) and self-catering cottage, The Rookery. Laurence and Jennifer Bristow-Smith, cooks, gardeners and interior designers, are the perfect hosts. They ensure there are logs for your fire and they serve delicious food inspired by their extensive travels. Accommodation is cosy and stylish, and you can wander in the garden and pick some vegetables for your supper – or even better, let Laurence prepare you a feast. The excellent Elizabeth MacGregor Nursery is two doors down.

➔ Tongland Road, Kirkudbright, Dumfries & Galloway DG6 4UU 01557 339422 glenholmecountryhouse.com 🍵 |O| 🏠

9 ALTON ALBANY FARM

Food

II THE RESTAURANT, KAILZIE GARDENS

This restaurant is set in the converted stables of Kailzie Gardens, with its unwild walled gardens and lovely wild woodlands. Stuart and Amanda Clink have created a relaxed dining experience using some of the best produce to be found in the Borders. Excellent home-made sourdough, focaccia and Scandinavian smorrebrod are topped with patés, remoulades and local cheeses or you can tuck into local sausages served with mustard and mash. There's also a deli, so you could pack a picnic to take into the gardens, home to Scotland's oldest larch and where you'll hear cuckoos in spring.

➔ Kailzie Estate, Peebles, EH45 9HT 01721 722807 kailzie.com ⏰ daily 10–5pm, to 8pm weekends (Sep–Mar Wed–Sun only) 🍵 |O|

12 GARDENER'S COTTAGE

I was excited at the prospect of eating at The Gardener's Cottage in central Edinburgh. I'd read some rave reviews and it didn't disappoint. The long, canteen-style tables are noisy and fun and a relaxed, happy ambience pervaded the renovated cottage restaurant. The two owner-chefs are committed to making everything with fresh, seasonal and local produce – and it really shows in the excellent food. Make a reservation as this place is deservedly popular.

➔ I Royal Terrace Gardens, London Road, Edinburgh EH7 5DX 0131 5881221 thegardenerscottage.co ⏰ daily (except Tue & Wed) lunch 12–12.30pm, dinner 5–10pm |O|

The canteen-style long tables are noisy and fun and a relaxed, happy ambience pervaded the renovated cottage restaurant.

10 GLENHOLME

11 THE RESTAURANT AT KAILZIE GARDENS

12 THE GARDENERS COTTAGE

13 THE COURTYARD CAFE

This is an attractive café on Knochraich Farm in the beautiful Campsie Fells outside Fintry. The farm is run by Robert Rodgers and the artisan dairy, was originally set up by his wife Katy. There they make wonderful yoghurts, crème fraîche and ice cream from the farm's Friesians. You can sample the dairy's produce at the café. An orchard and a kitchen garden designed by Arabella Lennox-Boyd are starting to take shape, which will supply even more wonderful ingredients.

Knockraich Farm, Fintry, Stirlingshire G63 0LN 01360 860132 knockraich.com daily 10–4.30pm (Nov–Feb until 4pm)

CAMBO

Fife, Perth & Angus

Explore dramatic coastal grasslands, wild woodland gorges planted with Himalayan exotics and flora-filled masterpieces that will take your breath away.

Fife, Perth & Angus

The highlights

›› Discover a colourful tapestry of planting hidden behind high walls and sea mist (1)

›› Find four species of cricket and over 250 species of plants in a warm micro-climate at Montrose Bay (8)

›› Enjoy buzzing hay meadows, toadstools and incredible floriferous flower borders at Pitmuies garden (5)

›› Delight in organic food and orchard camping (13)

Best for red squirrels

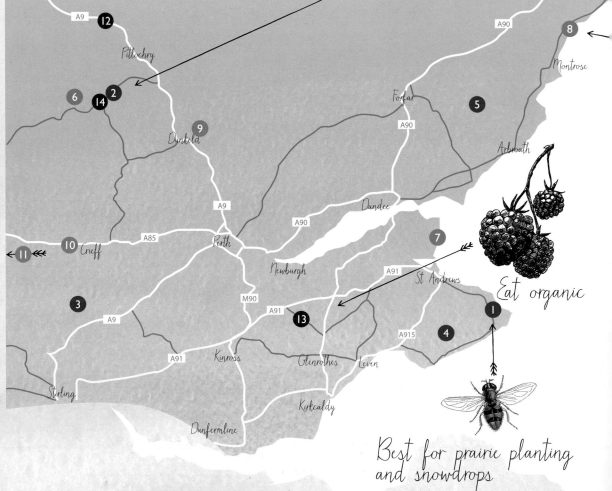

Eat organic

Best for prairie planting and snowdrops

This landscape is characterised by large estates and freshwater lochs fringed with woodland, a habitat in which red squirrels and ospreys thrive. Perthshire is known as 'big tree country' and the eastern area is dominated by its straths – wide shallow river valleys.

To the south, the Fife Coastal Path follows its sandy dune-backed way from North Queensferry to Newport on Tay. Near Montrose, the coast is dramatic, with huge volcanic cliffs soaring above the beach. Here in the St Cyrus National Nature Reserve, coastal grasslands harbour a wide diversity of insect and plant life, thanks to its sheltered micro-climate.

Further south, at Cambo Sands near St Andrews, we enjoyed a magical morning walk along the coast, the sea mist clinging to the wild flowers of the dunes. Nearby is the floral spectacle of Cambo Gardens, where the fog added a mystical air to the naturalistic planting. The walled gardens were a riot of colour and fruitfulness, with seas of herbaceous perennials, herbs and wildflowers. Near the old stables there is a stunning area of prairie planting and each February Cambo celebrates its collection of 350 different snowdrops.

Scottish collectors and plant hunters have had a great impact on Britan's gardening history. The plants they brought back from areas such as the Himalayas thrived in Scotland's climate, and many are now common to our gardens. The intrepid Scottish plant hunters' story is told at the six-acre garden Explorers near Pitlochry.

You can find many of the plants they brought back in a series of gardens in this part of Scotland. Many incorporate wild glens and it's easy to imagine yourself in the Himalayas. Not far from Explorers are the lovely Cluny Gardens, home to Britain's widest-girthed conifer and red squirrels. At Pitmuies we were surprised by a wild deer that leapt across our path as we wandered through the dappled woodland garden. My favourite secret garden can be found at Braco Castle, a wonderland of mossy paths wending through trees and meadows, before revealing, finally, a walled garden straight from a story book.

Many of these gardens have wonderful places to eat, and use produce that has been grown on the premises. Among these, the strangely named Pillars of Hercules café, based on an organic farm, stands out. It's the perfect place for a relaxed lunch under the apple trees. If you find it hard to tear yourself away, you can even camp in the orchard or stay in a cosy bothy.

Best for coastal wildflowers and crickets

Gardens

1 CAMBO

On our visit in late July, every plant shimmered with dew, the sun strangely illuminating the mist as it fought its way through. The prairie garden, with its backdrop of the old stables, felt quite ethereal. The tall stems of penstemons, echinaceas, veronicas and physostegias in muted colours waved gently amid a multitude of grasses – in the mist it was truly spectacular. I passed a fig tree and wandered through a door to find myself in the walled garden. There I found an explosion of colour, with gnarled trees burdened with fruit and weathered old glasshouses dripping with apricots and grapes. Whole sections of prairie meadows merged into high borders of rose arbours and exotic palms. Cutting through all this was a little stream, its steep banks thick with wild meadowsweet and marjoram. It's a well-stocked garden, and even holds the national collection of snowdrops, with a snowdrop festival each year. At Cambo, everything – from the four-poster beds of the B&B accommodation, to the sumptuous glamping, the secret gardens and even the little café – is simply delightful.
Kingsbarns, St Andrews, Fife, KY16 8QD Scotland 01333 450054 camboestate.com
⏰ daily 10–5pm 🍵 🏠 🍴 ⚘

1 CAMBO

garden was founded by Betty and Bobby Masterton in the 1950s and is now run by their daughter Wendy and her husband John Mattingley. Managed on organic principles, it's a work of love and dedication. The journey begins near the house where, in a quirky display, self-seeded bladder campion nestles among gravel and the skulls and bones of local sheep and deer. From a small lawn the path descends into a woodland garden. Himalayan and martagon lilies thrive in the dappled light. The well-named Chilean flame flower *Embothrium coccineum* crawls up into the tree canopy, and in late summer the beautiful hips of *Rosa omeiensis* were burning orange. I didn't see any of the red squirrels that live here, despite my best efforts to walk quietly.
→ 3 miles NE of Aberfeldy on B946, 1st L. Perthshire, PH15 2JT. Cycle Route 7. clunyhousegardens.com
⏰ daily 10–6pm (4pm in winter) 🍵 ⚘

3 BRACO CASTLE

Braco's gardens were a special discovery. The castle looks rather foreboding, with not a hint of the delights to come. I took a leaflet off the little table, put my money in the jar and started walking up the velvety moss path. It leads through an arboretum of monkey puzzles, oaks climbed by roses, majestic beeches, and rhododendrons – glorious in spring. In mid-July I was the only visitor and it felt truly mysterious. The woodland opens out into pasture, which had

winding paths mown through it. Without warning a beautiful pond was revealed. *Alchemilla mollis*, ferns and a stunning hoheria overhung the edge, admiring their own reflections. This is the entrance to the walled garden and with no one else around it felt like a secret garden – with the only sign of human activity being some recently clipped hedges. Paths lead in all directions, offering vistas of the 19th-century landscaped garden. There are a great variety of trees, shrubs and plants to discover, including, to the front of the house, a natural meadow, rich in wildflowers.
→ 1 mile N of Braco, W of bridge on A822. Braco, FK15 9LA 01786 880437 scotlandsgardens.org ⏰ Feb–Oct 10–5pm 🍵

4 KELLIE CASTLE

Kellie Castle is a lovely Arts and Crafts organic walled garden spilling over with fruit, tumbling rose arbours, vegetables and chickens. Surrounding the 14th-century castle, acres of wildflower-rich meadows, woodland and ponds all teem with wildlfe. The garden offers hours of happy discovery and there is a good café where you can relax right in the heart of a scented garden. There is a lovely circular walk through the woodland, past the fernery, pond, adventure playground and along the river.
→ Off the B9171, Anstruther, Fife KY10 2RF 0844 493 2184 nts.org.uk
⏰ daily 9–6pm (sunset if earlier) 🍵 🍴

2 CLUNY HOUSE

2 CLUNY HOUSE

Cluny House is a true wild garden, famous for its two magnificent 150-year-old Wellingtonias, one of which, at 36 feet, is the widest-girthed conifer in Britain. The

3 BRACO CASTLE

4 KELLIE CASTLE

5 PITMUIES

Prepare yourself for the colour explosion of
Pitmuies. We toured the area in July and
hot pink roses welcomed us to the gate. To
the right is the most extraordinary fern roof
covering the outbuildings. Once inside the
show begins and the vegetable garden was
a riot of colour and the formal garden was
spectacular. In the heart of the garden you
are squeezed through a long copper beech
backed allee filled with blue delphiniums,
white roseybay, silver echinops, golden rod,
pink geraniums, red velvety roses - their
colours intensified by the blue sky and
sunshine. In complete contrast is the cool
green woodland garden that runs alongside
the little burn. An old doocot (dovecot) and
a wash house that could have come straight
from a Grimms' fairytale highlighted our
walk. We were unprepared for the deer that
leapt out in front of us, leaping over the
fence and into the flower filled hay meadows
where it was lost from view. There are some
incredible ancient trees on the estate, a large
pond and many funghi. Unusual plants and
fruit when in season, are for sale.
  Guthrie, by Forfar. Angus DD8 2SN 01241
828245 pitmuies.com
Ⓒ Apr–Oct 10–5pm

Besides harebells and meadow cranesbill, more than 200 species of wild flowers can be seen at Balchroich and in the gloaming the meadow was a delight humming with butterflies and hoverflies

8 ST CYRUS NNR

Meadows

6 BALCHROICH MEADOW

Much of the Scottish Wildlife Trust's Keltneyburn Gorge reserve is inaccessible, – good for its resident pine martens. An easier part of this reserve to explore is Balchroich Meadow, both accessible and lovely for a wildflower walk. Its series of high knolls and damp hollows offer a stunning display from spring to summer. We missed the eight species of orchids that peak in June, but on our visit in late July the show continued. Besides harebells and meadow cranesbill, more than 200 species of wild flowers can be seen at Balchroich and in the gloaming the meadow was a delight, humming with butterflies and hoverflies.

→ 5 miles W of Aberfeldy off B846. Access via steep track next to General Stewart's statue in Keltneyburn village, 0131 312 7765 scottishwildlifetrust.org.uk 56.6223,-4.0046 ⚓

7 TENTSMUIR POINT

This is a windswept wild peninsula of shifting sand dunes backed by forest. Rich in history, it is a place of Stone Age settlements, Viking invasions and shipwrecks. The dune grasslands are a great place to see cowslips and early purple orchids in spring; pansies and delicate creeping ladies-tresses in June; and ragged robin, sea campion and massed northern marsh orchids in late summer.

→ Trail E along beach to Tentsmuir Point return via woods. 3.7 miles NE Leuchars, Fife, KY16 0DR tentsmuir.org 56.4078,-2.8139 ⚓

8 ST CYRUS NATURE RESERVE

Stunning volcanic cliffs tower over northern Montrose Bay creating a uniquely sheltered dune grassland that is a fantastic habit for wildflowers. Vibrant displays of clustered bell flower, and northern marsh orchids are just a few of around 250 species that thrive in its mild microclimate. The reserve is rich with invertebrates – amazing diversity, considering that it's only two miles long and 500 metres wide.

→ Visitor Centre 5 miles N of Montrose on A92. Nether Warbuton, St Cyrus, DD10 0AQ, 01674 830736 nnr-scotland.org.uk 56.7609,-2.4250 ⚓ 🍴

Accommodation

9 BAY TREE COTTAGE

The lovingly-renovated Bay Tree Cottage in the little hamlet of Butterstone is a delight. With its rose-covered porch, white-painted floorboards, woodburners, open fires and country garden, this holiday cottage is a perfect bolthole. Behind the house there is access straight out into woods and hills, so it can be the start of many lovely walks. Pets are allowed and the pretty village of Dunkeld is just four miles away.

→ Butterstone, Dunkeld, Perthshire, PH8 0HJ 01835 822277 unique-cottages.co.uk 🏠

9 BAY TREE COTTAGE

10 COMRIE CROFT

Set in a stunning wild landscape, Comrie Croft is a permaculture-croft using and sharing the land for sustainable tourism and local business. Accommodation is either in cosy Nordic kata tents, each with beds and woodburner, or in the bunkhouse, farmhouse or steading. If you like you can bring your own tent and have a campfire in the woods or on high meadow. It's as low impact as possible and rich with wildlife in all seasons. Aileen runs the on-site tea garden serving breakfasts and lunches as well as delicious cakes. It's a great place for cycling and walking.

→ 4.5 miles W of Crieff off the A85 Braincroft, Crieff, Perthshire, PH7 4JZ 01764 670140 comriecroft.com 🏠 🍴

11 MONACHYLE MHOR HOTEL

For a luxurious and stylish country getaway, with fantastic local food, head to Monachyle Mhor. Rooms are all wood, white linen and contemporary cosiness, with underfloor heating, fires and great views. The working farmyard is just next door so you really do know where your food comes from. The restaurant is open to non-visitors. Six miles away is its little sister, the funky Mhor 84 Motel also with excellent food and rooms.

→ Balquhidder, Lochearnhead, Perthshire FK19 8PQ 01877 384622 mhor.net 🍴 🏠

We ate our food in Strawberry Fields, shaded from the sun by the apple trees

10 COMRIE CROFT

10 COMRIE CROFT

Food

12 BLAIR ATHOLL WATERMILL

What a find this is. The mill dates from the 1590s and is one of just eleven working watermills in Scotland. It has been beautifully renovated and it's lovely to see the mill in action. Stoneground grains have a characteristic nutty flavour and a high nutritional value, and the wheat and oats ground here are sold by the bag and used in the superb café. Alongside some lovely cakes, fresh breads are served with delicious soups and salads and local smoked fish.

→ Ford Rd, Blair Atholl, Perthshire PH18 5SH 01796 481321 blairathollwatermill.co.uk ⏰ Apr–Oct 9–5pm 🍴

13 PILLARS OF HERCULES

For really delicious vegetarian food we loved the Pillars of Hercules experience. The name refers to the site, previously the Falkland estate's tree nursery. Since the 1980s, owner Bruce Bennett has advocated organic farming and the thriving farm, the orchards, the polytunnels, cutting garden, hens, farmshop, café and camping are all a testament to his beliefs. Happy campers set up tents in the orchard or you can stay in the bothy. We ate our food in Strawberry Fields, shaded from the sun by its apple trees. Inside, the café is cosy and full of laughter and at weekends it opens in the evening for Bistro nights.

→ 1 mile N of Falkland off A912. Cupar, Fife KY15 7AD 01337 857749 pillars.co.uk ⏰ daily 10–5pm, weekend evenings 7–9pm (farm shop until 6pm) 🍵 🍴 🏠

14 THE WATERMILL ABERFELDY

This is an award-winning independent book shop, but also an art gallery and a stylish vintage and contemporary home store. It has a café at its heart and is a great place for a relaxed stop in Aberfeldy. Lunch is home-made soup and locally-made organic bread. The cakes are delicious and there is a terrace with seating in the summer, and a cosy fire inside in the winter. Nearby are Cluny House gardens and Balchroich Meadow (see listings).

→ Mill Street, Aberfeldy, Perth PH15 2BG 01887 822896 aberfeldywatermill.com ⏰ daily 10–5pm (11am Sunday) 🍴

13 PILLARS OF HERCULES

13 PILLARS OF HERCULES

13 PILLARS OF HERCULES

LIP NA CLOICHE

West & Mull

The landscape of Argyll and Bute has some of the richest biodiversity in Scotland, complete with sea eagles on Mull and corncrakes on Tiree. There are wild shores, Atlantic oakwoods and coastal gardens waiting to be explored.

West & Mull

Discover alpine flora

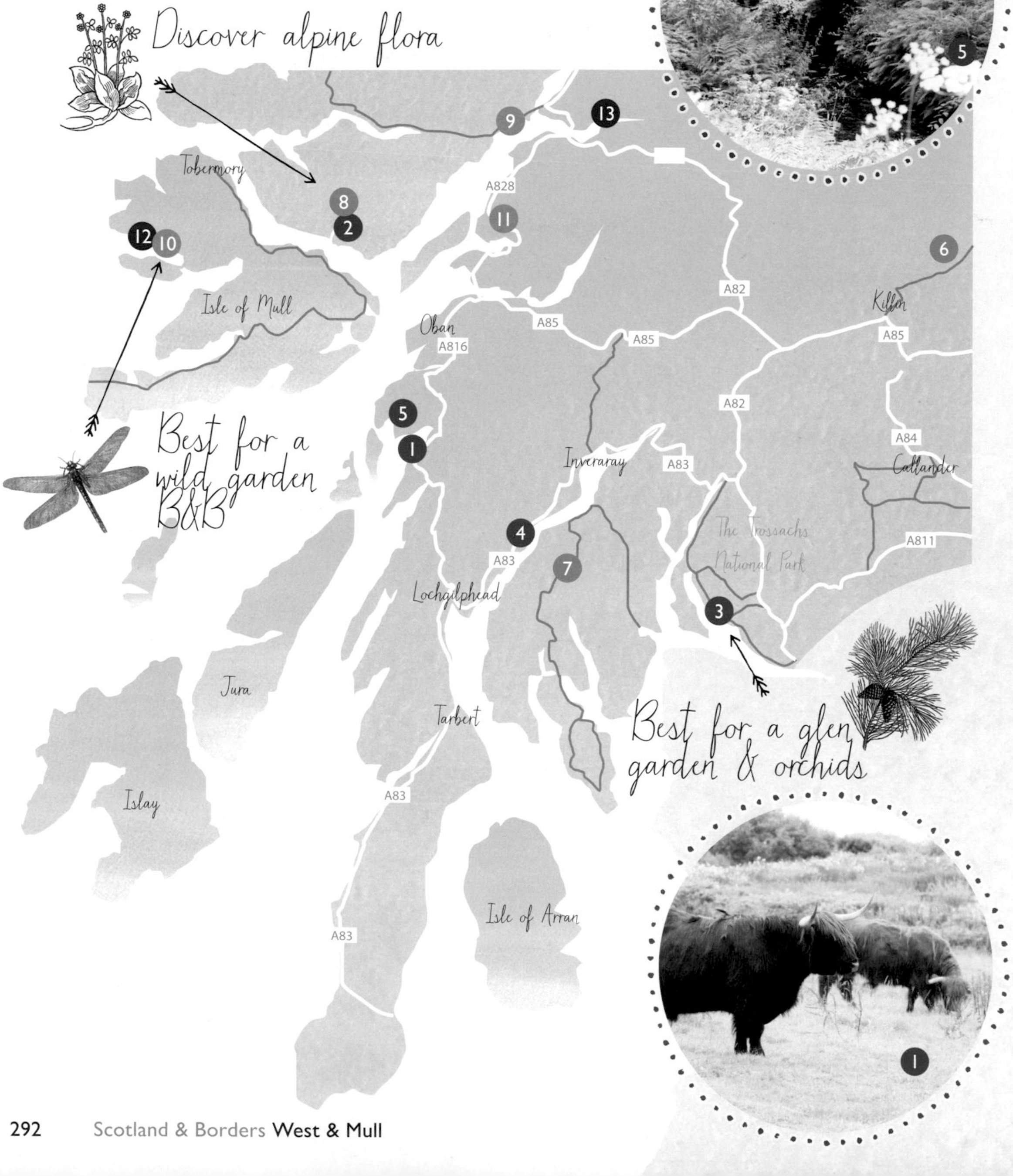

9

13

5

Tobermory

8

2

A828

11

12 10

Isle of Mull

6

Killin

A82

Oban

A816

A85

A85

A85

Best for a
wild garden
B&B

5

1

A82

Inveraray

A84

Callander

A83

4

The Trossachs
National Park

A811

A83

7

3

Lochgilphead

Best for a glen
garden & orchids

Jura

Tarbert

A83

Islay

Isle of Arran

A83

1

The highlights

›› Explore the romantic gardens of Ardmaddy Castle and keep an eye out for sea eagles (5)

›› Spot rare arctic-alpine flora at the top of Ben Lawers, Scotland's tenth highest mountain (6)

›› Enjoy a fresh fish supper served up with stunning views at Ballygown restaurant (12)

›› Stay in a stylish B&B and discover the secrets of marginal gardening at Ard Daraich (9)

This part of west Scotland has a varied landscape that offers a variety of valuable habitats for our native wild flora and fauna. Here you can see arctic wildflowers, magnificent sea eagles and rare Atlantic oak and hazel woods.

For our rare alpine flora head to the National Nature Reserve on the slopes of Ben Lawers or the Rahoy Hills wildlife reserve. At the foot of the Rahoy Hills are the rain-drenched woodland gardens of Ardtornish. The estate has been the home of the horticulturally inspired Raven Family for 80 years. John Raven wrote many books on botany, mountain flowers and plant-lore and with his wife Faith created Docwra's Manor garden near Cambridge. Daughter Sarah Raven is the well-known gardener, broadcaster and wildflower advocate and sister Anna Raven gardens at Ard Daraich (see accommodation listing) – all glorious and productive gardens that are covered in these pages.

South of here, looking out over the island-studded Sound of Jura, is the Arduaine peninsula and garden. It is a haven for wildlife and rare plants from California and the Himalayas. After touring the gardens we enjoyed a delicious locally-caught seafood lunch at the Chartroom Bistro (at Loch Melfort Hotel).

For more fresh fish and gardens, head to Loch Fyne where you will find the busy sea food restaurant at Clachan. Further west are the wild Himalayan gardens of Crarae Glen. For spring and autumn colour its rhododendrons and acers will not disappoint. I also highly recommend the incredible show of rhododendrons at Glenarn. This is a gorgeous private garden that's open to the public for Scotland's Gardens, the sister organisation of the NGS, from March to September, dawn to dusk. These opening times mean that you can enjoy the lovely woodland gardens at their most magical. I visited in mid-July in the golden light of early evening: the skies were deep blue and the garden felt like a secret labyrinth of sylvan pathways.

Taking the ferry to Mull, we headed straight for our destination, Lip na Cloiche, a garden and B&B in a wild setting. Early evening was falling and the views out to sea were calm and golden. Its sign read 'Please feel free to look round the garden – no entry charge'. It felt like another world. The cottage garden at the front of the house was a riot of poppies, sweet peas, frilly hollyhocks and delphiniums, set against the incredible view of Loch Tuath and the islands beyond. Everything here felt organic and fecund. Ropes and driftwood created soft fencing and handrails – much needed up the steep garden paths. It's a magical place and very intimate – such a contrast to some of the grander gardens that we visited on our trip.

Gardens

1 ARDUAINE

Arduaine was the home of James Arthur Campbell who started building a garden here on the south slope of Arduaine peninsula (meaning 'green point') in 1898. Building a rabbit proof fence and clearing the wilderness, he first planted trees for shelter, brought in from California and the Himalayas (rhododendrons were imported in tea crates). By the time of his death in the late 1920s there were more than 200 species here. Today the garden is managed by head gardener Maurice Wilkins who aims to provide a sanctuary for its rich wildlife and plant collections. Along the lower long border, spring is heralded by stunning drifts of rare Iberian *Narcissus cyclamineus*, then the grass is left to grow until it is cut in September. Many native orchids thrive here, appearing naturally when the cutting regime was changed. There is a beautiful shaded rockery garden, a kitchen garden, a cliff walk and ponds fringed in candelabra primroses and meconopsis. Otters have been seen in the garden and the ponds are brimming with life. We visited in summer, when along the Asknish shore wild flowers painted the grasslands white and pink and long-horned cattle bathed in the sunshine.
→ Signed off the A816. Arduaine, Oban, Argyll PA34 4XQ 08444 932216 nts.org.uk
🕙 daily 9.30–sunset 🥄 🐾 🍴

1 ARDUAINE

2 ARDTORNISH

2 ARDTORNISH

With an average rainfall of well over two metres a year, this is a wild and wet garden. With more than 25 acres of wild woodland, rocky hillside and river valley to explore, it's a place of stunning views, plants and wildlife. I spent a quiet summer's day wandering up Ardtornish's River Rannoch, through the stepped woodland gardens, immersed in its tranquillity. Thrushes were abundant, a good sign of its insect life, and every tree had become a little ecosystem, covered in moss, ferns and lichens. The focus here is on the trees, minimising the importance or even need of the herbaceous borders. A grand mix of exotic and native trees have enhanced the predominantly birch and oak woodland. Acers, several rhododendron species and cultivars and a number of prunus, hoherias and eucryphias deliver incredible colour throughout the year. Self-catering holiday accommodation available. Nearby is Rahoy Hills nature reserve (see listing).
→ Morvern, Oban, Argyll PA80 5UZ 01967 421288 ardtornish.co.uk
🕙 daily 10am–dusk 🥄 🏠

3 GLENARN

Amongst the grand oaks of this glorious 10-acre private garden live a serious collection of historic and endangered Red List rhododendrons – an incredible sight when they are all in flower. In July, when I visited, a few still held on to their large blossoms, their petals decorating the mossy fern lined paths that follow the little burn up towards the house. Pools edged in ferns and bog-loving plants reflected the tall trees and dappled light and the bird song was enchanting, even at this time of year. This garden, although not large, is not for the faint hearted: steep steps carry the visitor up through the tree canopy. The views from the top of the garden are stunning and orchids decorated the boggy meadow. I really enjoyed the kitchen garden where giant mullein stood straight as soldiers along the productive beds of fruit and vegetables. This is a wonderful secret garden with a rockery, beehives, glasshouses and a few plants for sale.
→ Park on street. Glenarn Road, Rhu, Helensburgh G84 8LL, 01436 820493 scotlandsgardens.org
🕙 21 Mar–21 Sep daily dawn–dusk 🥄

4 CRARAE GLEN

Reginald Farrer was a Victorian plant hunter who aimed to plant specimens in ways that recreated their natural habitat. The wild glen of Crarae owned by his aunt Lady Grace Campbell became home to plants from China, Nepal and Tibet. For three generations the Campbells experimented with exotic and specimen trees. There are more than 600 different rhododendrons, national collections of southern beech, bamboos and ferns to discover. The garden's rich wildlife includes otters and owls.
→ 10 miles S of Inveraray on the A83. Minard, Inveraray, Argyll PA32 8YA, 0844 4932210 nts.org.uk
🕙 garden daily 9.30–sunset (visitor centre only Apr–Oct Thu–Mon 10–5pm) 🥄

3 GLENARN

4 CRARAE GLEN

5 ARDMADDY CASTLE

On arrival at this castle on the Argyll coast, the first thing you see is a fairytale tower guarding a turreted house. Crossing the burn, you are invited to enter the garden. We found a little bothy there filled with information, weighing scales, hessian sacks of tatties, baskets of courgette flowers, jars of herbs, mangetouts, broad beans, rhubarb and lettuces – anything we wanted we weighed, paid for and put in our bag for our supper. The countryside was bright with sunlight in July and the walled kitchen garden was in full flourish. The garden sits in a shallow valley surrounded by deep woodland, adding to the charming setting, and a small gate beckons you out into the wilderness. The burn is planted beautifully with ferns, rhododendrons, and crocosmia spilling over its steep banks and there is an unusual stone bridge. Meadowsweet scented the air, filling it with clouds of hoverflies and bees. Orchids speckled the long grass and led to the richly-planted water garden that was on fire with more crocosmia, alstroemeria and candelabra primulas. The Ardmaddy estate, which has holiday cottages, is a great place for country walking and offers a rich coastal habitat for golden and sea eagles.

Signed S of B844 (E of Clachan Bridge)
Ardmaddy, Oban, Argyll & Bute PA34 4QY
01852 300353 gardens-of-argyll.co.uk
 daily dawn–dusk

On the high hills of
Beinn Iadain and
Beinn na h'Uamha, many
rare upland plants more
commonly found in the
Faroes and Iceland can
be seen living amongst
the ancient basalt rocks.

6 YELLOW SAXIFRAGE, BEN LAWERS

Meadows

6 BEN LAWERS NNR
The land around the mountain Ben Lawers is a National Nature Reserve and one of the best places in the country to see our rare arctic-alpine flora. At over 1200m high, the mountain's soft limestone and fertile soils create a unique habitat for delicate alpine forget-me-nots, Perthshire's county flower the alpine gentian, and drooping saxifrage. Listen to the calls of the curlew and black grouse as you discover spring displays of purple saxifrage followed by pink mounds of moss campion and then glorious displays of heather, autumn crocus and fungi in autumn. The views from this high mountain are incredible.
→ Main path and nature trail starts at visitor centre. Cycle Route 7. 6 miles NE of Killin on the A827, Killin, Perthshire, FK21 8TY. nnr-scotland.org.uk 56.5125,-4.2627

7 DUNANS CASTLE WALK
Dunans is an ongoing restoration project of both an 1815 bridge, designed by Thomas Telford, and a castle, which was ruined by fire in 2001. The waymarked one-hour heritage walk loops the grounds. Spring and early summer are the most colourful times, with diverse meadows rich with orchids and bluebells. There is a large rhododendron collection and Britain's tallest tree.
→ Off the A886 12 miles S of Strachur. Glendaruel, Argyll, PA22 3AD 01369 820115 dunans.org 56.0724-5.1495

8 RAHOY HILL WILDLIFE RESERVE
On the high hills of Beinn Iadain and Beinn na h'Uamha SSSI, rare upland plants more commonly found in the Faroes and Iceland can be seen living among the ancient purple basalt rocks. Norwegian sandwort, Lapland marsh orchid, roseroot and starry saxifrage are just a few of the alpine flowers that thrive here. It's a 10-mile circular walk from the car park to the summit of either hill and is steep, uneven and muddy. Bring a map.
→ Start N up track by river Black Water then E up Gleann Dubh. Car park off A884 0.5 miles N of Claggan, Oban, Argyll PA34 5XB scottishwildlifetrust.org.uk 56.5894,-5.7432

Accommodation

9 ARD DARAICH
Home of artistic Anna Raven and Norrie Maclaren, this is marginal gardening at its best. There's not much choice here. The landscape is harsh, there is hardly any soil and plants must fight for themselves. Once the holiday home of Constance Spry, specimen trees, special rhodendrons and a beautiful wild and productive kitchen garden thrive. The pink house is a stylish cosy retreat filled with flowers and offers B&B and self-catering accommodation complemented by delicious home produce.

8 ARD DARAICH

297

→ 2.8 miles SW of Corran off A861. Ardgour,
Fort William, Inverness-shire PH33 7AB 01855
841384 ardgour-selfcatering.co.uk 🏠

10 LIP NA CLOICHE

The garden of Lip Na Cloiche is glorious –
do visit even if you're not staying overnight.
Entry is refreshingly free and the plants on
sale are an eclectic mix superbly presented
in a tiny space – much like the garden.
A myriad of remarkably exotic plants,
colourful perennials, fruits and vegetables,
sea finds and driftwood crafts are
artistically curated along its steep terraces.
The use of space is inspirational and the
garden feels fun, a creative project crafted
out of love and with a deep knowledge of
plants. There are two B&B rooms and your
breakfast eggs come fresh from the little
bantams which live here.
→ Ballygown, nr Ulva Ferry, Isle of Mull PA73
6LU 01688 500257 lipnacloiche.co.uk 🌿🏠🌱

11 KINLOCHLAICH

Kinlochlaich offers a wonderful range of
self-catering accommodation in its western
Highlands estate. There is a luxurious tree
house with views over the tree canopies,
a lakeside cottage, or apartments in the
17th-century house. The gardens around
Kinlochlaich are beautiful and open
for charity under Scotland's Gardens.
Warmed by the gulf stream, they include
an octagonal walled garden filled with
fruit trees, vegetables and heavily-planted
borders. It has great woodland walks
across the estate, with bluebells and
rhododendrons in late spring, and its own
specialist plant nursery.
→ Signed off A828 at Appin, Argyll, PA38 4BD
01631 730342 kinlochlaich-house.co.uk
🌿🏠🌱

10 LIP NA CLOICHE

10 LIP NA CLOICHE

Food

12 BALLYGOWN RESTAURANT

Down the road from Lip na Cloiche (see
accommodation listings) is Ballygown, a
small restaurant with incredible views over
the loch towards Ben More. It's a friendly
place that serves excellent local food (with
as much as possible from Mull) and the
menu is small and changes daily. Bread
and pasta are home-made and it's excellent
value: around £15 for two courses. It doesn't
have a licence so bring your own alcohol.
→ 2 miles N of Ulva Ferry on B8073, Isle of
Mull PA73 6LU ballygownmull.co.uk
⏰ Apr–Oct Mon, Thu, Fri, Sat 5.30–10pm,
Nov–Mar Fri 5.30–10pm (Sun 12–6pm
booking essential) 🍴

13 LOCH LEVEN SEAFOOD CAFÉ

Despite an abundance of seafood in Scottish
waters, it's often hard to find places that
serve it fresh, locally caught and expertly
cooked at reasonable prices. This café
offers all this in a simple artistic space on
the shore of Loch Leven, with stunning
views over the Pap of Glencoe. It is next to
a shellfish company's dispatch centre and
the philosophy is to deliver it fresh to your
table. Its shop sells a wide range of seafood,
fresh and frozen, to cook at home.
→ Off B863, 6.5 miles E of Onich, Fort
William, Inverness-shire PH33 6SA
01855 821048 lochlevenseafoodcafe.co.uk
⏰ mid Mar–Oct lunch 12-3pm
dinner 6–9pm 🌿🍴

*It's a small remote
restaurant with
incredible views over
the loch towards Ulva
and Ben More. It's
a friendly place that
serves excellent local
food.*

12 BALLYGOWN

12 BALLYGOWN

10 LIP NA CLOICHE

CLIFF BEACH, LEWIS

Highlands & Hebrides

Discover the 'machair', the incredible flowering dune meadows, and enjoy Highland gardens filled with champion trees, colourful plants and birdlife.

Highlands and Hebrides

The highlights

>> Discover the incredible machair – dunes carpeted with wildflowers set behind white sandy beaches (5, 6 & 7)

>> Count hundreds of butterflies in the wild gardens of Cawdor Castle (4)

>> Enjoy a feast of langoustines and a glass of crisp white wine in the walled gardens of Applecross (11)

>> See choughs and even otters at the flower-strewn RSPB reserve on Uist (5)

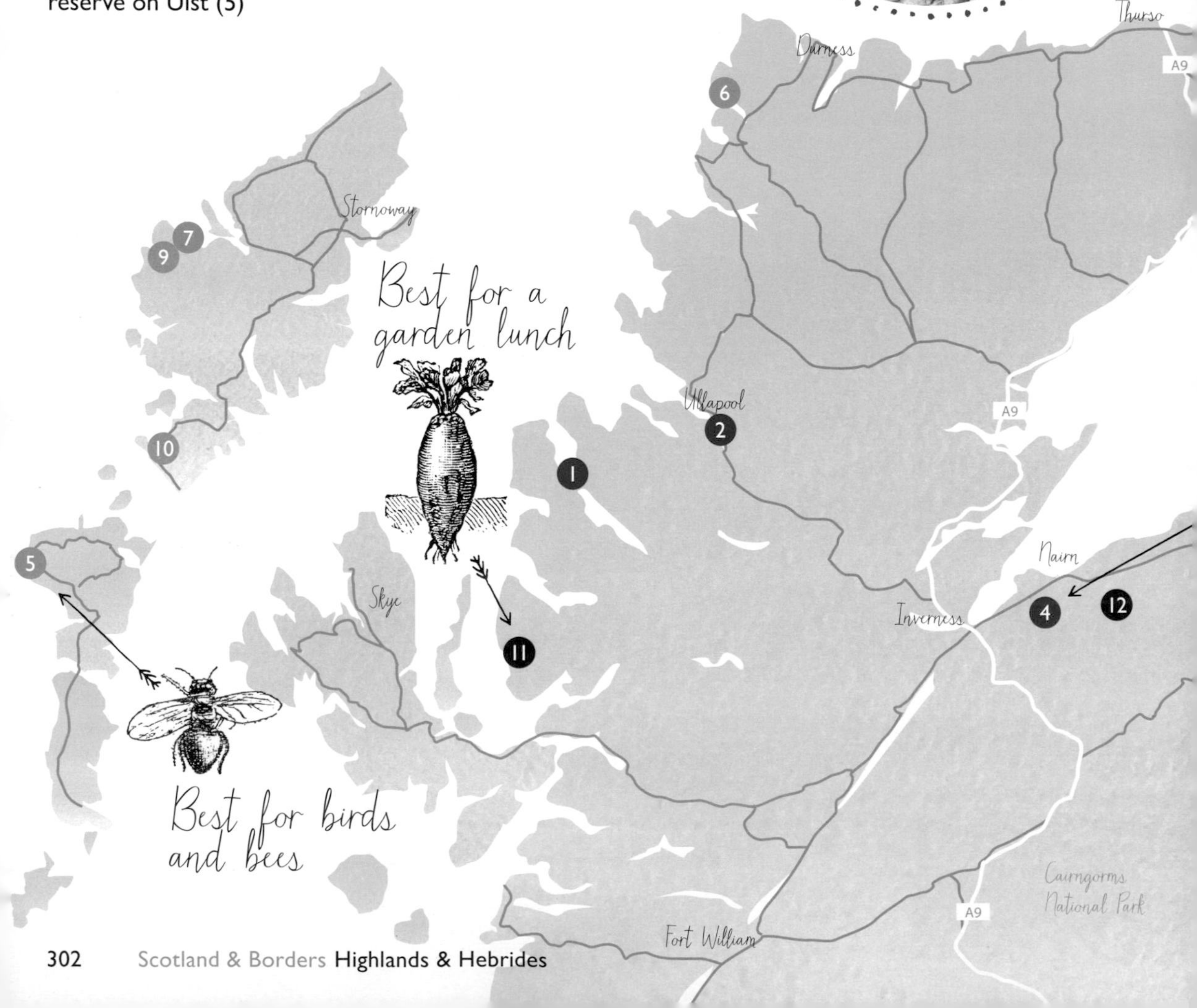

Thurso

Durness

Stornoway

Best for a garden lunch

Ullapool

A9

Nairn

Inverness

Skye

A9

Best for birds and bees

Fort William

A9

Cairngorms National Park

The machair (a Gaelic term now used to describe dune pastures) is one of Europe's rarest habitats and the rich floral grasslands can only be found in the north-western coastal areas of Scotland and some parts of Ireland.

I have always wanted to experience these fairytale flower carpets, so last summer we packed our cameras and headed west in our well-stocked campervan. The sand here, formed from ancient shells, is the palest pinky-white. When the sun shines, the clear water gleams such a bright turquoise you could almost be on a paradise island.

These extensive dunes along the coast, knitted together by tough grass, have existed for thousands of years. Some of the best machair in the world can be found on the John Muir Trust's reserve at Sandwood, particularly between Sheigra and Oldshoremore. The trust is dedicated to preserving Britain's wilder landsapes and is a great source of information on our wild places and their biodiversity. Our summer machair hunting on the outer Hebrides in July was blessed with glorious weather. The sun shone most days and the temperature gauge reached a staggering 26 degrees on Uist, although the water remained icy. Delicate harebells, orchids, clover, tormentil and lady's bedstraw bloomed in a beautiful array of yellows, pinks, purples and blues. We found stunning flowery tapestries fronted by white sandy beaches on Lewis, and I highly recommend a day spent at the RSPB reserve at Balranald. Here you can wander through

traditional arable fields dotted with corn marigolds and poppies on your way to the beach. The machair here is stunning – lucky birds!

The gardens will equally enthral you. I have never seen so many butterflies and hoverflies as I did on my visit to Cawdor Castle. Much-visited for its association with Shakespeare's Macbeth, we discovered a garden unbeatable in its obvious insect life and beyond its strong walls are wild gardens abundant with wildlife. At Inverewe the ornamental vegetable gardens intermingled with tumbling roses and southern hemisphere trees and the views over the loch were amazing. You can find more southern hemisphere treasures at Leckmelm, its a true secret garden and a lovely place to stop near the Ullapool ferry.

If the weather is good – there is just no beating this part of Scotland.

303

Gardens

1 INVEREWE

The scenery around the Wester Ross coastline is breathtaking. We arrived at Inverewe via the coast road from Applecross and it was an unforgettable drive, but the best approach is along the Kernsary path from Poolewe. It's about a two-hour, circuitous walk along Loch Kernsary through fairly wild territory, and in summer the displays of local wild flowers are incredible. Inverewe was bathed in sparkling sunshine, and the famous vegetable garden overlooking Loch Ewe glowed with intense summer colour. Vegetables were planted in long, radiating lines and were so plump and glorious that not even the heavy bowers of roses could compete. Further into the garden, the flowering dogwood (*Cornus kousa*) and the handerkchief tree (*Davidia involucrata*) looked stunning, while the flame creeper (*Tropaeolum speciosum*) was a vibrant scarlet. On such a glorious, still day it is hard to remember what a wind-swept, fierce place this headland can be despite the Gulf Stream. There are wonderful walks through woods, meadows, and along the rocky coastline of the 2,000-acre estate.
➔ Off A832. Poolewe, Achnasheen, Highland WV22 2LG, 0844 493 2100 nts.org.uk ⏰ Apr–Oct 9.30–6pm (reduced times in Apr, May, Oct) 🥪 🐾 🍽 🌷

2 LECKMELM

We had the good fortune to discover Leckmelm while driving from the ferry at Ullapool early one summer's day. If you like trees and tree ferns you will love this secluded little arboretum and may even

1 INVEREWE

have it all to yourself. Planted in the 1870s, Leckmelm's 12 acres slope gently down to Loch Broom. Abandoned from the Second World War, maintenance and replanting restarted only relatively recently, in 1985. Quiet paths winding through giant trees and shrubs create a colourful woodland walk and there are two 'champion' trees to admire: a huge drooping Lawson cypress native to the East Coast of the US, and an enormous multi-stemmed Japanese *Thujopsis dolabrata* that my daughter thoroughly enjoyed trying to climb. Many huge exotic specimens from the southern hemisphere thrive here in the damp, mild climate. There are also camellias and rhododendrons, and spring displays of snowdrops and bluebells.
➔ 3 miles S of Ullapool A835. Leckmelm, Garve, Highland IV23 2RH 01845 612662 rhs.org.uk ⏰ Apr–Oct 10–6pm ☕

3 LEITH HALL

Leith Hall, a 17th-century laird's house, sits deep in the Aberdeenshire countryside. Wild cats live in the woods and on the gorse-covered rocky hills, the summer sky was alive with swallows. We arrived late as the house was closing, and the gardens southern slopes were bathed in the early evening sun. The four acres of gardens display a random mix of styles. At the top of the garden the iconic Chinese moon gate was built in the 1900s. It is a stunning feature: the dark hole opening into the deep woodland that borders the garden. A snaking border, almost 100-feet long was crammed full of head-high herbaceous perennials, all out to impress. It made a dramatic contrast to the orchard and the Pictish stone circle located in a traditional hay meadow. These were my favourite areas – the old fruit trees a jumble of apples, nests of clematis, and lichen while the expanses of meadow grass were crisply bordered by perfectly mown paths.
➔ Kennethmont, Huntly, Aberdeenshire AB54 4NQ 0844 4932175 nts.org.uk ⏰ daily 9.30–sunset 🥪 🐾 🍽 🌷

The gardens were thronged with clouds of tortoiseshells and hoverflies

2 LECKMELM

3 LEITH HALL

3 LEITH HALL

4 CAWDOR CASTLE

4 CAWDOR CASTLE

Doubtful of its 'wild-garden' status, we visited Cawdor out of curiosity for its history. The castle is the 'spiritual home' of Shakespeare's *Macbeth* – there is no actual historical connection. It is a perfectly dark and looming place: solidly built with small turrets, thick, grey-stone walls, and small windows. Step into the garden, however, and the atmosphere is completely different. To the south, the gardens were thronged with clouds of tortoiseshell butterflies and hoverflies. Every flower seemed to have a visitor, and it was incredible and rather poignant to see such an abundance of insect life. The new slate garden is a triumph and fits surprisingly well with its backdrop of ancient woods. The old orchard trees were dressed in thick coats of shaggy lichens, and deeper into the ferny and mossy woodland walks we were to find even more evidence of rich habitats. Half an hour's walk from the Castle through Big Wood is Cawdor's dower house – Auchindoune. A Tibetan garden filled with plant-hunter treasures from the wild Tsangpo Gorges, this is a lovely, quiet and intimate garden.

Cawdor, Nairn, IV12 5RD 01667 404401
cawdorcastle.com   May–Sep 10–5.30pm

Miles of incredible machair cover the dunes backing the sheltered white-sand bays between Cnip and Traigh na Beirigh

5 RSPB BALRANALD

Meadows

5 RSPB BALRANALD
A perfect day can be spent wandering
the inner coastline of Balranald. Among
that day's sightings were rare great-yellow
bumblebees, painted ladies, red admirals,
choughs and otters. Many birds, such as
the corncrake and corn bunting, have
been decimated by intensive farming but
thrive here where the machair is cropped
on a rotational basis, seaweed is the only
fertiliser used, and there is no mechanised
harvesting. The machair is stunning and the
barley and rye fields are abundant with corn
marigolds and poppies. The Dunes food
shack near the little RSPB visitor centre
serves amazing soups and local crab.
→ 2 miles SW of Baleloch off A865
towards Hogha Gearraidh, North Uist
HS6 5DL, 01463 715000 rspb.org.uk
57.6056,-7.5166 ↘ IOI

6 SANDWOOD
Owned and maintained by the charitable
John Muir Trust, Sandwood covers over

11,000 acres and includes the stunning
machair between Oldshoremore and
north to Sheigra – it's probably the best
in the world. Here at the north-west tip of
Scotland over 200 different plant species
including eight orchids and mountain
avens – rarely found on any other machair –
flourish on the mostly ungrazed grasslands
behind the dune systems. Skylarks (a
declining species) nest amongst the flowers
and feed on the rich insect life and seeds.
Park at Oldshoremore Bay or at Sheigra; it's
about a three-mile walk between the two
beaches.
→ 1.8 miles N of Kinlochbervie.
Oldshoremore, Lairg, Highland IV27 4RS
jmt.org 01971 511259 58.4774,-5.0828 ↘ 🏠

7 ISLE OF LEWIS
Stunning machair covers the cliffs backing
the sheltered, white-sand bays from Cliff
beach, east to Cnip (Kneep), Bhaltos
(Valtos) and on to Traigh na Beirigh (Reef
Beach). Thick carpets of orchids, harebells,
meadowsweet, and clover reach as far as the
eye can see, enhancing awesome views of

the crystal-clear turquoise seas. We visited
in mid July and the flowers and weather
could not have been better. There are simple
community-run campsites with showers and
loos at Bhaltos and Traigh na Beirigh.
→ Traigh na Beirigh, Cnip, Uig, Isle of Lewis
HS2 9HS 07542 142750 ↘

5 RSPB BALRANALD

Accommodation

8 WILD CAMPING

If you want to wake up where a white crescent of sandy beach is within metres of your bed, then bring your tent or campervan and wild camp. Scotland's access legislation means wild camping is allowed as long as you are respectful, leave no trace, and follow the guidelines. Some community sites do charge a small fee and some have showers and loos. It's a great way to get really close to the native flora and fauna and a morning dip has to be the perfect way to start the day!

→ Scottish outdoor access code can be viewed at visitscotland.com

9 AUBERGE CARNISH

We discovered Auberge Carnish on the Isle of Lewis when photographing the machair near the sandy beaches of Ardroil. Overlooking the vast sweeps of white-shell sand, the small hotel and restaurant has five well-appointed rooms, a lounge with woodburner, and a glorious terrace overlooking Uig sands. Food is described as 'devoutly Gallic' using local island fare, the menu changes regularly, and non-residents are welcome. The beaches are stunning.

→ Near village of Ardroil. Carnais, Uig, Isle of Lewis HS2 9EX 01851 672459 aubergecarnish. co.uk 🏠 🍴

10 SCARISTA HOUSE

Scarista House is something of an institution on Harris. Across the road from this relaxing, small hotel with open fires there is a wild, white-sand beach, which is often deserted. Food is a delicious offering of island produce cooked according to the slow-food philosophy. Non-residents are welcome for dinner, but do book.

→ 15 miles SW of Tarbert on the A859. Sgarasta Bheag, Isle of Harris, HS3 3HX 01859 550238 scaristahouse.com 🏠 🍴

8 CLIFF BEACH, ISLE OF LEWIS

Food

11 APPLECROSS POTTING SHED CAFÉ

Applecross Walled Garden and its fantastic café come highly recommended. We enjoyed a delicious super-fresh seafood platter in its lovely vine-covered potting shed. The atmosphere is informal and fun and it's a great place for a locally sourced long lunch. Dinners are candlelit and I would love to try their eight-course tasting menu. The garden is open (donation requested) and filled with beds of vegetables and herbs destined for the café. Arbours are covered in cascading roses and there is an orchard and gravel garden to discover.

→ Applecross, Strathcarron, Ross-shire IV54 8ND 01520 744440 applecrossgarden.co.uk 🕐 Mar–Oct daily, serving food 10–8.30pm (Sun 4pm) 🍴 🍴

12 LOGIE HOUSE FARM SHOP & CAFE

Logie Steading is a great place to stop if you are travelling in the Findhorn valley. Logie House gardens are open daily (small entry fee) and there is a lovely walk along the beautiful Findhorn river as far as

picturesque Randolph's leap. The farm shop sells a range of succulent Logie longhorn beef, local smoked fish, and soft fruits from the garden. At the visitor centre, you'll find a plant nursery, whisky shop, art gallery, and bookshop, as well as the Olive Tree café, which serves lunches and teas.

→ Off the B9007, Forres, IV36 2QN 01309 6611222 logie.co.uk 🕐 Apr–Oct daily 10.30–5pm 🍴 🍴

The atmosphere is informal and fun and its a great place for a locally sourced long lunch.

10 SCARISTA HOUSE

9 BEACH NEAR AUBERGE CARNISH

11 APPLECROSS POTTING SHED CAFÉ

11 APPLECROSS WALLED GARDEN

Wild Garden Weekends
Explore the secret gardens, wild meadows
and kitchen garden cafes of Britain

Words:
Tania Pascoe

Photographs:
Tania Pascoe and Daniel Start

Editing and Proofing:
Anna Kruger
Sue Wingrove
Michael Lee

Design & Layout:
Tina Smith
Nicola Erdpresser,
Amy Bolt

Production:
Daniel Start

Distribution:
Central Books Ltd
99 Wallis Road, London, E9 5LN
Tel +44 (0)845 458 9911
orders@centralbooks.com

Published by:
Wild Things Publishing Ltd.
Freshford, Bath,
BA2 7WG, United Kingdom
hello@wildthingspublishing.com

wildthingspublishing.com
wildguide.net/gardens

Photographs

All photographs © Tania Pascoe and Daniel Start except the following (all reproduced with permission: p.11 © Andrew Montgomery, p.78 © Barnsley House, p.78 © Pauntley Court, p.97 © Tim ST Jones, p.97 © Feather Down Farm, p.123 © Nicola, p.126 © Wendy Tobbit, p.137 © Marcus Harpur, p.138 © Alde Garden, p.144 © Mike Powles, p.147 © David Hen, p.148 © Ling's Meadow, p.158 © The Coach House B&B, p.162 and p.198 © Jack Thurston, p.188 © Under the Thatch, p.188 © Gavin Hogg, p.218 © Farm on the Hill, p.218 & 219 © Talton Lodge, p.288 © East Farm B&B, p.233 © Damian Young @ Landlife, p.235 and p.238 © Stephen Rogers, p.243 © Rosalind Simon, p.247 © John Grimshaw Yorkshire Arboretum, p.249 © Kiplin Hall, p.256 © Ann and Steve Toon, p.263 © Barbara Roberts, p.266 © BENGNK, p.267 © Middleton Hall, p.268 © Capheaton Hall, p.278 (top) © Andrea Jones, p.278 (bottom left) © Laurence Bristow, p.279 © The Courtyard Cafe, p.279 © The Gardener's Cottage, p.287 © Unique Cottages, p.288 © Comrie Croft. CC-BY-SA: p.92 Adam Tinworth, p.124 AD Teasdale, p.207 James Loach, p.207 SA Ryan, p.224 Thomas Quine, p. 227 Christopher Hilton, p.288 Richard Croft, p.230 Upupa4me, p.233 (top) and p.237 (top) Alex Dixon, p.237 (bottom) Chris Moriss, p.267 and p.297 S. Rae, p.273 and p.276 Gerry Zambonini, p.287 Anne-Marie, p.296 Clive Giddis.

Acknowledgements

I would like to thank all the garden owners, gardeners, The Wildlife Trust and National Trust rangers who have shared their gardens, wild places and above all their knowledge with me. Thank you to Angela Whinfield, James and Caroline Weymouth, Mary Keen, John & Lynn Sales, Steve Oram and Lauren Alexander (PTES), Beatrice Krehl (Waltham Place), Sally Beamish (Brantwood) Andrew Excell & Vicky Whitaker (Suffolk Wildlife Trust), Helen Buckingham (National Trust), Toby Guise, Hannah Hargrave.

Heartfelt thanks to Sarah Price, Jack Thurston, Michael Lee, Anne Churchill and Will Smith, Jessica, Paul and Myla Rothwell, Yvette, Matt, Kaspar and Minna Alt-Reuss, Bee Carnac and Esme Rice, Vicky and Juno Peck, Emma, Eva and Oliver Heatley-Adams, Sara, Isabelle and Isaac Stewart, Sasha Ransome, Kate, Will and Jack Porteus, Karen Dora and Lotta Wilcox, the editors and designers and above all to Daniel and Rose Start, and Marijka, Tony and Ivan Pascoe, my wonderful travelling companions and family who have inspired and supported me.